C000243210

CLOGS WERE MY LIFE

CLOGS WERE MY LIFE

Frank Walkley

The Book Guild Ltd
Sussex, England

The Book Guild Ltd
25 High Street,
Lewes, Sussex

First published 1998
© Frank Walkley 1998
Set in Times

Typesetting by Wordset
Hassocks, West Sussex

Printed in Great Britain by

Antony Rowe Ltd,
Chippenham, Wiltshire.

A catalogue record for this book is
available from the British Library

ISBN 1 85776 233 9

CONTENTS

FOREWORD

Frank Walkley has certainly made his mark as one of the last colourful characters in a once great industry, the clog industry. His name will continue to be associated with clogs, one imagines, as long as any type of clog continues to be worn. His lifetime's experience, his love for the industry and his knowledge are probably unique. His book will appeal to all those people who want to look back and enjoy the nostalgia of a forgotten age.

Sir Ernest Hall, OBE, DL.

1

At Home and on the Farm

I was born at No. 30 Church Avenue, Crosland Moor, Huddersfield, on 20 February 1920, with one sister some six years older, our father having been abroad during the 1914-18 War. Church Avenue consisted of some 44 'back-to-back' houses with shared outside toilets situated at the bottom of the back houses' gardens, which also served as suitable places to keep dustbins, a dividing wall separating the two areas.

All the houses were on a weekly rental, those at the front paying 6s 6d weekly (32½p), which included our own house; the back houses were a little cheaper at 6s (30p). The houses themselves were all stone-built, probably due to the stone quarries being located less than two miles away. All had both attics and cellars, the latter being excellent for keeping food but also serving as a washing cellar and having a separate coal place.

At the far end of our cellar a three-legged table held a very large earthenware bowl used for the weekly bread-making, which invariably took place each Wednesday. Washing facilities for clothes consisted of a 'copper' (not made from copper) to heat the water by gas, a large zinc tub complete with a wooden 'posser', which had a long brush-like handle and was used to thoroughly wet the clothes, a rubbing board of metal corrugations fitted in a wooden frame and standing inside the tub on two short wooden legs and lastly a double wooden roller 'wringing machine' with an iron frame, worked by hand with a large iron wheel at one side to which a short wooden handle was attached. The stone sink with cold-water tap was fitted under the cellar window, half of which was below ground level but it still provided enough daylight for washing purposes. A single gas light with rather a long upright mantle lit the cellar when used during the hours of darkness.

To reach the toilets from the front houses we had to go through a narrow passage leading between the houses, which had four metal covers near the middle that had to be lifted up to put the sacks of coal down into each of the four houses served by the one passage. The coal cellar was merely a bricked off part of the main cellar and was fitted with a door to keep the coal dust away from the clothes and food. Deliveries of coal were either by the ton in bulk or in one-hundredweight sacks. When a delivery was in bulk this was deposited on the pavement at the end of the passage and had to be shovelled into a wheelbarrow to take it up the passage and shunt it down into the coal cellar. When delivered in bags it was one of my jobs to count each one dropped down into the cellar to make sure that we got the correct number ordered.

The ground-floor room was known as 'the house' with a 'cellar head' no more than four feet square at the top of the cellar steps, where a single gas ring provided the only means of heating water there. Lighting was almost non-existent, comprising a gas flame in a maple-leaf shape formed from a small horizontal slit in an upright piece of porcelain about the thickness of a cigarette and half its length. By this light, washing up had to be done using an enamel bowl standing in the stone sink. A single cold-water tap provided the only supply to the ground floor.

'The house' itself (a single room), as was usual at that time, was furnished with a sideboard, dining table, chairs and, for myself, a small round wooden stool. A piano fitted neatly into the recess at one side of the fireplace, the other side being cupboards in the top part and drawers in the bottom half. A large picture named *The Four-in-Hand* hung on the back wall. The title referred to the carriages which each had four horses pulling it.

There was, of course, no electricity in any of the houses but the gas lamp gave excellent light from its circular mantle. The 'range' consisted of a central coal fire with the cooking oven on the left-hand side and a 'boiler' to hold water on the right. A level 'rib' conveniently held two iron pans and was also used for heating the 'irons' for ironing clothes. We had two for this purpose, one small and reasonably light, and the other much larger and heavier. The 'boiler' was really a square-shaped iron container with an iron lid and handle all in one piece and had to be filled and emptied by hand using what was then called a 'piggin', an enamel ladling can. The whole of the fireplace was black-leaded every week and made to shine, using small oval-shaped black-lead brushes with a centrally placed handle for the fingers to grip tightly and put as much pressure on as possible.

As bathrooms were non-existent the method of taking a bath consisted of draping a large sheet or tablecloth round a clothes horse in front of the fire and filling a zinc bath brought up from the cellar with hot water from the boiler. The bath itself stood on newspaper to keep the floor dry. The linoleum, or oilcloth as it was known could easily become slippery if wet, hence the precaution. A list rug placed in front of the fire provided a little warmth to stand on when drying as lino was always cold to the feet. The accepted practice for having a bath was simply to wait until everybody else had gone to bed for the night, when privacy became unnecessary.

To complete the furnishing of the house a sewing machine, a vital part of life at that time, stood in front of the window.

The small bedroom where I was born had no heating at all, any extra warmth in winter being provided by the simple method of wrapping an old shirt or similar round the feet to get off to sleep easier. The large bedroom with a full-size double bed made from mahogany boasted a tiny iron fire grate and was used only in case of illness. The bed, wardrobe and dressing table completed the furniture and both bedrooms were fitted with a single gas mantle of a long and cylindrical shape like the cellar light.

The attic steps behind a wooden door on the landing were very narrow indeed and we had to walk up them sideways. The danger was obvious and resulted in me falling down them as a child, which hurt quite a bit as there was no such luxury as a carpet on the attic stairs. The attic itself did have a waist-high rail to prevent falling down the stairs but with a 90-degree turn at both top and bottom it was just a disaster waiting to happen. A bed and wash-hand basin completed the furnishing, apart from a large black box sent by my father from India which was used as a blanket box. List rugs, made by my mother, were placed at each side of the bed, making it slightly warmer than the bare wooden floor. A large skylight window, which was opened by a long flat iron handle with slots in it every few inches, provided what light there was, whilst a 'manhole' in the wooden side wall gave access to the underdrawing but I cannot recall it being used at all.

Our household, apart from myself, consisted of my mother, father, sister and grandma, the latter being my mother's widowed mother. Even at the age of 84 she was able to read the local newspaper without the aid of glasses and insisted on doing the weekly bread-baking herself. The annual jam-making was also her domain. Also, once a year, she made 'home brew' from dandelion leaves, nettles etc. which was stored in the cellar in large earthenware bottles. Some time after brewing the corks would fly out with a loud crack. Besides being a very proud person, teetotal of course, she was chided after making one particular brew about its alcohol content. At this time she was most indignant and adamant that there was no alcohol in her brew, saying 'there can't be because I haven't put any in!' To her this was logic and no one could convince her otherwise. Sadly she died in her late eighties, having been in charge of all her faculties up till the last two years of her life.

As I had no brothers and only one sister, our family was obviously a small one, with my uncle, his wife and his sister-in-law being the only relations in the area, as my father's family were Londoners. My uncle had a shirt and pyjama business located by Huddersfield railway station in St George's Street, the trade being done on a made-to-measure basis mainly for professional people and covering a fairly wide area. This necessitated regular calls on his clients, who were notified by postcard of his coming a few days in advance. The only help he had was an old soldier from the First World War who had been wounded and walked with the aid of a stick. The actual machining work was mainly done in the Leeds area, which had a large number of clothing firms making everything from men's suits to ladies' wear of all types. My uncle had to bus round the various towns where he did business, which was very time-consuming, so he eventually bought a Singer car together with his sister-in-law. During the week he would use this for business and

Miss Bamford drove it at weekends.

She was a teacher at Stile Common Road school at Primrose Hill and I remember that when she was driving the car she would grip the steering wheel as hard as she possibly could, which was even to me at that time obviously totally unnecessary, but that was her way of doing it. She was quite a character in her own right and certainly a person who could get a party going at Christmas, and she was always well liked by all who knew her.

Sometimes, on school holidays, my uncle would take me with him when travelling, which was very nice when we were on the move but rather boring to me when waiting for him making his calls. Having been brought up in a fairly strict Baptist household, my uncle did not believe in people having to work on Sundays, and so sincere was this belief that he would not travel by bus on that day but walked all the way from Crosland Moor to Primrose Hill Baptist Chapel at least once a day, which would take over an hour to do. Being a rather logical type even at that early age, I could not understand his action in doing this kind of thing, especially in wet or snowy weather, as surely he must have realised when he bought his Monday morning paper that this had been produced by people working on Sunday and through the night transporting newspapers all over the country to enable deliveries to be made the following day.

At my uncle's office there was an old typewriter and he allowed me to go there and teach myself how to use it, which was to be helpful later on. Both my uncle and aunt lived and died in Frederick Street, she from yellow jaundice, which was the first time I had seen skin go that colour. They had no family of their own. Miss Bamford, like so many teachers, had to be taken away to the 'Retreat' at York, where she stayed for a long time until unable to pay any longer. She was then transferred to Storthes Hall Hospital for mental patients at Huddersfield, where she died within a few days. I remember much bitter comment about this at the time but I was really too young to understand the true position.

Church Avenue is a row of some 22 houses on one side of the road only, the opposite side being the boundary wall of St Barnabas Church, after which no doubt Church Avenue got its name. At one end of Church Avenue was quite a large Co-op serving the needs of the many rows of houses round about; our check number was 709. Opposite the Co-op at the bottom of Yews Hill Road was the inevitable fish-and-chip shop, which became a meeting place for the children in the evenings.

All the occupants of Church Avenue were people who took a pride in both themselves and their houses and each weekend the doorsteps would be scrubbed and scoured with either a 'ruddle-stone' or a 'donkey-stone' to finish off the cleaning process. Invariably after any fall of snow everybody was quickly out cleaning their own 'flags' as they were called, so that within a very short time anyone could walk the whole length of the avenue on cleared pavement. Anyone unable to clear their own part because of old age or illness was helped by willing hands from nearby houses and a good community spirit existed.

From our house window could be seen a large metal sign bearing the initials DBS for David Brown & Sons fixed high up on the multi-storey engineering works on the far side of Park Road opposite. Every day at 5 o'clock hundreds of men would pour out of the main entrance opposite Church Avenue where I and other boys were waiting for them with the cry 'Have you got any cigarette cards, please, mister?' We must have said this thousands of times in a year but invariably I was able to collect a complete set of every issue that came out, whatever brand was giving them away. Any duplicates could easily be swapped with other boys. A lot of information was printed on the backs of the cards, referring to the coloured picture on the front, and much could be learnt from this source. On saving one particular series and sending it in, a full set could be exchanged for a beautiful picture ready for framing. This series included *The Laughing Cavalier, Mother & Son*, a lovely horse and foal picture and the historical picture entitled *And When did You Last See Your Father?* There were others equally famous.

At the age of five I was admitted to Crosland Moor council school situated in Blackmoorfoot Road some ten minutes' walk away. The workhouse was next door to the school on the approach side and walking past the entrance each day was a constant reminder of those unfortunate men in rough grey suits

6

who could be seen in the vicinity. Whilst attending this school I invariably received a full-attendance certificate each month and a differently coloured one every three months. Our class teacher was a Mrs Shaw, who taught us how to spell, add up, multiply and divide, and reading and writing. This latter had to be done with pen and ink using thin upstrokes and thick downstrokes for the letters. The pen nib had to be repeatedly dipped in the inkwell resting in a round hole at one corner of the desk and the task of refilling inkwells was given to everybody in turn. The standard of handwriting in particular was excellent, with everybody doing their best, and we were totally attentive at all times as Mrs Shaw was highly respected by all.

A Mr Senior came to the school from Stile Common Road school at Primrose Hill and he made us all parade each morning when he would inspect us for smartness in appearance; boots had to be blacked and shiny, ties neatly fastened and socks pulled up to the top. He taught us to have pride in our appearance at all times, irrespective of how poor anyone was. All the boys were proud to be under his tuition, and both education and sport, particularly cricket, soon improved beyond all recognition. I am permanently indebted to both these teachers for instilling discipline, obedience and self-respect in this primary school during those early formative years of my life.

When I was about eight years old our family, with the exception of Grandma, went to stay in London for a week with my father's family as he was born in Pimlico. My sister and I had been named after Uncle Frank and Auntie Molly, with whom we were staying. To go on this trip I was fitted out with a revolting bright green jacket, a white waistcoat with brass buttons and a black walking stick with a silver top. To me, this outfit was 'cissified' and I hated the green colour, but I had no choice in the matter and had to wear it, although not oftener than I could help. We took a full clothes basket of home-made bread with us to London, which was very much appreciated by all down there who were living on 'bought bread' considered at that time to be much inferior to the home-made variety. I cannot recall seeing many of the sights of London on that visit but will never forget the green jacket.

It was about this time in my boyhood that I contracted measles, which left me with a discharge coming from each ear. This was to continue in the years ahead and was, unknown to me at the time, to be destined to have such an impact on my later life. As a consequence of this *otitis media bilateral*, I had to attend the clinic in Huddersfield two or three times each week where the nurse carried out what was known as 'dry-mopping', which meant continually inserting cotton wool into each ear until all the discharge was removed. Unfortunately, this absence from school for an hour at least on each clinic visit naturally affected my time in school, and must have been detrimental to the learning process to some degree.

During my six years at Crosland Moor council school my boyhood leisure consisted mainly of riding my tricycle and playing football or cricket, according to the season of the year, in the recreation ground at the bottom of the adjacent May Street and only two minutes' walk away.

At Christmastime my usual presents, apart from the inevitable apple and orange stocking fillers, would include a Meccano set which could be upgraded each year and once I had a clockwork Hornby train set which needed endless winding up for it to run round the track laid on the floor. At home we all played card games, particularly whist and high, low, Jack, with a whist drive taking up at least half the evening at the annual Christmas Day party. About 16 to 20 people would be present on these occasions, with two sittings necessary to eat the dinner in view of the smallness of the house. My grandma, with her excellent appetite, always sat through both these sittings and thoroughly enjoyed the food, which had mainly been prepared by herself anyhow, with everybody else joining in and doing as they were told to help her. The party, after the full 24 games of whist had been played and duly recorded on the whist drive cards and prizes presented to the winning lady and gent, would continue with various games such as charades, the group being divided into two competing teams trying to beat each other in finding the hidden word being acted.

My father was employed as a boiler firer at Taylor & Lodge's mill in Folly Hall on the Lockwood road, and once every six weeks he had to work on Sundays to de-scale the boilers, by climbing inside them and clearing the boiler walls as best he could in that cramped position. On these occasions my sister and I had to walk to Primrose Hill Sunday School by a more roundabout route to take his dinner. Dad's daily work consisted of feeding the two hoppers high up at the front of the boilers by shovelling the solid fuel into them from the coke pile high on the floor behind him, thus keeping a steady supply to the fires fed by gravity from these hoppers. It was very hard work shovelling coal or coke above head height and as a result he developed muscles as hard as iron from this constant upward action. Like others doing this type of work, Dad wore clogs, which were ideal as the wooden soles were virtually unaffected by the heat if he happened to tread on a hot piece of coke that would have ruined a pair of boots.

After Sunday School was over, my sister and I sometimes called at nearby Prince Street in Primrose Hill where Dad had for some time been brought up with the spinster sisters and their brother who lived there. During this time, although some of the details remained obscure to me, I was told that some of Dad's relations came up from London to take him back there and this attempt to 'kidnap' him was only foiled when they were at Huddersfield station with him, on the point of leaving. In the event it was thwarted and Dad was brought back to 'Uncle Sam's', were he stayed until joining the regular army for a seven-year stint in the local Duke of Wellington's regiment. After serving his time and the ensuing period on reserve, he was not eligible to be called up again when the First World War broke out, but nevertheless, like so many others, did so after a while. Patriotism was very strong at that time, with the billboards full of such pictures of Kitchener pointing towards the reader with the caption 'Your country needs you' and provoking a sense of duty to join up. Fortunately, he came back unharmed after the war and resumed his former work.

On Sundays he attended the Pleasant Sunday Afternoon at the Queen Street Mission in Huddersfield and I well remember him coming home with a large red book as a prize from the PSA entitled *Britain's Best Pictures*. Inside, it was in loose-leaf form, each picture held in place by the smallest amount of glue so that it could be easily removed and framed for hanging on the wall. One happy memory of my father was when he brought me some sweets home, after going to town, which were really a form of biscuit made in the shapes of the letters of the alphabet and not sweets at all.

My mother had a friend who married a 'gentleman farmer' as he was called, and moved away from Huddersfield to Galphay, a small village some five miles or so from Ripon in North Yorkshire, and I was to spend many happy hours of my childhood during school holidays at their farm. I thoroughly enjoyed being there and did learn quite a lot about the day-to-day running of the farm by driving the horse and trap, feeding the hens, collecting eggs, milking the cows by hand – this latter art no mean achievement as among other things it is necessary to know which side of the cow to sit on otherwise the cow would soon object by lifting one leg up all the time and knocking the bucket away.

Haytime in particular was very hard work, especially when I was not very old, as the rakes seemed enormous in size and cumbersome to use. Every two hours all the workers helping with haymaking had 'drinkings' brought out to them in the fields and, apart from the tea, a whole range of home-made scones and other types of food. This was most welcome and everybody was always ready for them as the work was hard to do with the wooden rakes and somewhat primitive tools available in the 1930s. In the evenings I set up a lot of snares or 'snickles' as they were called, to catch rabbits, which lived in the nearby wooded area in large numbers. This work was quite an art as the snare had to be both set in the right place on the 'run' and also at the correct height when the rabbit was jumping. Rabbits always ran and jumped in exactly the same place, which could easily be seen by looking along the run and noting the level of grass in between each jump.

Thursday was market day at Ripon, with the weekly collection of eggs being taken there for sale, along with such other items as farm-made butter and cheese. One of my jobs was to haggle with the market men to obtain the best price for my rabbits, which the farmer had already cleaned for me before I went to the market. Naturally Thursday was the highlight of the week, when I would have the pleasure of driving the horse and trap back and forth to Ripon.

Making butter with a churn was slow and somewhat boring work, especially on occasions when it seemed never-ending waiting for the butter to solidify. This farm butter was white in colour and tasted quite nice on either bread or scones. I shall never forget the gorgeous plum pies in particular, topped with the farm cream and really delicious to eat. Similarly the lovely scent of sweet peas on the table on entering was a welcome not easily forgotten. Skeefe House will always be remembered with affection and happy memories.

One way of spending a day's holiday at home was for us to walk to Blackmoorfoot Reservoir, about three or four miles away, then on to Helme and finally end up in Meltham, returning either by bus or train to the nearby Lockwood station about five minutes' walk from home. The 'ramble' as it was called, was a very healthy, cheap way of spending a day in the open air, of which there certainly was plenty on these moors by Blackmoorfoot. Our doctor recommended the air on these moors as being in his opinion just as good as going to Blackpool for the bracing offshore breezes there, and certainly much cheaper. The only holiday I can remember having as a boy apart from the farm at Ripon, was at Blackpool for a week. Other trips out would be on a daily basis by weekly rail 'runabout' tickets which gave unlimited travel over a small area but including the coastal resorts.

2

Huddersfield College

Despite missing part of the lessons at primary school due to the continuing visits to the clinic, I was able to pass the entrance examination to go to high school. My first choice was to attend Huddersfield College, which was considered by most people to be the best secondary school for boys in the town. Again I was lucky to be accepted, being of only average ability. Accordingly I arrived there to commence the new year in September 1931 at the age of approximately 11½ and was placed in Form 1B situated on the ground floor of this rather foreboding-looking building, built with large black rectangular stones, on one side of New North Road about a quarter of a mile from the town centre.

The system of dividing boys into various forms was on the basis of the brightest ones being allocated to Form A, and the B form, in the first year only, taking all other boys except Catholics, who were put into Form C. Indeed, the Catholics went into 2C and 3C as the years went by, irrespective of academic achievement. Each form had its own form master, with pupils being divided equally between the various houses on arrival at the school, thus making six different divisions keeping together during the whole of their school career. Each house had its own name and colour, which was reflected in the two stripes on the front and back of the caps. I was allocated to Kelvin House and my cap had red stripes, with a similar colour for my football jersey, whilst other houses wore yellow, green, mauve and blue. The college colours were green and yellow. The school ties were made with these colours in a diagonal pattern and broad stripes, although another style had a self colour background and the

12

Huddersfield coat of arms on it.

New boys needed a school blazer and a complete football kit of jersey, white pants, boots and shin pads. The playing fields for both cricket and football were just a short walk away along Highfields and they also served on the annual sports day for the various races, which besides giving individual prizes awarded points to the house of the winners. The main prize was called the Victor Ludorum, which when I studied Latin in the second year I was able to translate into meaning the person who gained most points taking all games into consideration.

The main building at the college contained the gymnasium, form rooms all round it and separate rooms for such activities as chemistry, physics, art and so on, with classes moving from one room to another as required. The morning session consisted of four periods of 40 minutes' duration with a short break halfway through to enable the boys to visit the tuck shop and the toilets. Three periods took place in the afternoons, with some subjects such as football taking two consecutive periods. This also applied to some morning subjects.

As I lived some two miles or more away from this new school this entailed quite a long walk from Crosland Moor to Paddock foot triangle and then up Gledholt Bank, through Greenhead Park and down to New North Road and the school there. In view of both the time taken to make this journey and the fact that to go the town way seemed such a long way round and meant paying bus fares as well, the only thing to do at dinner times was to stay in school and take something to eat with me. This more often than not consisted of bread and bananas and only on a very few occasions was I able to pay for the hot meal that was provided for pupils who could afford this luxury.

In the first year all forms had to do two homeworks, each of the two subjects being supposed to take 30 minutes for the average student to complete, whilst in subsequent years three of similar duration had to be done. Books, pencils, pens, rubbers, drawing materials etc. were carried to and from school in a leather schoolbag which had one large pocket and a second smaller one sewn on the outside for textbooks. Two straps and buckles fastened these bags and on the small pocket were the initials of

13

the student, printed when the bag was bought. A good leather schoolbag formed an excellent substitute for a sledge down Gledholt Bank after a fall of snow but unfortunately this was detrimental to the bag itself. However, the damage was hidden from view, being on the underside.

Nearly all the college masters wore their black gowns all day when teaching, and on the first day looked a very awe-inspiring sight to the new boys, who had never seen anything like it before and arrived there wondering just what to expect. Our form master in 1B was a Mr Leonard Fouracre, and as the boys invariably had a nickname for all the masters I will resist the temptation to say what his was. There was a Mr 'Piggy' Blake, so named because of his piercing eyes and disapproving look which could send shivers down anyone's spine, whilst 'Billy' Marsden, another English teacher, had exactly the opposite temperament, being a very mild-mannered man. His riposte to me personally, on asking me a question to which I did not know the answer, would be, 'Walkley, the things you don't know would fill a big book.' Suitably admonished, I would sink still lower in my desk. The headmaster, Mr H.E. Atkins, was naturally referred to as 'Tommy' by all the boys and was a very slim, grey-haired man of unknown years who was never known to raise his voice, such was the esteem in which he and the other masters were held. Once a year he would take on all challengers at chess, which was one of the popular games at the college and one which gave points to the winning house team in their competitions. Moving round from one table to another he could quickly make up his mind which piece to move, and proceed to the next opponent.

At the annual Speech Day held in Huddersfield Town Hall all the masters wore their best gowns, decorated round the shoulders with various colours according to the degree in which they had qualified, and presented a colourful display compared with the normal dowdy-looking black worn during daytime school lessons. Our school song was called 'Forty Years On' and had rather a rousing tune with words to match, and it was sung with gusto by all the boys, probably in the knowledge that the proceedings were coming to an end and we would soon be able to stand up after two hours sitting listening to speeches. It was the custom for either the headmaster or the principal guest speaker to announce either a day or half-day holiday to follow the Speech Day, which always raised a cheer from the rows of bare-kneed boys sitting in front of the organ.

During my first year at the college I continued to have the same treatment for my ears at the clinic, which was now somewhat nearer than when I had to go there from Crosland Moor on the other side of the town. These visits obviously continued to disrupt my lessons to a certain extent but at the end of the term I usually obtained a result somewhere in the middle of the form for most subjects but near the top for mathematics and languages.

My worst subjects were geography and history, the latter being almost a waste of time in my opinion as what has happened is dead and gone, and although it naturally affects the present and the future, it is these that are more important to me. Our history master, nicknamed 'Bessie' Baldick because of his nature, could be persuaded to talk about any subject on the slightest pretext and was egged on by the boys themselves. Chess and football were the main themes guaranteed to leave history completely lost and forgotten. This situation occurred so regularly that I decided to analyse a 40 minute period on the different subjects talked about and the length of time spent on each, with the rather expected result that history took just ten minutes of the whole lesson. Small wonder that I lost interest in the subject, as I have a very strong feeling about waste of any kind, whether time or materials. He was the only master, in my opinion, who seemed to deviate from the very high standard of the otherwise excellent staff but perhaps others who like history might take a different view.

It was about this time that I joined Lockwood Rehoboth Boy Scouts, which caused a conflict of interest as I had been attending the Primrose Hill Sunday School for such a long time. Being in the Scouts, I was expected to go on Scouts' Parade on the first Sunday in each month, after which the Cubs and Scouts would occupy the two front rows of the chapel for the morning service. No doubt, looking back, they would be able to keep an eye on us better and avoid any mischief that might otherwise have occurred. After much heartache my mother allowed me to leave Primrose Hill and go to the Rehoboth chapel, which was only some two or three hundred yards away, and naturally I liked this far better than the long walk to Primrose Hill and back.

One of the advantages of being a member of the Rehoboth was the fact that a building next door, owned by the chapel, had a billiard table, which later I was able to use free of charge during Wednesday afternoons when the institute, as it was known, would normally be closed. The hall was used for adult afternoon meetings on Sundays, with guest speakers from all walks of life coming to give talks. One of these was a Mr Douglas Clark, who kindly gave me his autograph, attaching the words 'World's champion wrestler, undefeated'. This was a great thrill to me as Mr Clark, who was a coalman, was reputed to be the only man who could hold a sack of coal in each hand at arms' length; these sacks always weighed one hundredweight each. I never saw this feat myself, or indeed met anyone who had, but the story was certainly believed by the boys.

At the start of my second year I found myself in 2D which was the lowest second-year form, there being no D form in the first year – doubtless due to my own failings and the effect of time lost from lessons. Latin was taught in the second and subsequent years, our Latin master being a certain Flying Officer W.B. Cass, RAF, which at my age sounded very impressive and was no doubt due to his wartime service. He was a small, dapper man, well liked by all and I learned quickly from him, having some aptitude for and interest in languages. For some reason that I still do not know examination marks for Latin were set at 200 whereas all other subjects had a maximum of 100 marks. To me the only consolation of being in 2D was the fact that I became top of the form every odd week whilst another boy, Ashcroft, took the top place on alternate weeks. It was almost uncanny how this situation developed but it occurred consistently throughout the year. Better to be top of 2D than bottom of 2B, I kept telling myself – at least it sounded better.

Towards the end of my second year, in the May of 1933, my father died in his early fifties, and as my sister had been recently married and left home to live in Lockwood this left only three of us at home. The shock of his death seemed to have the effect of stopping me growing for a while, or at least I thought so at the time. My mother's widow's pension was 37½ pence weekly and together with Grandma's old age pension of 50 pence was the sum total of our household income, apart from anything that I could bring in to help. On Saturday mornings I ran errands for a lady in Lockwood, receiving some small payment, the amount of which I cannot remember now. At that time every penny counted more than ever. I applied for what I think was then called a maintenance grant, a type of £25 scholarship payable over a two-year period with three payments of £3.33 in the first year and three of £5 each in the second year. To the best of my knowledge this grant was intended to help needy people and had no test or examination involved.

Certain weekends during the summer the Scouts would hold a camp in a field at Healey House in between Netherton and Meltham some three or four miles from the Rehoboth, and we had to push or pull a trek cart loaded with camping equipment to get there. This involved a long hill climb through Big Valley before reaching the village of Netherton, from where the road was either level or downhill. In fine weather we enjoyed these camps but we had a bad habit of wakening up at about three or four o'clock on Sunday morning, probably after a not very comfortable sleep. On one occasion when this happened the monthly Scouts' Parade fell due and on arriving at the chapel for morning service we all fell asleep on the two front rows, to the consternation of the Rev. Colin Edwards delivering his sermon. At least no one could say that we hadn't been quiet.

Another way of bringing in some money was to have a Christmas Club a few months prior to the occasion and this was quite successful with neighbours and friends paying in small weekly amounts and ordering their boxes of chocolates in advance. I also did a similar idea with Christmas cards and calendars, the latter from a very attractive album and printed with the buyers' name to make a more personal type of card. I extended this club idea by having a chocolate club with supplies purchased at wholesale prices from a town shop and carrying this on all the year round. The profit was either ploughed back to increase the selection of stock or saved up in a little round money box supplied by the Yorkshire Penny Bank, as it was then known, or it was

17

simply passed along to my mother to swell the pension money.

Once a year at hot cross bun time, I worked for Heeley's the local baker's situated on the corner of May Street which adjoined Church Avenue. The method of selling these buns was to call round as many houses as possible beforehand to get orders and then deliver them on the great day, collecting payment at the same time. Heeley's paid me 1½d per dozen buns sold, which was all grist to the mill so to speak but could only be done once a year.

My mother was appointed a part-time organiser for the Liberal Party (she was Secretary of the Crosland Moor Women's Liberal Club for about 25 years) and the work entailed knocking on doors in various districts, trying to persuade people to join the party and, hopefully, to pay an annual subscription of 4s 4d, the rate then being one old penny per week for the full year. I believe there was also a cheaper membership fee of 5 pence per annum for another category known as 'shilling members'. The pay was not very good but it all helped in our position at that time.

The next year at Huddersfield College found me in Form 3D with much the same routine as in 2D, both these years' classes being taught in a separate building from the college main building called 'the House' – probably it had been used for domestic reasons in times gone by. The fourth and fifth years at the college were in a sort of intermediate level and called Remove A and Remove B. The 'A' classes continued as before until the sixth form. The ultimate examination was called the Matric, an abbreviation of the official title of the Joint Matriculation Board Examination, and this necessitated passing with five credits from specified categories of subjects or groups. As geography and history were in one group I considered that I had no chance of passing my Matric, but there was a lower level called the School Certificate, whilst at the other end of the scale the best pupils could pass with distinction, which would no doubt help some to decide whether or not to stay on till the age of 18 and go in for the Higher School Certificate.

Life carried on mainly as before in my last two years at college with the exception that, in order to sit for a Civil Service examination, I had to study for an entirely different syllabus which I found most difficult. My aunt, Miss Bamford, coached me in her spare time. The end result was that I did not do as well in either examination as I might have done had I not been swotting for both at the same time. From memory, I obtained either one or two credits in the Matric but came fourth out of all Huddersfield in the open Civil Service examination. This was most disappointing, bearing in mind that only two candidates would be successful in obtaining a job. I would point out that in the 1930s any Civil Service position at all was considered to be just about the ultimate one could achieve, firstly as it was a job for life and secondly because there was a pension at the end of it. This situation was reflected by the fact that examination candidates were willing to pay 50 pence just to sit the examination. To show just how much 50 pence was worth at that time, the first weekly wage I received some two or three years later was a princely sum of 60 pence for a full week's work of about 50 hours.

During the summer of 1936 I spent about six happy weeks at the farm previously mentioned, awaiting the results of both the examinations with some trepidation and certainly not a lot of confidence but nevertheless enjoying the farm life for this last opportunity. On hearing the result for the Civil Service exam I was naturally deeply disappointed, but this was short-lived and spirits rose dramatically on receiving a letter to the effect that the list of successful candidates had been extended to include my name. Deliriously happy, I completed the medical questionnaire form sent with the letter and in reply to the question, 'Have you ever suffered from running from the ears?' I naturally and truthfully answered, 'Yes', having been brought up to be strictly honest at all times.

Some time later I was asked to attend a medical at Leeds by an aurist by the name of Dr Munby for his opinion on my ears, and this was to be at my own expense. I dared not miss any opportunity at this stage, so I duly paid the fee and went to Leeds. The outcome was that the offer of employment was turned down on medical grounds so that all the studying and expense had been completely in vain. Devastated by this decision, I wrote a bitter letter to the local paper explaining the position as I saw it and pointing out that the suggested treatment of the ear specialist was exactly the opposite to the 'dry-mopping' treatment given to me over such a long period of time. The crux of the matter was simply water. On one side the advice was on no account should water be allowed to enter the ears and on the other side syringing (with water) was put forward as the correct treatment. Naturally I was confused with the conflicting advice and resentful of the lost opportunity to join the Civil Service for which (rightly or wrongly) I blamed the Huddersfield Clinic. I well remember signing the letter 'Despised and Rejected', so bitter did I feel at that time, realising just how much I had lost through no fault of my own. When visiting our family doctor I related what had happened, and he gave me to understand that if I had not mentioned the running from the ears the medical people would never have known. I had had one of my first lessons on the effects that honesty can have on a person's life.

I now felt I was at a crossroads in life, having reached the age of 16½ by the time I left school and with only a School Certificate to show for it. A decision had to be taken on my future, although I can say that at that time I had a completely open mind on the matter and no real preferences. Previously I had tried to obtain work in a local architect's office where my Sunday School teacher, a local alderman, was in a high position, but I was not accepted. Having taken art and architecture at Huddersfield College instead of the physics and chemistry grouping, I had done some extremely neat, tidy and accurate work and spent some of my spare time at home drawing scale plans of the roads in the area round our house. Mathematics were, of course, my forte as I had learned from experience the value of adding up and multiplying during my various attempts to make money for home.

I now started seriously to look for work through the local paper as their advertisements seemed to be the best medium for trying to obtain work even in the Depression of the 1930s. There were many unemployed so that inevitably a large number of applicants chased every vacancy on offer. One evening my uncle came to the house asking if I had seen the advertisement for a boy to train in a clog making, boot repairing and retail shop which I had already seen and passed over as not really being what I was hoping for. I thought that I could do better if I got the chance, but chances were very few and far between then. My uncle pointed out to me that, should I ever go deaf in later years, if I had a 'trade in my fingers', to use his words, then I would always be able to make a living. The logic of this was patently obvious and I slowly and reluctantly warmed to the idea.

Accordingly, before eight o'clock the following morning when the shop opened, I presented myself with boots blacked at 29 Northgate at the bottom end of town near a very rough area, to be interviewed by the proprietor. Mr Herbert Hays was a man in his sixties with a reddish face somewhat marked on his neck, the result, I was later to learn, of a motor accident when he had been so badly injured as to be left for dead. His first action after looking at me was to lean over the shop counter and take a good look at my boots, which were, thanks to the lessons learnt from Mr Senior at primary school, absolutely shining, and this no doubt immediately gave a good impression. The fact that I was almost too old at nearly 17 can be gauged from realising that in the 1930s most boys left school at 14 years old, and this age gap certainly went against me. However, a few days later Mr Hays must have decided to give me a try. He offered me 60 pence for my weekly wage, as if I took the job of a 14 year-old I could only expect to receive that level of wage. The hours were from 8.00 a.m. to 8.00 p.m. on Mondays, Tuesdays and Thursdays, with early closing at 1.00 p.m. on Wednesday. Friday's hours were from 8.00 a.m. to 8.00 p.m. and Saturday 8.00 a.m. to 9.00 p.m., making a total of just over 50 hours per week after deducting the one-hour break at lunchtime and a half-hour at tea-time, both of these breaks being dependent on whether anyone happened to come into the shop during these times, when obviously they had to be attended to. Being the last one to be employed at the shop, it fell to me to deal with customers calling during breaks whilst the other two men had an uninterrupted meal. It is quite surprising how quickly one can chew food running up a flight of stairs, through the trapdoor and into the shop behind the counter. Unknown to me at this time, this was to be the start of a whole lifetime in the clog trade which was to bring me finally to having the complete monopoly of clog making in the United Kingdom.

3

A First Step in Clogs

Having obtained work at long last, I threw my heart and soul into learning all I could, encouraged as time went by when Mr Hays said he wanted me to be able to take over when he eventually retired. The shop itself was an old building in a row of shops and was rented from a Mr Raymond Cockcroft, who had a chemist's shop further along Northgate on the same side of the road. Clog making was done in the cellar and a trapdoor from one corner of the shop behind the counter led into it down a wooden staircase. Another cellar reached out under the pavement at the front of the shop and this was full of old tea chests which held the stock of wooden clog soles, separated in their styles and sizes. A low bench for clogging was sufficient for two men sitting side by side, with myself at the end.

At my side was a large empty tin can with a long piece of string tied to it passing upwards through the floor and fastened to the shop door so that when anyone opened the door this tin can would rattle upwards, and then downwards as the door closed again. Customers must have wondered how we knew anyone had come in when one of our heads appeared through the trapdoor. A neat lesson from the boss in making something costing nothing and yet completely effective for its purpose. At least it was so until the string eventually wore thin and broke and had to have a knot tied in it.

At one side of the cellar a wooden rack held the stock of made-up clogs in their various types and sizes. At the far end of the cellar stood an old iron stove, heated by coke and used to heat the room and to keep a bucket of water warm enough for dipping

22

clog uppers in to soften the leather ready for lasting. Nearby stood a 'knocking off' machine, a cast-iron contraption on three legs which was used, as its name implied, for knocking off the soles before replacing with new ones. It was worked by means of a long iron handle moved up and down, forcing a vertically held chisel end to break the wood away from the welt, taking care not to damage the upper leather in the process. The machine was also used to perform the same function with men's heavy boots, which were mainly made at that time by the 'screwed and stitched' method of manufacture. The pressure that could be exerted by this very simple method reminded me of the principle of the lever, about which I had been taught at school.

Knocking off the soles of clogs ready for re-clogging became my first task on Monday mornings, the clogs having been brought into the shop the previous Friday or Saturday. Once the wooden soles had been removed from the uppers, any necessary patching or stitching would be done prior to replacing new soles onto the uppers, making them almost as good as new. After soles had been removed from working boots the upper had to be trimmed round by hand, using a rather long-bladed knife to cut the surplus leather away to take the shape of the wooden soles. Cod oil was then brushed onto the upper, which was immersed in the warm water bucket, and with both hands I would work the leather by rubbing and flexing it so that the cod oil soaked into the pores of the leather. Good working boots could be bought for $2\frac{1}{2}$ pence per pair when they were worn out and past repairing as the uppers were still serviceable. After making up into clogs these were sold at $27\frac{1}{2}$ pence and were known as 'old tops'. Some buyers preferred these to buying new clogs as the uppers were usually made from softer leathers and needed no breaking in. I learned that after the First Word War when surplus army boots were being auctioned off, the worn ones were bought by Mr Hays at one halfpenny per pair and delivered to Huddersfield station in three large railway trucks. How long it took to make them all up into old tops I do not know as I arrived on the scene some 15 years later.

The clog uppers were cut out by Mr Hays himself in one corner of the cellar which had been fitted up as a cutting bench with a shelf underneath to hold the leather. On the top of the bench lay a large marble slab similar to that used by fishmongers and on which a piece of cardboard was placed. This cardboard arrived at the shop in cartons with the boots and shoes and provided an unlimited free supply, necessary as the knives would soon render the cardboard unusable when a lot of cutting had been done. Most of the clog patterns had also been made from this cardboard but a few were made using zinc sheeting, which, although it would last almost indefinitely, could easily damage the knife blade if care was not taken during the cutting process. The skill in cutting, or 'clicking' as it was known in the trade, was in the handling of each side of leather and being able to decide by feeling it just which part of the upper should be cut from any given part of the side. An apprenticeship of five years or more was necessary to be fully acquainted with the many and varied types of leather used in some footwear manufacturing firms and the only local one big enough to train any apprentices was the Co-operative Wholesale Society's Heavy Boot Factory at Heckmondwike.

After cutting out the various shapes to make the uppers the next process was 'skiving', which means thinning down the leather wherever two pieces were to be sewn together. To do this the cardboard was removed from the cutting bench and the skiving done on the marble slab, which was ideal for this purpose, enabling the four- or five-inch-long blade of the skiving knife to make a perfect skive according to the hand pressure exerted on it. The parts of the simplest kind of clog uppers comprised the back, vamp (front), tongue and stiffener, which was also called a 'counter'. The backs were then ready for eyeletting, that is, first punching holes for the laces and then inserting the brass eyelets. This was done in two separate operations on the eyeletting machine. Two pedals, foot operated some three inches or so from the floor, were made with one longer than the other to enable them to be used individually for each of the two stages in eyeletting. Spacing was done automatically by a simple hand setting to suit all men's sizes and starting the punching from the edge accordingly to make an even matching row on each side. The operator had to stand on one leg, use both hands to steady and hold the back level, and use the other foot to depress the foot pedal to punch or eyelet according to the pedal used. Great care had to be taken operating this machine and one Saturday morning I put the punch through my thumbnail by mistake, which was very painful but taught me to treat the machine with much more respect in the future. It never happened again. Looking on the bright side if I had been using the other pedal I might have had an eyelet through the thumb instead of just a hole.

After eyeletting, the backs were now ready for closing. A half-moon-shaped stiffener was sewn centrally inside, with a small amount of it showing below the back to be trimmed off later. Two rows of good waxed linen thread were sewn onto all parts of the uppers as clogs were mainly to be used for rough work and this saved much stitching and repairing later as the clogs were usually brought back for repair to the shop where they had been purchased originally. Having sewn the stiffener into the back, a tongue was then sewn onto the vamp and finally back and vamp were sewn together to complete the clog upper. The type of sewing machine used in those days was a treadle-operated 45K heavy-duty Singer, which was placed centrally in the remaining space in the cellar.

It will be noted that in a small clog-making business in the 1930s virtually all the work had to be done by hand without any electrically driven machines available to us. This obviously was unnecessarily time-consuming and made production a slow and laborious task only tolerated because of the low wages paid to cloggers. I might add that as far as the boot repairing side was concerned, a large number of war-wounded soldiers were trained for this purpose after demobilisation as the trade was considered as not being particularly skilled and men could run their own one-man shops to make a living; but this was only done by working extra-long hours which quickly became the norm.

Having made the uppers, or 'tops' as they were more generally known, they had to be attached to the clog soles after lasting, but the wooden soles themselves had to have some form of material nailed to them to provide the wearing qualities. Wood clog soles, although made from beech, would not last long otherwise. The accepted materials for 99 per cent of clogs made at that time were called clog 'irons' and made from a mild steel strip, bent and cut to shape and forged in a furnace before having the nail holes punched in them. This was again a trade in its own right, with many clog iron manufacturers even having their own association. Heel irons had four holes and sole irons either seven or eight according to the size. Children's sizes had only three holes in the heels and six in the sole part. The measurement for the length of sole irons was taken from the centre of the toe end to the end of the longest leg of the iron as they had to be made with the longer part fitted to the outside of the sole. As an example, a size 7 inch clog sole iron was the most popular men's size as this fitted a size 8 in boot sizes. Incidentally, for some unknown reason clogs were numbered three sizes higher than boot sizes, which caused a lot of confusion for people who were not aware of this. For measuring clog soles a wooden 'size stick' was calibrated in both boot and clog sizes and had a small metal end on it to be held against the toe end of the clog sole in the 'grip'.

Special nails called tip nails were made with a groove along the length and I was taught to pick them up from the nail tin on my bench, holding the groove to the inside of the clog iron, which helped to eliminate or minimise cracking the wood. Any cracking was a complete disaster as there was no way to close up a crack satisfactorily. Nails of differing lengths had to be used for the different nail holes in the irons, the large one-inch ones, six in all for the sole iron had two each at the toe end and the waist, where the strain or pull was the greatest in wear, and two in the heel iron at the front part of it; all other holes needed only smaller nails to bed the irons neatly and firmly round the rim of the wooden sole. As the grain of the wood was always from toe to heel, care had to be taken when hammering the tip nails in and it was necessary to have a solid base for this purpose.

When ironing, cloggers used a 'stithy', also called a 'stiddy', made from cast iron with a round base where a man's foot could be placed on either side to hold it steady, an upright rod of some inch and a half in diameter and with the top, usually rounded. larger than the stithy itself after constant usage. An 'S' shaped piece for inserting into a clog to re-iron the sole part was fixed from the main rod at a height just above the knees of the clogger in the sitting position. An alternative to the stithy was a 'peg-leg', similar to a stithy in shape but without the curved section for sole ironing and enclosed in a circular wooden piece held between the thighs when ironing clog soles.

Having secured the clog irons firmly to the wooden soles, the next step was to attach the upper. As already mentioned, some types of leather uppers, mainly the waxed split leathers, had to be dipped in warm water prior to lasting. The method of hand lasting taught at that time was to use wooden lasts which were 'straight', that is, neither left or right feet in shape. The upper with the wet vamp was held by the clogger on his apron between his thighs and the wooden last slipped inside,taking care to keep it straight. A two-inch-long nail was hammered into the last near the toe end of the upper, the last was then knocked down lower into the upper and finally lasted using lasting pincers and fixing two further nails at each side. If not lasted completely to the wooden shape, a nail would be taken out and the upper re-lasted by pulling it tighter by hand and then re-nailing when it was satisfactory. This continual holding of the clog upper by hand whilst hammering the nails into the last made a clogger's handgrip almost like a vice.

The upper was next 'slickered', using a two-handled steel tool some 15 to 18 inches long and kept warm by resting on a cradle over a Bunsen burner. The backwards and forwards action of this tool with its semi-circular working shiny steel surface produced a gloss to the leather very quickly and set it in shape as it dried out. The five nails were then taken out of the last to release the upper, which was then placed in the recess, or welt, at the back of the clog sole and, after checking for being centrally placed, secured by a welt nail $1\frac{1}{8}$ inches long.

By trial and error and experience, over a period of time a learner became proficient at making a slight adjustment when putting the upper on to form either a left or a right foot. The shape of the left or right clog sole helped to do this by the contours of its manufacture. After fastening the upper at the back, the toe end was nailed down and, using a very short-bladed knife, the upper was cut neatly round, following the shape of the grip. It was then tacked down, using two or three nails at each side, usually spaced to enable a nail to hold the end of the stitching at the waist and stiffener for extra security.

The clog was then 'nailed round', which was one of the apprentice's first tasks before being allowed to do any lasting. A vast range of metal toetins in brass, iron or copper was available for use on the various types of clogs made, with the cheapest having an iron toetin and better-quality ones having brass ones. The brewers' clogs invariably had a large copper toetin to match the copper welting. The toetins were nailed into the welt using similar metal clog welt nails, leaving the last hole open to enable the clog welting to be slid under the toetin to form a neat joining. The leather welting was skived about a quarter of an inch at each end of the nailing-round process for this purpose. Short nails were used for the fore part of the nailing round, and the longer ones from the waist right round the back where all the pull took place in wear.

The making of the clogs now completed, they were then 'sized' by using a small sponge soaked in a black jelly-like substance, called Tip Top Dressing to give it its correct name, thus producing a shiny finish to both the upper leather and the wooden sole, the latter having been blacked round the edge with edge ink before sizing. Once dry, the clogs were tied up in pairs ready for sale.

The leather welting had to be prepared for use in two separate stages, first cutting the leather to the width of the clog sole grip and then skiving one edge only, which was nailed to the top part of the upper, leaving a right-angle section in the welt. In order to perform both operations, a flat piece of wood was placed on the knees with the grain of the wood running from side to side, which enabled the knife blade to cut into the wood easily, and by placing the thumb and forefinger correctly, holding the knife upright, the welting could be cut to width with the right hand holding the knife and the left hand pulling the strip of leather sideways to the left hand side. This could take two or three pulls as the material used would be about four or five feet long. A 'V' shape about half an inch in depth was cut out of the middle of the same board on the far edge of the sitting position of the clogger and, by holding the knife blade in a position across the cut-out, the welting strip was pulled through the aperture, causing one of the edges to be skived all along the length. When welting the clog the skived section would be away from the welt edge of the clog sole and form a very neat joining against the upper, thus creating a waterproof bond.

We were indebted to the textile trade for supplies of corrugated and rubber leathers, and the welting material was originally used by the cardnailers in their work for fastening the carding to the machines. The strip cut off as excess was in the region of two or more inches wide.Only the very best oak bark tanned leather was used for this purpose but as scrap it was sold to us at threepence per pound. The bulk of carding was tanned by Holdsworths, one of the oldest Huddersfield firms, who sent it all over the world wherever textile machinery was used. Whilst we in the north of England had a plentiful supply available, clog manufacturers in the south used copper welting, made in the same width as the clog sole grip of course. This latter became traditional welting for the then very extensive fish-dock trade all around the coast of the United Kingdom.

The clog irons had differing names in various parts of the country, being called 'caulkers' in the northeast and northwest but 'tips' in the London area. A slightly narrower section of mild steel was used in the making of clog sole irons compared with the heels, which tend to have more wear. In order to fit the various shapes of clog soles, the irons were similarly made in shape as required. In Huddersfield we used the 'duck' toe shape on nearly all clogs except the 'old tops', which, originally having been boots, looked better with a round or 'common' toe. The London toe clog sole had a squarish toe shape and a 'boot' heel about half an inch longer than the common toe sole and needed a boot-shaped heel iron very similar to the heelplates fitted to men's working boots, which were, incidentally, made on the same clog iron machine, known as the heel bender. The 'Lancashire' clog sole had a rather short heel and rounded toe, the 'Leeds' toe was somewhat squarish like the London toe.

Some special patterns of clog soles were made for specific trades, such as the brewers sole used in both breweries and on the fish docks. These soles were thicker than the average patterns due to the excess water involved and measured one inch below the grip. Naturally these were heavier and cost more, in view of the extra timber used. Very often both these industries preferred the soles to be dipped in oil to make them extra waterproof and this was done at a small extra charge. Working on the fish docks, there was a constant stream of water running off the bottom of the apron onto the clogs below and even the brewers sole had to be made in yet a thicker pattern, called 'clumpers', which again because of the extra weight was really far too heavy to wear comfortably. Fortunately not a lot of actual walking about was necessary as most of the work was done by men standing in one position.

The 'bath sandal' sole had no grip at all but, being made without any heel, was simply contoured to the shape of the underside of the foot. A single strip of either leather or canvas about an inch wide was sufficient to hold the bath sandal on as men were only walking a short distance to and from the showers and the 'dry area'. The nailing of the instep strip was either brass or copper to avoid the rusting that would have been caused by iron nails. These clogs were called 'pattens'.

The most clumsy clog sole of all, made in various shapes, was the 'overshoe' clog sole, which was cut across the width to insert a steel hinge, similar to a door hinge and at least three inches wide, to give some flexibility. These were worn under their working boots by men on the slag heaps. The upper consisted of a strip of white duck canvas some four inches high nailed into the side of the clog sole, or into the grip if there was one, and only protected the back part of the foot. At the front another piece of canvas just wide enough to take a large sail eyelet was nailed on each side so that this could be tied up over the front of the boot while the back part was laced across the instep. This overshoe clog was also made from corrugated leather, according to the customer's choice. Another overshoe pattern had straps and buckles for their fastening instead of the sail eyelets and lacing method, and this style was liked most in the north-east and Sheffield areas. The heat on the slag heaps was such that conventional safety boots would have been ruined in no time at all and the overshoe clog, although very clumsy indeed, was proved to be satisfactory in use as there was only minimal walking about necessary.

It is impossible to put the 'nature' back into leather once it has been burnt, no matter whether the heat be a constant one like footwear being left to dry by a radiator or by sudden heat like boiling water. You will notice that when we used water for clog lasting this was warm and never hot, for this very reason.

I have explained in some detail how I was taught to make clogs by the methods used and the equipment available in the 1930s, bearing in mind that the accepted method of selling them was over the counter to the buyer himself. Accordingly they were made as attractive as could be by blacking the edges of the wooden soles and sizing them at the same time as the leather upper.

Just as different parts of the UK preferred their own shapes of clog soles, so varying styles of uppers appealed to the wearers in each area. In the West Riding of Yorkshire nearly all the clogs were of the 'Derby' pattern, where the back of the upper is sewn onto the vamp and with the tongue visible in between. These were made in different heights of back and had five, six or seven eyelets in each side accordingly. The 'pit' clog had a four-eyelet low back and in addition to the toetin often had both sideplates and backplates round the heel as wear took place all round the clog sole when miners were working in a sitting position with one leg under the other. In South Wales, Tyneside, Teesside and London the most popular style of upper was called the 'blucher' or 'flap and buckle blucher' and this style was also worn in the navy. The blucher had a low back, the stiffener being sewn on the outside and a fibre counter fitted in between for extra strength and fastened by the flap, which had the strap as well all in one piece of leather, and the 'chape' or buckle bit nailed under the welt on the outside of the foot. The strap part had three holes punched in and was set to fasten by the middle one. This style was made without the flap, which was riveted on by two bifurcated black japanned rivets after the clog had been made to ensure a perfect fit for the strap and buckle. Some blucher clogs had the stiffener pattern right up to the top of this low back in a shape known as the 'jockey back' from its obvious shape when sewn on. Other London clogs were the high-back Derby, at least six inches in height measured from the grip upwards and the wellington clog, which had a warm lining made from old army blankets for cheapness.

As men's clogs were usually worn for menial or hazardous work of some kind and were the cheapest form of footwear, clogmakers tried to obtain their raw materials as economically as possible, resulting in the use of 'residual' or second-hand leathers from the mills as the main source of supply. The textile industry provided these in the form of 'gill leathers' or 'combing leathers'. The gill box leathers were the wider ones and the combing leathers anything up to four and a half inches in width. Both types were driven by rollers with ribs on them to give a positive drive and prevent slipping, the strands of worsted or silk being fed through the machine by this action. Over a period of time the leathers of both kinds became uneven and were known as 'corrugated leathers'. Even with tons of pressure applied to make these leathers smooth again this was impossible and the corrugations remained during the life of the clog. Nearly all corrugated clog leathers were made from 'chrome' leather, which was quite dry, having no oils, waxes or dressing of any kind in it. A single skived joining about two inches wide formed the endless belt needed to stay on the machines and this joining had to be cut out as waste before we used them on clogs. One other type of corrugated leather was called 'sleeves'. Sleeves were much wider still than the gill leathers, probably in the region of 18 inches square, and were much sought after as they were invariably a lot softer than the gill or combing leathers. All chrome leathers were greenish in colour with one exception; when the leather used was not chrome it was brown and often quite hard in comparison.

The second-hand leather from the woollen mills provided the other cheap residual leather and these endless belts were in various lengths and widths but normally about five feet long. Invariably black in colour due to being fed with high-grade oils during their working life, they were known in the trade as 'rubbers', a most confusing misnomer if ever there was one but perfectly descriptive of the action as opposed to the material of these leathers. 'Rubbers' were used in pairs on a large machine about six or seven feet high incorporating four pairs of rollers on which the rubbers had been fitted, and the strands of wool would be driven through the machine about an inch or so apart. The rubbers thus got their name from the rubbing action of two leathers rubbing against each other by an oscillating sideways motion of about an inch. That part of the woollen mill engaged in this section of clothmaking was known as the 'scribbling' department. The slight indentations caused by the movement of these scribbling machines made a little difference to the surface of the leather but were hardly visible and certainly not detrimental to its use or appearance when made up. Only the very best leathers were made into rubbers as it was difficult to obtain an area of leather some 60 inches or so in length where the variations in the animal's skin did not have some parts liable to stretching, rendering it useless for this special purpose. Consequently, new rubbers were extremely expensive and if a firm was engaged on cheap shoddy clothmaking, they would use the rubbers until they almost dropped off the machines and were so thin as to be useless for either clog making or anything else.

The supplying and fixing of rubbers in the mills was the province of the cardnailers already mentioned as supplying the carding to us for welting purposes. This trade was usually performed by one man working for himself who was quite skilled in his trade. Apart from the cardnailers, our other suppliers of scrap leathers of all kinds were the very numerous 'tatters' who would go round the mills buying anything in the scrap line for cash, including old rope, rags, scrap metal etc., and then selling it to buyers such as ourselves for leather and scrap merchants for any old metal. A steady stream of these men called at the shop throughout the year offering leather to us. The carpet trade also used the corrugated type of leather but in their case the leathers were many feet wide and far too heavy and bulky to be used in clog making and rarely seen. Due to a plentiful supply of rubber leathers in the West Riding, we at Hays never used the corrugated leathers at all, considering that rubbers were far superior both in making and wearing.

The R/L clogs were sold at 25 pence per pair over the counter and this was the very cheapest the clogs were sold at. A 'chemical' clog for that trade was priced at 30 pence per pair, being made without any leather upper at all but using a

33

rubber/canvas material known as 'printers' blankets', another scrap material. Though excellent in quality for our purpose, it had been used in the new state for printing colour advertisements on cardboard cartons. Apparently any slight variation in the thickness due to wear resulted in the blanket being discarded. Had any type of leather been used for a chemical clog this would not have stood up to acid etc., as this rubber/canvas material did. The blankets, with holes down two opposite sides where they had been held on the rollers, were in the region of four feet square, which was about as big as could be easily handled during the initial cutting process, and were quite heavy relative to their size. The most popular leather of all for countrywide clog making was the waxed hide butt split, the word split referring to the original hide having been split through its thickness. Splits were made in three thickness grades, $2/2^1/2$, $2^1/2/3$ and $3/3^1/2$ millimetres, also in three selections of quality and two different dressings, firm or mellow. These variations resulted in a large variety being available. In the north of England the mellow dressing was favourite, being softer and more comfortable to wear, whilst the London manufacturers always used firm-dressed splits, which in my opinion were far too hard and I thought that anyone wearing them for the first time could easily be put off clogs for life as they would assume that all clogs were as uncomfortable.

Most waxed split dressers, or curriers as they were also called, tended to operate in the north or in the Bristol area, which was a highly productive area for men's heavy boots, some of which had waxed split leather uppers. The leather dressers could make differently finished leathers from the original splits so that in times of heavy fashion demand for suede leather they would make more of this and less into waxed splits, with the prices of each fluctuating according to the supply-and-demand situation.

Following the split clog retailing at 30 pence, the next higher price range was $32^1/2$ pence for a clog made from black grain leather, usually called the 'mill clog' as this type of leather readily absorbed the oil used profusely in the textile mills. Often mill floors looked as if they were soaked in oil accumulated over a period of time.

The very best quality of all for making clogs was kip leather

imported from eastern India and sold at the weekly auctions as EI
kips, followed by the weight range such as 40/60s and so on. Kip
is the whole hide and easily recognised by the pimply surface on
the flesh side of the leather. Imitations of kip were called 'kipola'
and made to look like kip by pressing a grain onto the underside.
We, along with many others, never used this material at all. Kip
clogs sold at 40 pence per pair and the uppers were fitted with a
half bellows tongue, also called a half-watertight tongue as it was
sewn half-way up the eyelets to make the clogs more waterproof.
These uppers, along with a similar style made from waxed split
leather which also had the half-watertight tongue, had a long
stiffener sewn into the back right round from one side to the other
and finishing at the waist, which made a better quality of upper.
Both these were bought in by Mr Hays because they needed
different machinery to make them and it was cheaper to buy them
rather than attempt to make our own, especially as the bulk of our
sales were for the lower-priced clogs.

Clasp clogs were mainly worn by women especially for
laundry work. This pattern had no tongue but a whole front,
which made them very difficult to last into shape despite being
soaked in warm water and lasted two or three times. The
fastening of the clasps, made from either black japanned iron or
brass, was made by inserting the male clasp on the right-hand side
of both feet through a slot cut on the instep of the leather and then
inserting the female clasp, setting it in position to fasten in the
middle of three holes. A right-handed person would simply use
that hand to fasten each clog, easier than fastening the clasps one
with the left hand and the other with the right, although when
fancy patterns were pressed onto the brass clasps they could look
odd if not done in lefts and rights. The black clasps had very little
pattern on them, which tended not to show up anyhow.

Other patterns for women's wear were the 'bar' clog, again
made from waxed split, having an open instep part and an integral
strap and back all cut in one piece. Because of the bar clog pattern
having the strap touching the back when cut from a flat piece of
leather, there was no way that a longer strap could be provided;
anyone with a higher instep than normal had to choose some
other pattern. The bar clog was fastened by means of a slot

punched by hand tool near the end of the strap and a black button riveted onto the back in a suitable position to fit the wearer's foot. To ensure a perfect fit this was done at the time of selling the clogs, literally in one minute.

For ordinary wear not needing a waxed split leather, a soft brown grain leather upper was made, ranging in size from the largest women's down to the smallest babies' size 3. Although never popular in our area, a pattern somewhat similar to a lace-up was made but instead of using eyelets had a narrow strap-and-buckle fastening, and this pattern was called the 'Dershu' an amalgamation of the words Derby and shoe.

For men a Sunday best clog, a whole-front low-back pattern made from waxed split, had an attractive pattern crimped into the thickness of the leather both on the vamp and on each side of the backs. The brass eyelets were inserted close together in a triangular 5, 4, 3, 2 and 1 formation to make a decorative pattern contrasting with the black of the leather. If a whole-vamp pattern was not used, a very long tongue was sewn upside down onto the vamp and turned over to reveal the outside of the leather and also decorated with a row of four eyelets down each side of the tongue, which could be laced as required to hold centrally onto the vamp.

Of these two variations the whole vamp pattern proved to be the more popular and I spent many of my Wednesday half-day 'holidays' designing attractive patterns for crimping. These were mainly butterflies or birds as opposed to a pattern design. After carefully crimping the pattern into the thickness of the leather, the pattern showed up quite well and it always seemed to me to be rather an anticlimax when the clog upper was sized, thus making the pattern less readily seen; time and wear would soon have done this anyhow, but they looked much better when first done. The hand-crimping tool was made from steel with two legs like a pair of dividers or compasses, one leg performing the cutting action by having a bent over curved part at the end. The waxes and oils in split leather tended to lubricate the cutting edge so that, with this type of leather, sharpening of the crimping tool was reduced to a minimum. Great care had always to be taken when crimping as one little slip cutting the leather in the wrong place would ruin the design and it could not be rectified in any way.

So far I have dealt in some detail with the clog side of the business, which was to become by far the most important to me in the future. When I joined H. Hays there was only one man clogging apart from the boss and myself, the boot repairing needing also just one cobbler. I had very little opportunity for practical learning in the boot repairing department but did learn a lot by watching and was able to use the finishing machine to scour the soles and edges, ink them and then polish on the revolving brushes fitted at one end of the machine.

It was customary to finish clog making at teatime on Fridays, have a quick wash and a snack, and then serve on in the shop till the 8 o'clock closing time. Similarly on Saturdays work ceased at dinnertime for the same reason, to leave all three of us available to serve customers till the 9 p.m. closing time. At certain times of the year there would be no one coming into the shop after 8 p.m. but the boss steadfastly refused to let me put the gates on so we had to wait till 9 p.m. to close, which thoroughly annoyed me as I had already worked the clock round by 8 p.m. and it seemed pointless staying open and wasting electricity, apart from our time.

I quickly learned the prices and location of the 3,000 or so pairs of footwear, which comprised a vast range for all the members of a working family. Babies' shoes in white, blue and champagne made like a slipper from a cloth patent material sold at 5 pence per pair, whilst the very dearest top-quality men's boots cost just under £1 per pair. Although joining as an apprentice, it fell to me to deal with the working-class customers, I soon found the best way of both addressing and dealing with the different ones. It was amazing how many wives came for their husbands' footwear and they would buy the same colour, style and price, time and again. I was able to remember these details, including the size that regular customers bought, so that at times it was rather embarrassing for me as a teenager to hear a customer being served by Eric (the clogger) or Harold (the cobbler) say, 'Where's Frank? He knows what I want.' In any case I doubt if either of them were bothered in the slightest, as if I was serving the customer they would not have to do it themselves.

It soon became obvious to me that the situation at 29 Northgate was not a very happy one insomuch as Mr Hays did not pay a very good wage, resulting in sales not being fully recorded when they should have been, so that a loss occurred when there really wasn't one. There was a time when Mr Hays was paying out more for his supplies than he was receiving through the till, to the consternation of his accountant, who advised him to stand there and take the cash himself even if others served the customers. He did not take this advice and it seemed to me that stalemate would continue so long as Mr Hays would not pay better wages and the employees would not stop their dishonest ways. I cannot recall the final outcome of this stupid situation but, in order to check on sales, I had to take a complete stock every Monday morning. From this I could list the type, size, price etc. of every unrecorded sale for the previous week, but there was no real advantage in knowing what was missing if at the end of the day nothing was done to remedy the situation. It was quite easy to leave an empty box on the shelves along with the others as it was impossible to check literally every individual box. Realising the hopelessness of this weekly checking, I told Mr Hays that there seemed to be no point in doing this check each week and for me at my age it was a very unpleasant task checking on people twice my own age and created an atmosphere in the shop.

However, my learning of the business continued and I became responsible for the window dressing of the double-fronted shop. One side was for ladies' wear and the other for men's wear, each having a side window to the shop doorway. Northgate was the main road and bus route to Bradford and the traffic made quite a lot of vibration in the windows. This caused the glass shelves to move gradually, requiring constant watching to make sure they did not fall off their supports. I learned to put light-coloured footwear in the top part of the ladies' window as one's eyes tend to be naturally attracted to white and lighter colours.

Mr Hays lived in a room above the shop and besides doing various errands for him I had to clean up his room once a week. Among other things, this entailed replacing the newspapers from the dining room table as Mr Hays never used tablecovers but lived very frugally, apart from his annual Continental holidays.

When I had been sufficiently trained to make clogs from start to finish without supervision I was sent up to Lindley, some two miles away, to a retail shop run by a Mrs Cliffe in Lidget Street. She sold clogs from there retail and also had an arrangement with a nearby works to supply them wholesale. Mr Hays went there each Tuesday afternoon to do any work that could not wait till Thursday, when I had to go and do any repairs or make new clogs to keep her stock of all sizes up to the required standard. Officially I was to work there till the normal 7 p.m. finishing time and then go straight home. When any re-clogging had to be done this was most difficult as there was no knocking-off machine there; in order to remove the wooden soles I had to place a heavy steel plate on my thighs in the normal sitting position and knock the soles off using a very heavy short-handled knocking-off hammer. This meant that every hammer blow had to be accurate in hitting the joining of the welting and the wooden sole. Occasionally when learning this way, a badly directed hammer blow would cut through the leather upper, in which case I tried to hide the effect by putting a neatly skived patch of leather on the underside to cover up the hole and make it as near waterproof as possible again.

Mrs Cliffe, no doubt because she was a widow living on her own, was a great talker and many times persuaded me to work till ten o'clock making clogs if she thought that her stock needed it, and no doubt took advantage of my own nature in wanting to help if I could. Fortunately for me a cross-country bus service had been started up from Lindley to Newsome, passing the end of Church Avenue on its way from Milnsbridge to Lockwood, so after leaving Lindley I was soon home. This service was an outstanding success and was routed through all the busy mill and factory roads. Naturally any work after normal 7.00 p.m. was unpaid. This twice-weekly service for Mrs Cliffe was the result of a debt of gratitude which Mr Hays felt for her as, during the First World War, her husband had been a clog sole maker for Mr Hays. He could easily have left to start on his own but chose to stay on, so that after he died Mr Hays felt obliged to help her in this manner. However, there was some benefit to him as well, insomuch as Mrs Cliffe was officially employing Mr Hays and put a weekly stamp on his employment card, thus enabling him to qualify for a pension which, being self-employed, he would otherwise have been unable to do at that time.

When Mr Cliffe was making clog soles by hand, the method used in those days was to have a low wooden bench fitted with an iron ring at one end through which the long-handled stock knives were secured whilst cutting. These comprised a full set of three knives, known as the hollower, sidecutter and gripper. Suitable blocks of wood had already been dried out to a suitable moisture content prior to shaping, which was done by 'eye' and watching it progress with each cut. It was, of course, a skilled job, and whilst some clog sole makers did nothing else but shape clog soles, others would be able to make the actual clogs as well. Like anything hand-made, it was not a quick process, but speed came with practice and in any case in those far-off days life went on at a much more leisurely pace and accuracy of work and the pride in doing it counted far more than any slight increase in production.

At the age of 18 I had saved up to take a holiday in Belgium, the ticket from Huddersfield station to Brussels and return being £3.33, which also included the ferry journey lasting three hours and twenty minutes from Dover to Ostend. Being tired out by the time I arrived in Belgium, I fell asleep in the train, waking up just in time to see a sign 'Gare du Nord', not knowing at that moment whether we were arriving or leaving. As the next stop would be in Germany I was really worried for a while until the train stopped and I realised that it was just arriving. I heaved a heartfelt sigh of relief and spent a few happy days in both Brussels and Ostend. Everything abroad seems to be different, especially on the first visit. My best-remembered impression of Ostend is the lovely coloured lights in the park which reflected in the water in the centrally placed duck house. Brussels had some fine buildings, including the Palace, the floral clock, and the memorial at Waterloo an hour's tram ride away at Laeken, a large statue of the British Lion set on a huge stone base resting on a man-made mound of earth brought from all over the battlefield. The story went that when the Germans invaded Belgium they put a rope round the lion's tail to pull down this symbol of British victory but the tail, or part of it anyhow, simply broke off and the Germans gave it up as not worth bothering with further. The tail was replaced after the war and the statue restored to its former glory.

The trams, usually in a set of three, provided the best way of getting round Brussels, the main street of which was supposedly the most brilliantly lit in the whole of Europe. The outdoor pavement cafés were very popular and relaxing to use.

Having had my appetite for foreign travel whetted, I saved up to go to the Rhineland on a ten-day holiday the following summer with International Summer Schools at an inclusive cost of £5.25, but when the time came my mother insisted that another war was in the offing and it was better to stay in England than risk being caught up in Germany should this happen. As I had been studying German at the Huddersfield Technical College in the evenings, this was all the more disappointing.

Work continued at Northgate as normal until that fateful Sunday morning at 11 o'clock on 3 September 1939 when the announcement of the declaration of war came over the wireless. At the time I was listening to the broadcast in Mr Hays' room at the shop. Immediately calls were made for volunteers to form the LDV (Local Defence Volunteers), which I joined the day it started. At first there was no uniform but we were issued with an identity card giving us the power of arrest. Subsequently the LDV was changed on the formation of the Home Guard, by which time we had been issued with a battledress, a side hat and the badge of the local Duke of Wellington's Regiment.

First World War rifles were issued for both drilling and bayonet practice, which took place at our headquarters, Crosland Heath Golf Clubhouse, where we assembled and went out in pairs to various points on the moors to look out for any signs of aerial invasion, considered at that time to be a very real threat especially at times of full moon. Through-night duty occurred on a rota basis, with volunteers doing their normal daily work as well. A bandolier made from canvas held 50 rounds of .303 ammunition and was quite heavy to carry over one shoulder. Whilst on guard, the sound of bombs falling in the Sheffield direction could easily be heard from the Crosland Heath vantage point and the flashes accompanying the explosions were quite visible on the skyline. Huddersfield was lucky as far as air raids were concerned and the

41

anti-aircraft battery stationed in Leeds Road behind the the Peacock Inn did not have to open up very often.

Our instructions, when on guard duty were to challenge anyone on sight with the words, 'Who goes there?' to be repeated if there was no reply. If there was no reply to the second challenge we had to say, 'Halt or I fire'. As this situation never occurred to my knowledge on our section, I could not help thinking what would actually have happened if we had been invaded. I couldn't imagine any Germans on being challenged answering '*Freund*' – or anything else for that matter. Surely they would just have opened fire and been glad that their target had identified itself. I began to have a dim view of our methods of defence. There was a story going round our section at the time about our counterparts on the neighbouring high ground at Outlane to the effect that one of their men went through this challenging procedure without reply, saw something moving in the mist and decided to open fire. A dead cow was found in Outlane the following morning.

Since beginning work I came up with another method of making a small amount of cash. I made a wooden stand with shelves to hold a small display of footwear, and stood this in the window at home to sell boots and shoes on a commission basis. A repair service also helped and was publicised by means of handbills and prices pushed through the letter boxes of all houses within easy reach. Apart from printing, no outlay was necessary for this venture as I took repairs to work and brought them back along with any new footwear required.

Government regulations governing call-up to the services allowed me to have a 12-month deferment, during which time I was, of course, doing my duties in the Home Guard. At that time I was classified as a shoe shop manager.

Although working till 9 p.m. on Saturdays I became very keen on ballroom dancing and on finishing work, being dressed up for Saturday shop working, I was able to go straight out to Fox's Academy of Dancing in Trinity Street near Greenhead Park, where Jack and Doris welcomed us. The ballroom was relatively small, with more of a family atmosphere. Jack Fox got everybody involved even if they were at all stages of learning the various dances. Records provided the music for dancing with strict tempo from the bandleaders of the day including, of course, Victor Silvester, whose book on ballroom dancing was very informative for anyone really interested in its finer points. As there was often some reluctance to be first on the floor for a dance, Jack would invariable say, 'Just one more couple in the centre please!' which always had the desired effect. The Cambridge Road Baths, which had a marvellous spacious dance floor, were the venue for the International Dancing Masters' Association competitions. These were held for a number of different age groups and the under-ten-year olds had the same evening dress as the men wore and looked really nice, as did their partners in their ballroom dresses. This event was a wonderful sight to see from the balcony. Professionals from all over the country produced a very high standard.

In spite of the war, not a lot had changed during the first year or so, apart from the introduction of food rationing and the black-out, which ensured that no lights were visible at all from the outside.

Before my deferment came to a close I had to go for a medical, along with others due for call-up. The position with my ears cropped up again, as expected. After the examination by the medical board I went back into the changing room to dress. Whilst doing this one of the men said to me, 'Are you Walkley? They are asking for you.' Accordingly I went back in to the board, who immediately sent me back again. Apparently calling my name was just a ruse to see whether I could hear it or not and, of course, I had not heard them at all. No doubt the person who told me that they were calling for me thought he was helping and did it in good faith, but if he had not spoken I would most probably have been rejected on medical grounds as I had been for the Civil Service. Those few words were to change my whole life.

Following the medical examination I duly received my call-up papers instructing me to report to Catterick Camp on Thursday, 7 November 1940 and enclosing a warrant for rail travel to Richmond station. By this time I was 20 years and 9 months old. Like others before me, I left home with a heavy heart, not knowing what to expect or if I would come back again and, naturally, worried about my mother having to live on her own.

4

Service in the Second World War

Arriving at Richmond station along with other recruits I found the duty truck doing a shuttle service by meeting each arriving train and transporting us the few miles to Catterick Camp. Being a permanent army barracks, the accommodation had been purpose-built with good road surfaces joining the various lines of barrack rooms. Most basic amenities such as washing, toilet and dining arrangements had been catered for to accommodate the full complement of men able to be stationed there.

On arrival the first action taken was to insert our personal details in the Army Book 64. This brown-backed book measuring some five inches by four inches fitted neatly into the battledress blouse pocket and had to be carried at all times as proof of identity. The AB 64 had two parts. Part two merely contained details of payments made to the soldier. On opening the AB 64 the inside cover gave a full page on instructions for personal decontamination of anti-gas, covering the clothing, body and equipment processes. The next page of the soldiers' service listed eight instructions to be followed whilst serving in HM Forces. Paragraph four gave details about making a will (on pages 15 to 20), which seemed somewhat ominous to a 20-year-old. Pages two and three were completed, allocating me my number 7924662, personal details such as date of birth, service 'for the duration', height, weight etc. with particulars of any army training courses entered on page four. Page five was reserved for the record of employment as an army tradesman. Records of special significance such as promotions and demotions followed next, with records of 'privilege leave'. Medical classification, vaccination and protective inoculations took up the next two pages. Next of kin details were listed on pages 10 and 11, with soldiers' wills taking up no less than 11 paragraphs on pages 12, 13 and 14, followed by army form B2089 –'form of will' – with suitable examples on pages 15 to 20 at which point the AB 64 part one finished.

Having read and inwardly digested the implications of our AB 64, we were then briefed on our training programme, which was to take 13 weeks to complete. The training method was to form a new squad each week as the next intake arrived. Ours, numbered 81Y squad, was composed of about 30 recruits. We were all billeted in one barrack room with a small partitioned section at one end for the NCO in charge.

The next day we were introduced to our squad sergeant, in our case Sergeant Marsh from a cavalry regiment. We had to parade in threes outside the barrack room and marched to the MI room, as it was known, to have two inoculations and one vaccination. The ATT and TAB inoculations needed a second jab some ten days later. We were kitted out with two sets of underclothes, battledress, overcoat, black beret, kit bag etc. and four blankets and a pillow to make our beds with. Army socks were thick grey and the boots, which I recognised as being the Sir Herbert Barker shape and last, were to receive much 'spit and polish', or the other name which we quickly learned. The toecaps in particular were 'beezed up' to look almost like black patent, this being the effect of cavalry staff as opposed to the tank regiments, who couldn't care less about such matters. The weekly laundry allowance consisted of one pair each of socks, vests, underpants (army designation 'drawers cellular', shirt and towel, rolled up and tied in a bundle with the soldier's name labelled on it. The other set of laundry followed the following week.

Training and drilling (or square-bashing) was done in denims, a loose-fitting type of battledress intended for any dirty work to save the more expensive battledress. Denims were not tailored in any way and it was a matter of receiving the nearest size to the soldier's shape and height.

In the first four weeks, besides the inevitable square-bashing, we received instruction on the army rifle, which was literally thrown at us with the brisk comment 'It's only six and three-quarter pounds' and was invariably caught by a natural reflex action. Bren gun training included the command 'mount for ack-ack', for which a maximum time of 60 seconds was allowed. I got down to 42 seconds by constant practice, speed being essential for anti-aircraft use when being attacked from the air. The Bren gun was mounted on a tripod, whereas for normal use on the ground it only had a two-leg section to hold the front steady. Being in the Royal Armoured Corps as opposed to infantry, all trainees had to pass out on 'wheels' within four weeks – wheels referred to any kind of truck and 'tracks' to the caterpillar tracks on tanks.

Besides being taught to drive, with double declutching being necessary to engage the gears, we received basic training on the operation of the internal-combustion engine and the procedure to follow in any breakdown to trace the likely fault as quickly as possible. Driving any of these army vehicles was totally different from the synchromesh gearboxes on private cars, and after revving the engine in neutral the gear lever had to be eased into the next gear as the revolutions died down. One instructor took no more than four of us so that one man was learning to drive whilst the other three waited for their turn and listened to the instructions.

The men in our squad tended to be much older than myself, no doubt as a result of the 12 months' deferment that I had. The majority of the men seemed to have had a secondary education. Some were in business, some schoolteachers and all possessed average or higher intelligence.

Apart from training all day, any leisure time was spent in the NAAFI, where food, drink, cigarette rations, soap (on coupons, one bar per week) toothpaste, shaving cream etc. and all personal needs were on sale. I used an Ever Ready safety razor at that time and these blades had also to be bought by ourselves in addition to the above-mentioned items. It was quite surprising how much all these things added up to in a week and were all essential for normal living. A piano in the NAAFI provided some relaxation with 'Tombola' – the army name for bingo – being played two or three times each week end. Tombola, or housey-housey, was the only gambling game legally allowed in the army, the sessions being organised by sergeants or sergeant majors or both, who took their share of the takings before paying out any winners. Previously unheard-of phrases like 'kelly's eye, before you come up, clickety click, top of the shop, unlucky, shiny ten' and so on took on a hitherto unknown meaning.

Following the basic training, each member of the squad was interviewed separately to be allocated one particular job for special training. The three main types of work in the RAC were the tank driver, gunner and wireless operator, and it was to one of these sections that most of the squad were invariably allocated. The others, commonly known as the 'odds and sods', were given a specialised job in various trades such as joiner, equipment repairer, technical clerk, butcher, cook, electrician, storeman etc., with only one man per squad given these duties.

In my own interview I was asked about previous experience of sewing and mentioned the types of sewing machines that I had used, only to be told that sewing machines could not be taken into action and all sewing had to be done by hand. In the event they decided to make me an equipment repairer, no doubt because they had got to the letter 'W' in their interviewing – everything in the army was done in alphabetical order – and there was hardly anyone else left to see. After this segregation of trades had taken place, each section trained according to their newly allocated duties, with such as myself waiting to go away somewhere as there were no facilities locally for this type of training.

The course for equipment repairers turned out to be in London at the Cordwainers College. London at that time was not a very peaceful place to be in, with daily air raids a constant threat, and as I was billeted on the fifth floor of the Royal Hotel that did not help much either. A class of perhaps 20 or so from various regiments were assembled, with the vast majority of them coming from various sections of the Royal Artillery, who were issued with all their equipment made from a grain type of leather, whereas in the tanks we had only webbing equipment. The training had to cover both. The course started on 11 January and finished on 10 February 1941, as duly entered in my AB 64 on page four of my particulars of training.

47

All the basic methods of making and repairing personal equipment were demonstrated, including such varied sewing as split-stitching, back stitching, double hand sewing and French-bound seaming, and instructions given on the various hand tools used for inserting eyelets, rivets and press studs, all of which were used in making straps and bags of various sizes.

One of the most important things to learn was how to make thread using strands of either flax or hemp. I already had a knowledge of making a three-cord wax thread using the boot repairer's method with black wax known as cobbler's wax, and found that the only difference between this method and the saddler's way was in the 'breaking' of the strands. One way was to gently roll off the end on the thigh standing on one leg, whilst the other method involved twisting the end section in opposite directions to open up the thread and then breaking it with a quick pull. Each method produced a gradual thinning of each strand tapering off to nothing at the end. The saddler's method always used beeswax of a neutral colour, compared with the jet-black wax ends made by cobblers. There was no particular advantage in either way of making thread as the skill was in making the three strands of slightly different lengths so that when they were rolled together before waxing the three strands became one. By inserting a garnishing awl with a smooth circular blade into the bench, the three lengths were rolled together one half at a time by rolling the hand forward until the strands were tight enough to be waxed, after which the thread was passed between the fingers and thumb to make a smooth finish to the thread. After making one half of the thread the process was repeated for the other half, again rubbing the beeswax by hand along the whole length till satisfied that it was ready for use. A length in these terms was the length of a man's outstretched arms from one hand to the other, which made quite a lot of sewing able to be done with one wax thread. I was to spend two hours every day for a full day's usage when later I was employed as an equipment repairer in my own regiment.

Other training included rope splicing using a steel marlin spike, which I found very interesting and which was to become very useful later on. Several methods of joining two ends of rope together were taught and after each had been done the end of the rope had to be whipped to stop any fraying. The main method was to use 'palm and needle whipping', which made a very neat job on the three-cord sisal rope used throughout the training. Sisal is one of the roughest types of rope and widely used. I was taught the definition of leather, which is 'the preserved outer covering of any animal, bird, reptile or fish', and to emphasise the point a sample of human leather made from the knee of a middle-aged woman was on display.

I still have my five samples of rope splicing, including the 'grommet', which is a full circle of the same thickness throughout and similar to the rope quoits used for deck games on cruise liners. When a piece of rope was spliced back into itself at one end, this was called a crown dog knot, whilst if a loop end had to be made and then spliced back into itself this splicing was done on a gradual basis with each of the three strands spliced in turn. The loop end was very strong indeed and was used to hold ships at anchor alongside the dock when a stronger rope was needed. The principle of splicing was exactly the same as our small samples. It could easily be seen why different methods of splicing were necessary for the various uses to which they were put, particularly with regard to the way in which either gradual splicing or same-thickness splicing were best for any given situation.

The leather samples we had to make were a round flax box to hold a ball of flax or hemp, with a central eyelet in the lid part for the strands of thread to pass through when being made, and several flat pieces of similar size and shape also forming a roughly round shape using the split-stitching method, with the stitches only being visible from the outside – merely to show the method of sewing and not for any practical purpose. To do this type of sewing the leather had to be held in position leaving both hands free for the double-hand split-stitching. This was done by having a round horizontal piece of wood fitted to the bench, protruding over the edge far enough to take whatever length of leather was to be sewn, on which the leather was held in position, by a long loop of leather reaching down to the floor and secured there by one foot. I had experience of this type of thing from boot repairing, where the boot or shoe had to be held on the last and the leather or rubber sole held in position by this stirrup until fastened by the rivets. Any sewing on flat leather was done sitting down, with a pair of clams resting between the legs, with one end on the floor, which opened up at the jaws to hold the leather or pieces of leather being sewn together.

The final piece of work on the course was to make a holdall for the tools used in this work. This was made from webbing material, single warp and double weft, with a large pocket the whole width fastened by two press studs and bound all round by a binding of brown leather double hand sewn, which had to be very neatly done as both sides were visible in use. Although really not very big, it was adequate for holding a flat knife, needles, awl blades etc., with suitably shaped leather sewn onto the inside of the holdall to hold these items in position.

All hand sewing was done using a diamond-shaped awl and 'blunts', that is, needles which did not have a sharp point like domestic sewing needles. When sewing, the needle would temporarily rest on the side of the diamond shape to guide the needle through the material and the thread, then pulled slightly backwards whilst the second needle was inserted from the other side, carefully avoiding cutting into the thread in the process, after which each needle was pulled sideways to the extent of the arms or the length of thread itself till tight enough to form a stitch. Every stitch had to be done this way but speed did come with practice.

In one corner of the holdall I put my initials *FW* by inserting cardboard letters underneath thin brown leather and then sewing round the letters to make them raised up above the surface; using yellow thread made them show up quite well.

The course was interrupted almost daily when the air raid sirens started wailing with their foreboding noise, and we had to all go downstairs into the basement until the all-clear sounded.

The food we received at the Royal Hotel was deplorable, mainly consisting of one large baked potato and something else besides, but many times I could not guess what the 'something else' was. Consequently I spent my money buying scones and jam from a shop which we passed every day walking to the college. As there was nothing at all to do in the evenings at the hotel due to being in separate rooms with nowhere where we could gather together, we tended to risk going out to a snooker club in Tottenham Court Road, which meant walking all down Southampton Row to the BBC Bush House, turning right and then right again, which took about 20 minutes or so. The alternative was to use the Underground, but as the Piccadilly Line was fairly near to the surface this invariably closed for the night immediately the sirens sounded in the evening.

One evening, making our way back to the hotel, we had just reached the corner of Southampton Row when a bomb dropped on the corner we had just passed a few moments before, and this gave us the impetus to try to break the sprinting record back to the hotel and up the fire escape to the fifth floor as we were not allowed to use the front door at ground level. Climbing five flights of stairs up a fire escape in an air raid situation was not very nice. However, on the brighter side, being so high up presented a marvellous view of the balloon barrage, especially when they were all lowered during the day and it almost felt as if we were floating at the same level. It certainly was an unforgettable sight.

A freak accident had already occurred in the Tube system when a bomb had actually gone down the escalator – its trajectory must have been exactly at the correct angle when falling for this to happen. One morning at breakfast time all the talk was about a 'land mine', which had dropped about a half-mile away from the hotel, fracturing a gas main and wakening everybody up by the explosion. Apparently some of the lads had been banging on my door to try to waken me up but eventually gave it up as hopeless and went downstairs for safety. My partial deafness coupled with being a heavy sleeper must have had its reward in giving me a good night's sleep.

On Sunday afternoons a show was put on for servicemen in London at the Hammersmith Palais de dance which was thoroughly enjoyed by soldiers, sailors and airmen able to go there. Robin Richmond was the resident pianist with dance bands varying each week and numerous entertainers doing their various acts for us.

Our course at Cordwainers College finished on 10 February 1941 and I returned to Catterick along with another equipment repairer from some other regiment in the garrison. The rest of 81Y squad were also finishing their three months' training about this time and shortly afterwards we all went on privilege leave, which in my case coincided with my twenty-first birthday on 20 February. Unfortunately there was nothing and no one to celebrate with so the day passed off like any other and I cannot even remember anything of interest happening at all either then or any other time during the leave. Most of my pals were also away either in the air force or the army.

On returning to Catterick I found all the squad awaiting posting to one or other of the many regiments of the Royal Armoured Corps stationed in many parts of the UK; notification of postings were on the daily regimental orders pinned up outside the office for all ranks to read. When my own posting came up on orders, I was to report to the 1st Lothian & Border Horse Yeomanry, which I had to admit I had never even heard of at that time. They were a former Edinburgh Territorial regiment who had already been in France before the Dunkirk evacuation. The Lothians, as they were known, were stationed at Whitby, occupying a row of some 20 or more former individual hotels in the Crescent which had been commandeered by the army. I was amazed to find that the Lothians' cap badge was a wheat-sheaf, which naturally resulted in other regiments asking if we were in the Land Army. I would much have preferred to keep my old RAC badge but this was not to be.

On arrival I was issued with a rough pillowcase and palliasse to be filled with straw to make as comfortable bed as possible as we had to sleep on the wooden floors. Each day we had to make our beds up with the usual four blankets and the army overcoat on top if not warm enough, but even though there were no actual beds it was incredibly comfortable on the wooden floors and I slept well. At times the straw was somewhat of a nuisance making its way through the pillowcase but it soon broke up into a smaller, more comfortable size. At least you can't fall out of bed when sleeping on the floor.

As regimental equipment repairer, like a few other tradesmen joining the regiment, I came on the staff of and under the command of the Captain Quartermaster, who had a staff of some 15 or so including clerks and other odds and sods. The quartermaster's staff, technical stores staff, orderly room staff and so on formed the headquarters squadron, along with cooks, pipe band etc. My AB 64 records 'trade equipment repairer, Group C, Class 3' as all army trades had different groups and classes, which affected the pay of each accordingly. Being in Group C as an equipment repairer, I had the lowest rate of pay for the three groups A, B and C but there was nothing I could do to alter this, and I took consolation in the fact that the one single stripe of a lance corporal tradesman in my grouping had a higher rate of pay than a duty sergeant with three stripes who was not classified as an army tradesman. My record continued with the words 'trade tested as such, Catterick Camp, February 7th 1941 Regimental Orders Part 2 February 19th 1941' (the day before my twenty-first birthday, what a present!). It continues by saying 'Mustered for pay in that trade accordingly'. The structure of pay for a lance corporal was some 30 pence more than a duty sergeant. I never did find out just which trades were in which groups or how many classes were in each but it would have made no difference, the knowledge being purely academic. I did try my best to better myself by going in for Classes 2 or 1 but nothing came of it and perhaps there was no class higher than Class 3 for my particular trade.

The months spent at Whitby are perhaps best remembered by the dancing at the Spa, the dive-bombing by the Germans on the ship convoys out to sea and the never-ending call-outs for fighting peat fires on Fylingdales moors. These would be beaten out to surface somewhere else nearby, helped by the wind and fanning out in a swathe blown along in whatever direction it was blowing.

During 1941 the 11th Armoured Division was being formed, constituting two armoured brigades, the 29th and 30th, each having three regiments. Ours was in the 30th Brigade. Other units such as the Royal Corps of Signals, LAD (Light Aid Detachment) Royal Engineers and Pioneer Corps were commanded separately but attached to each brigade. The two others in our brigade were the Fife and Forfar Yeomanry, usually referred to as the 'knife and forkers', and the Westminsters. Tank training took place on the moors inland from Whitby.

Being billeted in so many small hotels without any central facilities for such things as eating resulted in our being marched about a quarter of a mile or so into the harbour and to a former restaurant. One remarkable dish served up to us here still stays in my mind. This was a large slice of thick white bread with jam spread on one side and then deep fried in batter. At first glance this looked exactly like fish until it was tasted and it was some time before the exact composition of the meal could be decided. I reckon that the army cook who thought this one up should have been awarded a prize for originality.

The Lothians had by now formed a pipe band, much detested by the non-Scottish troops but very good to march to for keeping in step, although probably the drums rather than the pipes were responsible for this. Besides all the day-long army calls played on the pipes from reveille to lights out, the band would play for the evening mounting of the guard. This parade, done at the slow march pace of 16 inches to each stride, was perfected by the training of the sergeant major and his 'pacing stick' and was quite an impressive sight to watch, especially if the regimental tune was being played. The sounds of the strain of 'Come bonny boat' had a meaning all of their own and one could almost visualise the boat on its way to Skye. This was probably the most-liked tune of all that they played and perfect for the slow march time. The pipe band seemed to be called on for almost every parade from church parade to casting parade, perhaps to give them practice.

It was at Whitby that I made my acquaintance with a soldier posted up from the south who originated from Eastleigh in Hampshire, near Southampton, and was to become my best pal for the next three years or so. He was Lance Corporal Edgar Charles Doggrell, No. 7911518, who had been appointed the Technical Adjutant's clerk, so like myself was one of the odds and sods of the regiment. Having similar interests, except that southerners dance differently from northerners in certain dances, we got on extremely well together and became virtually inseparable. He had been called up a few weeks earlier than I had, hence the difference in our numbers. The southern depots for the RAC were Tidworth and Bovington. His posting to Yorkshire was his first visit to the north of England and, seeing more of the open spaces than towns, he made the remark to me that there must be more miles of nothing (there is an army expression for this word) in Yorkshire than anywhere else on earth.

Information was a commodity in short supply for security reasons but eventually obvious signs revealed that some movement was about to take place. Our time at Whitby, about six months in my case, had come to an end, presumably a full complement of soldiers having been assembled over this period to form the division. The tanks carried their crews whilst the rest of the men were packed into trucks and transported to we knew not where.

We eventually arrived in Duncombe Park at Helmsley, some 25 miles north of York. The park housed nearly all our brigade, with other units in nearby wooded locations similar to ours to give cover from air reconnaissance planes which might be looking for signs of army camps. Numerous Nissen huts had been constructed under the huge trees growing there and providing good camouflage, but making it rather difficult for us to see when walking about in total blackout conditions. Some larger huts called Tarran huts were used for mess rooms, hospital etc. Each Nissen hut housed about 30 men, each having a low single bed quite handy for sitting on when playing cards. The walls and roof were corrugated iron sheeting forming a virtual circle except for the concrete floor. Three 40-watt bulbs had to provide what lighting there was, which was not helped by the fact that they were secured in the roof fittings. A large iron stove in the middle of the hut provided the heating. This was to be our home for the next 18 months.

Here I must pay tribute to the high standard of my fellow occupants of K11, as our hut was numbered. When going for a wash, there being no baths even in this newly constructed camp, this necessitated in our case walking quite some distance, and a man would throw his towel round his neck and carry his toilet essentials with him, leaving all his personal belongings, including money, on his bed for all to see. The honesty and integrity of everyone in K11 was such that nothing ever 'went missing' in spite of what would have been quite a temptation to a weaker-minded group of men. With the exception of the cooks, who were at the other end near to the cookhouse, all the men in K11 were the odds and sods of the Headquarters Squadron and a great camaraderie developed between all being thrown together for many hours each day and night.

With the exception of the one 'brag' school formed by a few better-off men who could afford higher stakes, three or four games of solo would occupy every evening on a basis of one penny for solo, twopence for mizaire and three-pence for abundance, all these being in pre-decimalisation money of course. No one wanted to walk into Helmsley, some two miles or so away, as there was nothing to go there for in the evenings when no dancing was taking place, and the blackout could be very depressing when there was no moon. Each hut had a wireless, usually playing suitable music for men away from home to keep morale high; the inevitable Vera Lynn was the most popular singer, with her sentimental songs touching the right note and striking a chord between parted friends and relations.

Now that the regiment was in a more permanent camp, I was given one end of a Nissen hut for my equipment repairer's workshop. I was issued with a large wooden tool box, partitioned off near each end and with a drop front held by two chains which permitted it to open level. A padlock and key secured the contents when not in use. For double hand sewing a pair of saddler's clams were supplied, which because of their length could not be kept inside the tool box. Palms – sailmaker's sewing was the army name – were the hand pieces to protect the hands from being cut by wax threads when pulling stitches into position. All repairing equipment had to be indented for on a weekly basis through the regimental stores. My stock consisted of many sizes of brass Ds, buckles, duck canvas, flax or hemp, beeswax etc. and semi-circular pieces of leather to be sewn at the back of anklets to give more wear and help to stop the inevitable fraying of the gaiters due to scuffing against the army boots when walking. Other materials included steel helmet elastic chinstraps, rope, sail eyelets of various sizes, bifurcated rivets and washers, and anything needed for repairing the personal equipment or for the covers of tanks and trucks.

Altogether I estimated that I had about 500 vehicle covers to look after as the tanks had three each, the numerous Leyland, GMC, and 30-cwt trucks and PUs having at least one each. I was able to obtain a huge roll of leather cloth which I found ideal for inserting under the joinings of wagon covers, under two rows of stitching where each section had originally been sewn together, when making new and extending the leather cloth to cover the tear needing repair. This method made a very neat job indeed, making the covers as good as new again. The first two hours of every day were taken up making thread to last the day, but the constant rolling of the threads in time produced a horrible wart on the middle finger of my right hand. Most repairing was a matter of using common sense and innovation, with trial and error in some cases being the best way to tackle any given problem.

The Lothians, now at full strength, consisted of four squadrons: A, B, C and HQ, the first three being the operational squadrons of tanks and support vehicles. Large quantities of petrol were needed for the tanks and this is where the famous 'Jerricans' came into their own, holding several gallons each, carried on the tank itself and easily discarded after emptying. They presented a much lower risk than the normal petrol tankers, which if hit could explode and hundreds of gallons would be lost in one go.

An increasing amount of repair work, due mainly to the wear and tear of anklets, gave me plenty to do but my business mind was already working on using any spare time to make money. As my pal Eddie said when twisting my arm to do some sewing for him, 'Frank, you wield a nifty needle,' which seemed a good complimentary way of putting it – and getting the desired result. On seeing the way some of the men were attempting to do their own sewing on of insignia, stripes etc. I was determined to put my own experience to good use and accordingly worked out a charge for each of the various items which had to be sewn onto both sleeves of the battledress blouse.

I was now in business again, with increasing work as the news of my service spread around. Actually, when receiving a new battledress blouse there was quite a lot of sewing to be done. At the top of the sleeve the regimental nameband in light blue carried the letters in yellow, below this a narrow strip half yellow and half red for the RAC, with the divisional sign of the black bull lower down the arm still. This meant a minimum of six separate items to be sewn on, with other work such as stripes of rank, the tank badge in white on black being required by some in addition.

In order to make a first-class job I bought reels of the yellow, red, blue and khaki coloured thread, which made a vast difference to the finished work compared to the more amateurish method used by individuals using the thread provided by the army in the 'housewife' – a small packet containing black and white thread, needles, pins and buttons. Naturally this issue did not contain any of the coloured thread. The black bull symbol of the 11th Armoured Division looked very impressive in contrasting colours. Soon a whole row of blouses awaiting attention hung around my workshop and when my boss, the Captain Quartermaster, happened to walk in and see them all, he merely admonished me in a semi-jocular way, saying 'What's this, Walkley, a bleeding tailor's shop?' Looking round the finished work with approval, he knew that he could rely on me to do his own sewing when required (free of charge) and made no attempt to stop me in this work, which in any case was only done in my own time or when all army work had been completed first. I gathered that he had a sneaky feeling of pride in seeing the enterprise and the opportunity that I had seized with both hands, knowing that there was no one employed in the capacity of regimental tailor as at the training camps.

Besides sewing insignia on battledress, I turned to making 'attachments, brace', which were short webbing straps with brass fittings and part of the issued personal equipment, as I had stocks of the webbing in rolls and the three brass parts needed to make them. However, there was very little demand for these as the completed straps could be supplied from the regimental stores. A far better proposition was in making braces by using the elastic from steel helmet chin straps, making a small leather part to join the three strips of elastic together and buying the leather brace ends from Woolworth's to be slotted through the D rings of the braces. These were really excellent and much better than the army braces, which seemed to have no give in them at all compared to elastic ones.

Having acquired an electric iron, I next started shortening trousers, having been shown the correct method of sewing them by one of the men in K11 who had been the manager of a Burton's shop in Edinburgh. For some reason which I never did find out, the elements in the electric iron were constantly blowing and needing replacement, so I kept spares in readiness in order not to stop 'production'. A steady trade soon developed, with no shortage of paying customers.

After I had been sent to see another ear specialist in York, a medical board at Helmsley considered his report and downgraded my medical category to B1 instead of A1. This was on 12 February 1942, the effect of this being that officially I was no longer able to serve in the Royal Armoured Corps as only men in A1 or A2 were eligible. However, the farce of my medical categories was to continue; the 'old man', Colonel Crabbe, the Commanding Officer, simply used his authority to stop my transfer as he considered my work too valuable to lose me. Accordingly the Lothians' MO duly upgraded me again, this time to A2, in direct contradiction to the medical board, which was a much higher authority. Such was the absolute control exercised by the Commanding Officer that if he simply put N/A to anything at all that was the end of it. I do not know whether the Medical Officer himself had actually the authority to do upgrading or simply did as he was told by the CO.

As it was a Scottish regiment, all the officers and most of the NCOs tended to be Scotsmen even though the vast majority of the 'other ranks' were either English, Irish or Welsh. This resulted in a situation where racism and animosity thrived with glaring injustices becoming the norm. In Headquarters Squadron, where there were a lot of NCOs – either lance corporal or corporal – a total of perhaps 40 or more in all, at least 90 per cent of them were excused doing the corporal of the guard night duty. Tradesmen were considered not to be eligible, having their own special work to do but on the Quartermaster's staff both the joiner and myself were detailed for this duty, as also was my pal Eddie from the Technical Adjutants' office, all three of us being Englishmen. Things got so bad and feelings ran so high on this night duty issue that there came a time when I was doing this guard every five nights, which was ridiculous when so many others were excused even for such reasons as playing in the pipe band, where they were all NCOs. My strong sense of fair play was roused to such an extent that I applied for an interview with the Squadron Leader, as I was entitled to do, and explained the position to him in detail. It must have gone against me when I mentioned about the whole of the pipe band being excused guards, and I more or less got a telling-off for my efforts; at least, nothing changed. It was so humiliating to be treated this way and I felt so incensed at the injustice that I would rather have been fighting against the Scots than the Germans at that time. Besides doing night guard we had to work both the day of the guard and also the following day.

As there were no baths at the camp all ranks were taken in trucks at least once each month to York, where we were able to use the baths there. Afterwards we duly signed the bath book – we had to sign for everything in the army – and had the rest of the day free until returning at 11 p.m. There was a tea dance in Lendal in the centre of York which attracted me, and it was followed by another in the De Grey Rooms not far away in the evenings. This opportunity to get away from Helmsley was more than welcome, apart from the luxury of being able to get into a proper bath for a change. The journey home in the blackout, with headlights virtually blacked out apart from the smallest of clear glass, was one continual sing-song to pass the time away as the journey of 25 miles took quite some time. This truck became known as the 'passion wagon', which seemed to have a different meaning to different people.

On one occasion, after waiting a few extra minutes after 11.00 p.m. when two men had not turned up, the truck left without them. The following day we learned that they had walked all the way back through the night, arriving before reveille at 6.30 a.m. Their efforts were rewarded by being put on a charge – 'a 252', as it was called – and marched before the Squadron Leader for sentence. Section 40 of the Army Act is an all-embracing one to cover just about any and every eventuality and was invariably used before pronouncing the usual seven days' CB or 'jankers', as it was known. However, the outcome of these charges was that one of the men was awarded seven days' CB (he was an Englishman) whilst the other, a Scotsman, was let off scot-free. Now I knew what that meant. Both these men had done exactly the same by missing the truck and had walked together all the way back and now were treated as if only one was guilty of an offence. As news went quickly round the camp, the non-Scotsmen were absolutely livid but could not do anything about it.

It was probably this latest injustice that finally drove Eddie and myself to try to find any way we could to get out of this Scottish regiment. There were several ways that this might be done but in the last analysis every one could be prevented by the CO using his absolute discretion. However, we were determined to try anything to get away. By studying the soldiers' 'bible' *King's Rules and Regulations*, which was often quoted by barrack-room lawyers – we first of all applied for a transfer to a regiment of our own nationality; this was refused. Next we volunteered for overseas service, with the same result. After that we asked to join the Commandos and again were refused. The CO simply put N/A (not applicable) on any application and that was that. Lastly I applied for a commission and got as far as being interviewed by my former headmaster at Huddersfield College – a prerequisite in the application process, his recommendation was necessary in order to go to OCTU (Officer Cadet Training Unit). Failure once more, so at this point we finally accepted defeat and stopped trying. The word of the Commanding Officer was law as far as his regiment was concerned.

New Year's Day 1943, when all the Scotsmen were recovering from the previous evening's celebrations, which included the haggis having to be piped in to the enjoyment of all concerned and the consumption of large amounts of whisky, was to be a holiday. Eddie and I were walking up to the NAAFI for a cup of tea and cake at about 10 a.m., when we were confronted by the regimental sergeant major, who ordered us to 'volunteer' to give a pint of blood, there being a blood donor unit at the camp on that day of all days. What a way to celebrate New Year!

For a short while I was loaned to Divisional Headquarters to do some work there as I believe I had by this time acquired a name for doing some rather awkward jobs at the instigation of high-ranking officers. These soldiers were marvellous to be with and work with, a complete contrast to the treatment I received at Helmsley, and I would willingly have gone anywhere in the world with them if only I had the chance. Naturally I did my best to get them to keep me at Division but I knew from previous experience that it was rather hopeless and did not have much confidence in it happening in spite of the fact that the Divisional Command was certainly a much higher authority than a regiment. It was at least a straw to cling to until I had to go back again. At headquarters there was none of the 'spit and polish' of the cavalry half of the RAC and it was noticeable that none of their equipment had to be blancoed or brasses polished as had been the case up to then.

By coincidence a similar situation arose at our brigade headquarters, where the Brigadier had seen some of my regimental work and wanted something doing at their HQ. This did not entail leaving the Lothians as Brigade were stationed not far away in the same park.

Having been so critical, genuinely and honestly, in my opinion of the Scotsmen in higher positions treating us the way they did, I must say that others – a small proportion – were the nicest people that one could meet. This section, being fair-minded individuals, realised only too well our resentment at the treatment meted out to other nationalities and considered it patently unfair and completely unjustified. It was perhaps because of this understanding among the more intelligent men that we became even better friends with them as a result. You can't blame one man for what another does.

A regimental dance band was formed with an excellent group of former dance musicians, of which certain ones are particularly remembered. Taffy Jones with his huge chest and lungs was a marvellous vocalist besides being an expert bass saxophone player, whilst Jimmy Saville, a very quietly spoken man, played alto or tenor sax, doubling up with the clarinet, as was usual in those days. The pianist was absolutely outstanding, with a repertoire in classical music besides dance music. Once when he was playing the piano in the NAAFI I noticed one of our troopers, a Dutchman by the name of Van Hoorn, standing enthralled listening to him playing the *Flight of the Bumblebee*. The dance band played regularly at the court house in Helmsley market place, roughly two miles or so from where we were billeted, and a gang of lance corporals, including Eddie and myself, took every opportunity to go even if we had been on guard all the previous night. After feeling rotten all day long due to lack of sleep it was amazing how energetic and awake it was possible to be in the evening.

All our officers, if they did not already know it, had to learn the eightsome reel which was a good laugh for us Sassenachs but nice to watch when it was performed correctly. Pity we needed the pipes and drums for this purpose in such a small ballroom. The dance band played in other local villages such as Harome and Kirkbymoorside and the only way to go to these places was in the band truck along with the instruments. By dint of helping load and unload these and by volunteering to be 'doormen', which was hardly necessary and only lasted about half an hour, Eddie and I were able to have a good night out.

Part of the training in 1942 was for the action to be taken in the event of a gas attack, the method being for several of us at a time to wear our respirators and walk round in the back of a truck fitted up as a gas chamber, which was supposed top give us confidence that the respirators did actually work satisfactorily. After a short while we had to remove the face mask, whereupon we were instantly attacked by the gas and jumped out of the truck just as fast as we could. Page four of my AB 64, under particulars of training, duly states 'passed DM gas test November 4th 1942'. I have no idea what DM means to this day.

As training for the tank crews continued, the old Valentine tanks were being replaced by Centaurs and Centurions and Covenanters, these latter having no less than 17 separate faces on their turrets. I remember this quite well because our regimental joiner made a scale model of one for me in return for a large 'bit case' that I made to hold all the many sizes of bits for his brace. When they were finished they were really works of art, although I say it myself, as we both gave of our best, in the tradition of craftsmanship, without any money changing hands.

New inventions for tank attachments were now coming into use along with the newer tanks. One of these, known as the 'flailer' consisted of a thick steel horizontal axle fixed at the front of the tank about halfway up in height and having a lot of heavy chains perhaps four feet long which flew round when the axle rotated, making a terrific noise when in operation. This idea was to clear a path through minefields by blowing mines up with the pounding of the earth and the vibration of the rotary action of the flailers. The ground must have taken a terrific pounding and no doubt produced the required result.

Another huge iron structure resembling a short bridge was fastened over the top of some tanks so that when it was moved forwards and downwards it would provide a more or less safe surface for the tank when negotiating trenches or streams, considered to be obstacles for normal track movement. I never saw these in operation but they certainly looked impressive.

It was somewhere about this time that the 42nd Armoured Division was formed and a new insignia of a red and white diamond shape replaced the bull as the divisional sign. This provided more welcome work for me, although the former black bull was far better liked in general. Having been in the rather depressing environment of the camp for about a year, the powers that be decided to send us in small batches on a 'stand-down' week to Scarborough. A stand down is the army equivalent of a holiday; there was only one short PT parade in the morning in the Valley Gardens, leaving the rest of each day to spend as we pleased. Naturally this was a well-liked idea and no doubt thoroughly deserved, particularly by some units who perhaps did not even have as good facilities as we did. I remember on one occasion having to go to Carlton Highwoods on the other side of Helmsley, where the troops appeared to have a much more depressing environment than our own at Duncombe Park. I am not sure but think that it was the Pioneer Corps who were stationed in that part as most of their work was of the rough labouring type, hence their name.

In early 1943 preparations started for Exercise Spartan, so named because foul weather could be expected at that time of the year. Previous exercises had usually taken place with the duty squadrons being away for a few days while the remaining Headquarters staff like myself simply had to stay at the camp. However, Spartan was to be different, with all personnel taking part, giving rise to rumours that perhaps we were going on the invasion of Europe. However, at dawn on 1 March the whole convoy of vehicles climbed the hill outside Helmsley, heading southwards. The equipment repairers' truck contained all my repair equipment, stock and tools and carrying many men as well. Being in Headquarters, all our trucks tended to follow the other three squadrons, and our main job at the end of each day's journey was to park round the perimeter of a field and put the camouflage nets over the trucks to make them blend in with the countryside and be as inconspicuous as possible. Both trucks and nets were painted with camouflage paint. There is quite an art in spreading nets out in such a way that no one would think that a truck was there at all. Nearby hedges and trees naturally helped enormously to do this.

Each evening after dark there had to be no lights showing at all, with the result that everybody made their beds and got in them a lot earlier than they would otherwise have done. By using old canvas wagon covers cut to a suitable size almost the width of a truck roof I made a few hammocks with a sail eyelet in each corner and a rope spliced through and fastened at each end to the iron frame of the truck itself. My Cordwainers' training was coming in useful here. Whilst it was very awkward to get in and out of the hammocks, being so high up they were quite comfortable to sleep in and formed the perfect hiding place for anyone scrounging out of the way when men were wanted for fatigues. When not sleeping in a hammock the alternative was to sleep on the ground under a truck, which was really warm even when there was a white frost on the blankets the following morning. I had long since learnt the art of making a bed like a sleeping bag and sliding down inside it so that all the warmth was kept inside. Invariably the army greatcoat lying on the top would provide extra warmth and it was big enough to be able to be tucked in at each side.

It was to be ten days before we finished the exercise and during the whole time the weather had been abnormally mild and sunny even if there was a night frost. We were very thankful severe cold and snow did not materialise, as had been expected when the exercise was planned and named. The almost summer-like weather had definitely taken the spartan out of Exercise Spartan.

Finally we arrived at our destination. Warminster Barracks in the case of the Lothians, previously occupied by the Guards. Like Catterick, Warminster in Wiltshire had been a purpose-built barracks and was even equipped with central heating, something which in my previous life I had heard of but never seen. A complete contrast to the conditions of the previous 18 months at Helmsley but not necessary healthier, as I immediately caught one running cold after another. However, my own quarters were comparatively private and quite nice to live in. A wireless provided the most welcome entertainment with regular broadcasts of dance music for the services featuring the leading bands such as Ivy Benson and her all-girls band etc. The music at this time was very relaxing to hear and life in general better than had been experienced for some time.

During the months of service with the Lothians I had acquired a taste for their national product, whisky, which was readily available from Scotland to the regiment. My personal preference was to mix this with dry ginger, but the latter seemed to have more burps to the bottle than anything else I knew, so I changed to peppermint instead. This latter mixture was considered sacrilege by the Scotsmen as most of them drank the spirit neat, which did not appeal to me at all.

There was one relaxing occasion when the Americans and Canadians joined us in a day of various sporting activities, ending up with a dance in the evening. As all these nationalities liked their whisky, it flowed freely and I remember counting 17 including doubles before it was time for the last waltz, when I was on the floor (vertically) as usual. A good time was had by all and I had not far to walk back to my billet.

One of the doubtful advantages of being on guard all night is the opportunity to think with no-one to disturb the thoughts, and after three years in the forces I had plenty to think about, both happy and otherwise. Army life had promoted self-discipline and the ability to take a more objective look at things that happen. With the thousands of personalities around me this was an ideal opportunity to study human nature from one of its extremes to the other, the contradictions being enormous. My thoughts turned to one of the most vile personalities I ever met, which happened in London's Underground when the stations were crowded all night with people trying to rest. I met a French Foreign Legionnaire who looked as if he would as soon kill anyone as look at them. For some reason he said to me, 'I want to get back to Morocco, where everything I steal is mine.' I didn't doubt for a moment that he really meant it. It is on occasions like this that it is natural to wonder just what sort of life a person has led, to talk and act in this manner. What hope is there in life for people like this who will always be lonely even in a crowded railway station?

Experience had taught me that, without in any way being selfish, a soldier had to look after himself to the best of his ability, and early on at Catterick I found that if I sat next to a Jew at breakfast time on those rare occasions when bacon was served I was able to have two rashers instead of one, which I thoroughly enjoyed. Religions, in my experience, all seem to have a habit of either forcing believers to change their natural bodies in some way or other, or to change eating habits by fasting or feasting at certain times of the year, or to deviate from what would be the normal, sensible lifestyle. Anyhow, the bacon tasted good to me. For myself, if I had to have a motto it would be 'Eat well and work well', with the former helping the latter. I think a man needs both these equally if he is to fill his ambitions in life in a satisfactory manner. I have been blessed with an excellent appetite for both.

On 7 July 1943 I was issued with the War Office ID for vehicle drivers (Army Form A2038). This was granted on an annual basis and in my case for the classification 'Light vehicles', which in practice meant anything up and including 30-cwt trucks. Having passed out on wheels using a 15-cwt rather open type truck, I liked the driving cab of the GMC or Leyland much better and they were far more comfortable to drive.

As equipment repairer, I was well known to all as invariably everybody in the regiment needed my services at some time or other. This helped me to have the use of an army bicycle which I could use in the evenings to go to dances at nearby villages such as Frome (pronounced mysteriously by the locals as 'Froom') and Trowbridge, which was easy riding because of the level countryside there. Apart from this relaxation, a special train ran for us on Saturdays to Bath at a cost of 2½ pence return, which Eddie and myself took at every opportunity. Bath seemed to us to be a very attractive town but dominated by American troops as they had at last joined in the war.

The uniform issued to the Yanks was similar in quality and style to our own officers' uniform service dress and made our battledress look distinctly dowdy. However, not to be outdone, I acquired a service dress of my own which I was allowed to wear when off duty. It looked rather smart, having blue lapels on the shoulders, an honour apparently conferred upon the Lothians by Queen Victoria in appreciation of their musical rides. Regimental brass buttons completed the individuality of this uniform with 'collar dogs' of small wheatsheaf motif fastened on each side of the collars.

Naturally the girls all went for the Yanks at the dances as they all appeared to be rolling in money compared with our service pay. On enquiring, I was told that some of the medal ribbons that they wore were for such things as swimming. As they had only been called up a few weeks it seemed strange to us to see a row of ribbons and in complete contrast to our own idea of active service or bravery, or both, being the requisite for any medals. Resentment against the Americans was considerable for these reasons, and because of their perceived advantage over our own troops and their rather disrespectful manner in general, chewing gum all the time and speaking with such a drawl.

Tank training continued at Warminster on the nearby Salisbury Plain, which had long been used for this purpose. The former types of tanks were being replaced again by the American Sherman type, considered to be better or newer and being supplied in readiness for the forthcoming invasion of the Continent.

After some months at Warminster a series of moves took place, the first being to Adderbury, near Banbury, where they have the famous cross and a scantily clad woman on a white horse. She was not around when I was there. Here my workshop was in a building surrounded by apple trees. When ready for eating, the apples were freely available and I sent some home on one occasion. No doubt the previous occupiers of these properties would be far away somewhere and it was a shame not to put them to good use, especially when the country was crying out for any home-grown food.

The next move came quickly and this time we moved the fairly short distance to Henley-on-Thames, where the regatta is held, and were billeted in modern buildings something like a hospital, which probably started the story off that it was a VD camp, but with hindsight this was most probably not true. The conjecture arose from the fact that every toilet was being flushed constantly and only stopped when someone sat on the seat, which was rather strange experience the first time that it was tried. Our own communal knowledge of these diseases was limited to having been shown an army film on the subject in our early training and learning the effect of bromide in the tea every Friday. (The tea was never drunk, just thrown away.)

We were on the move again not long after arriving at Henley, this time much farther away at Wickham Market in Suffolk, where the nearest town of any size was Ipswich. This was to be the first time I had seen a modern pig farm, a far cry from my childhood memories at Galphay. This particular pigsty was so big that the whole regiment could be seated in it for concerts when ENSA came along to entertain the troops in isolated places. In the event I never saw a single pig there, so the farm must have been taken over by the military some time before.

The building that I had to use for my equipment repairing was shared with the three regimental boot repairers none of whom, incidentally had been in the trade before joining up. One had been a grocer, the second I have forgotten and the third, Jack Poulter, worked in a chemist's shop, Thompson & Capper in Huddersfield, and one of the very few men I ever met from my own home town. He had a considerable knowledge of his former trade and it was he who advised me to obtain some corn and wart solvent to clear the horrible wart that I had on my right hand from making thread every day over a long period. Anyhow, it worked and the wart completely disappeared in time, much to my relief.

Jack had a very dry sense of humour (any type of humour was an asset in the army) and one night when we were all in bed after lights out, one of the other boot repairers insisted in talking when everybody else wanted to go to sleep. Jack, having heard enough, suddenly said, 'Shut up, I'm reading,' and bearing in mind the pitch-black of the hut this raised a laugh and had the desired effect. It is amazing what a suitable word or phrase can do in certain circumstances.

Some 20 or 30 yards from our workshop we could see pheasants going about their daily non-military service and they presented a simple target for the .22 rifle that had come into my possession. If anyone wanted a brace to take on leave, this could easily be arranged, although I never attempted to take any the 200 or so miles home when my leave came round.

I have already mentioned our experience in the gas chamber, and as part of the continuing training in gas warfare it was decided that our respirators were to be worn for a whole hour once a week, progressing weekly to two, three and finally four hours. Wearing them even for a short while with anti-mist having been applied to the eyepieces was not pleasant, and if anyone could avoid wearing them at all they did so. It was on occasions like this that our workshop became a haven of refuge for anyone wanting to take their respirator off for a while. With one man standing at each end of the workshop, we could see if anyone in authority was approaching, giving us plenty of time to put the respirators back on. In practice even the Regimental Sergeant Major was glad to come in and scrounge out of the way for a while. Officers seemed to be conspicuous by their absence, probably having found their own bolt hole to hide in. Thankfully the last of these four weeks came and went and things came back to normal working, as it was absolutely impossible for me to do any work at all wearing a respirator on my face and the respirator bag tied on my chest.

Christmas time came round again, with the usual routine of officers and NCOs serving dinner and beer flowing in generous proportions. Again, as usual, I ended up on all-night guard duties, being one of the few sober individuals due to my dislike of any type of beer. During my service I actually was on guard four of the five Christmases. This particular year we had four days free of duties and the four of us played cards for literally the whole of the time, there being nothing better to do.

The occasional trips to Ipswich, where, like York, I had the luxury of a normal bath, were few and far between but the change was always welcome. There was a tea dance there as well but I cannot remember its location.

The air bombardment of Germany and the occupied countries was by now in full swing and the never-to-be-forgotten sight of a thousand bombers roaring overhead in wave after wave, filling the whole sky, became a nightly occurrence. Obvious preparations for the impending invasion could be seen and in my own case I was detailed to attend at the famous Addenbrooke's hospital in Cambridge for yet another ear examination. Following the report of this I was called before another medical board at Saxmundham in Suffolk, where they decided to downgrade me to 'permanent C2', which was the lowest medical category still allowed to be in the services at that time. This was on 19 April 1944. Having been A1, B1 and A2, I was now C2. The medical boards were engaged in weeding out all the low-category men ready for the invasion and this was the final act of my service in the Lothians as I was now to be sent to Oxford, where all similar low-category troops from all regiments were being assembled prior to onward posting to their respective bases. Having said my goodbyes to my pal Eddie and the other friends that I had made, it was with many mixed feelings and innumerable thoughts of times both good and bad that I made my way from Wickham Market for the last time. One lesson one learns is that, after a long period of confined living with a small community with all its faults, it is better to try to remember the good times and forget the others.

At Oxford there was little in the way of parades as there wasn't a fit man in the lot of us. I palled up with a low-category man with eye trouble by the name of 'Happy' Greenman, so called because he invariably had a smile on his face with lovely white teeth showing up well against his fresh-faced complexion. As a Londoner he was quite a character. Once, when we were walking along the road in Oxford, we noticed an officer approaching on the other side. Happy said, 'Have we to salute him or not, being so far away?' and I did not see much point in it so we didn't bother. The result was that the officer was not concerned and Happy said, 'If he says anything I'll tell him I couldn't see him and you say you couldn't hear him.' At this we had a good laugh, walked on and did not salute.

Having mentioned the marvellous sight of the thousand-bomber raids, we were to witness another just as spectacular at Oxford. One night all eyes turned to the night sky to see an armada of aircraft towing gliders flying southwards to invade the Continent. After all these years this was it and history was being seen in the making. There was no need to ask if this was actually the invasion as it was so vast and took ages to pass overhead. My thoughts were with my former men in the Lothians, wondering where they were as the whole of southern England was teeming with British, Canadian and American troops all massed in readiness to attack.

From Oxford I was posted, along with other Royal Armoured Corps personnel, back to the base at Catterick where I had joined up as a trooper in 1940. My lance corporal's stripe was withdrawn on leaving the regiment on 29 April 1944; I had held that rank from 3 November 1942. In view of my previous comments re the treatment of us Sassenachs in the Lothians, the reader will not be surprised to hear that my replacement as regimental equipment repairer was immediately made up to full sergeant on appointment, even though he had virtually no experience of the work involved. He was, of course, Scottish. On hearing about this later, I could not help wondering what my fate would have been if only I had been born Jock McWalkley. Food for thought!

Back at Catterick, I came under the orders of a certain Sergeant Joe Charlton, a man with only one eye who had been in the 7th Hussars as a regular soldier and was about finishing his time, usually 21 years service. He ran the saddler's shop in the camp and employed five or six similar to myself, including another time-expired sergeant from another cavalry regiment. The main occupation appeared to be making ladies' handbags from saddle pigskin, which had a lovely rich colour, and using a brown smooth goat leather for the inside pockets. These were of absolutely first-class quality and being hand sewn were in much demand from the officers. Any work of a regimental nature that needed to be done was done by myself or one of the other 'stooges', whilst the sergeant carried on with his 'private' work.

Private work was not frowned on at all as there was so little army work needed, the base being full of men who had already done their training and it was ready for the eventual repatriation of overseas troops arriving from Africa, Italy and Burma. I soon realised the opportunities in making handbags and shopping bags, so when I was able to go home on leave I bought as much leather as I could afford and carry, brought it back to camp and started to make my own bags in the evenings after finishing my ordinary day's work. I found a ready outlet for all the bags I could make, a department store with branches in Darlington and Middlesbrough. Either a train or bicycle ride was all that was needed for delivery at weekends.

Here I must mention 'Cook's tea', which was a twice-daily ritual in the cookhouse when the cooks made a real cup of tea for themselves and anyone lucky enough to be supplied by them. It became one of my routine jobs at the saddler's shop to fetch this tea from the cookhouse with the appropriate container, a former seven-pound jam tin fitted with a wire handle for carrying which held just enough for the few of us in the workshop. I have always tried to treat people in the same way that I myself like to be treated, and having gained quite a lot of experience firstly in the shoe shop and afterwards in the army, I was always able to approach others in such a way that they wanted to oblige with whatever was needed and in a pleasant and willing manner. This way of dealing with all sorts of individuals, all in their own way differing from one another, can be most helpful – as was the case with the cook's tea. None of the others in the saddler's shop were ever able to get any if they went to collect it, and yet I had absolutely no problem at all. The tone of voice, the correct approach and a pleasant manner can work wonders with most people.

Whilst at Catterick I received just one letter from my former pal Eddie in the Lothians, just before they were to attempt to cross the Rhine, but as nothing else ever came I never knew whether they actually made it across or not, nor what happened afterwards if they were successful. In my case for most of the time the war had seemed so far away, with the exception of my month in London, and most of the news we got came from listening to the wireless.

Catterick became the receiving depot for foreign serving men from the Eighth Army, from Italy and later from Burma and the Far East. Although literally hundreds of men from the Eighth Army passed through, as time went on and more were being repatriated I can honestly say that I personally never heard a single one have a word of praise for their leader, General (later Field Marshal) Montgomery. This seemed incredible to me after reading so much in the papers and hearing the news broadcast by the BBC on his exploits in North Africa. Seeing all these veterans of recent desert battles in camp with their medal ribbons, some having five in all, made me feel extremely embarrassed about having nothing to show on my battledress, because at first sight it looked to others coming into the camp as if I had been there all the war doing a 'soft job'. Not true, of course, but an obvious conclusion to jump to. Like over 90 per cent of all servicemen, I am neither a natural hero nor a coward but simply do the duty demanded where and when it comes. Spending all my time sewing equipment hardly seemed to be able to be compared with what these veterans had gone through during the same years, but for everyone in the front line many more are needed to provide the necessary back-up to keep them fighting.

I remember going into the washhouse one morning and noticing no less than four glass eyes on the washbowls where the men had taken them out before their morning wash. These men, often placed in Category B, had lost something irreplaceable in life and it was a very sobering experience to see this sort of sacrifice.

Besides the British soldiers returning to England, there was a fairly large contingent of German prisoners of war who, like ourselves, had been conscripted into their war and were also previously just ordinary workmen and a far cry from the arrogant SS types portrayed in the films. Within a very short time any feeling of animosity towards the enemy had completely disappeared as we all got to know one another, and I took the opportunity to further my learning of the German language, which had been cut short in 1940 when I joined the army.

One other brief opportunity occurred when they asked for volunteers to go in the army of occupation, but I had no wish to stay in any longer than necessary.

Eventually, on 8 May 1945 the Germans surrendered, signalling the end of the war in Europe, although the Japanese war was to continue for another three months or so. With the help of my bicycle, I made my way towards Huddersfield on that memorable day and even got a lift in a truck (complete with bike in the back) and arrived sometime during the hours of daylight. A half-bottle of whisky helped with the celebrations, for this was to be a very special day for me personally.

Some weeks later, after the dropping of two atomic bombs on Japan, the Japanese surrendered and the war was finally over. Thoughts naturally turned to wondering how long it might be before we were released from the army and we soon learned that a scheme had been worked out putting men into groups, the formula for which included both the age of the soldier and the length of service and, I believe, took into account any overseas service. My group was to be No. 34, which meant that at the rate of releasing I would still have to serve another 12 months or so. As I was called up at the age of 20, the weighting of the formula for grouping gave precedence to older men even though they had actually served a far shorter length of time than I had.

With the war over and the lights coming back on again, the atmosphere at Catterick Camp changed. There were relaxations to some of the rules and regulations, giving more freedom – particularly to going out in the evenings if we wanted to. A Northern Command exhibition of our hand-sewn craftwork was held in York, where I think six different exhibits were warmly commended. An education unit was set up and I was asked to stay on in the Education Corps in the rank of sergeant, but I declined this offer as I thought it better to make my own way in life in Civvy Street. Whilst at Catterick we had a visit from a miniature mass X-ray unit, which is recorded in my AB 64 stating No. 23248 negative. The last inoculations, typhus 1, 2 and 3 with TTs and TAB were performed in 1944, which just about filled the requisite page.

On the Quartermaster's staff when applying for a 36 or 48-hour pass it was the procedure to complete a pass form, have this 'backed' by the QM and present it at the orderly room for either acceptance or refusal as the case may be. Only a certain proportion were allowed each weekend but supply and demand did come into it as well as if a soldier lived a very long way from the camp a weekend leave was hardly worth while in view of the travelling time involved. If a pass was granted, the orderly room messenger, 'Geordie', would deliver them personally to each successful applicant in the late afternoon on Fridays and he, like everyone else, knew me quite well. For some reason Tynesiders seemed to always call me Wakley instead of Walkley but no matter. On one of these occasions when I had applied for a pass Geordie told me that it had been refused, and I was naturally disappointed but amazed when some little while later he came back to me holding a pass for Walkley. Containing my own surprise at this puzzling development, I made myself ready and got away just as fast as I could. I had noticed the words 'Compassionate leave' in red ink at the top of the form and, although quite intrigued by this I had learned not to ask silly questions; you live and learn in the army. However, on arriving back in camp the following Monday morning, or should I say 23.59 hours Sunday night, all was revealed. Another Walkley should have had my pass, or at least I should not have had his. With having a rather uncommon name, a mix-up occurred when Trooper Walkley 7924622 applied for compassionate leave to visit his wife at York, who had quinsies, at the same time that I had applied, and by a strange coincidence we had identical army numbers except for one single digit. Afterwards he was known as Walkley 22 and I was, of course, Walkley 62, which were the last two digits of our respective numbers.

When going on leave after the war was over it was not obligatory to carry arms, whereas when in the Lothians I had to go home with a .38 revolver strapped round one leg and resting in a webbing holster looped round my belt, making it most awkward to walk normally. The idea was, of course, that a soldier must be able to defend himself at all times, even though it was almost impossible to extract the bullets from their individual pockets on the front of the holster and we had never been able to practise doing this either. On arriving with this equipment at a dance, I had to hand in my black beret and revolver at the 'cloaks' before going in to the dance hall and collect them afterwards on the way out.

Entertainment at the camp was still the inevitable housey-housey, but not being confined to barracks we could now go to a dance in the nearby village hall, which had hitherto been just outside the actual camp itself. When time permitted I would cycle as far as Northallerton, Darlington or Stockton-on-Tees, all of which had very good dance floors.

When Group 34 eventually became due for release in July 1946 the final farce in my medical classification took place and is recorded in the AB 64 on 23 July showing yet another regrading, this time upwards to B1. So starting at A1, I had been B1, then A2, then C2 and finally B1, when probably my ear condition had been very little different during the whole six years. Obviously there must have been some reason for the final upgrading on the day before my release. My best guess would be that having been accepted as A1 on joining the army and ending up at 'permanent C2', it could possibly be argued that there was a case for compensation of some form or other on these grounds. My AB 64 was now finished with and the release leave certificate duly completed. It is perhaps interesting to note that a separate receipt had to be given when the man's greatcoat was surrendered, with another receipt on the back to be forwarded to the regimental paymaster at Bradford if the coat was not handed in.

My 'testimonial' states 'military conduct – very good' followed by 'the above mentioned has been employed by me for the past eighteen months as equipment repairer, he has given satisfaction in his work which was up to army standards. He is a willing and hard worker'. It was duly signed both by myself and the Camp Commandant on 24 July 1946. Army Book X 801 was handed to me and I went to No.2 military dispersal unit at York to be supplied with civilian clothes and my final railway warrant back to Huddersfield. The 'thank you' comments and a sum of £225 were all I had to show for some seven years in khaki, including the time spent in the Duke of Wellington's Regiment (Home Guard).

5

Setting Up on My Own

I had now to take a decision on my future work. Mr Hays informed me that on his doctor's advice he had sold the business to a consortium of three local men who formed a company, H. Hays (Huddersfield) Ltd for the purpose, Under the sale agreement he was to be allowed to live rent-free for the rest of his life in a room above the shop, exactly as he had previously done before the war at No. 29 Northgate. The move actually was from No. 29 to No. 39 Northgate, on the same side of the road but on the far side of Northumberland Street. This situation obviously meant that I would never be able to acquire the business as had been intended when I first went to work there, which was really quite a devastating blow to me personally as I had worked like mad to achieve that objective. However, obstacles are made to be overcome and I just had to try to put the past behind me and try to make up for what I thought should have been the best six years of my life. Thousands of others would, no doubt, be in the same position and at least I had come back in good health apart from my ear trouble.

Mr Hays was not as happy at No. 39 as he had expected and hoped to be and, following some harsh words, he moved out of his room into 'digs'. For the good of his health he decided to live in Torquay for the winter six months, hoping that the weather in the south would be more beneficial for his bronchitis. I took him there by car and brought him back afterwards, so that in the summer months he was quite prepared to help me if he could. Even if I had been asked, which I wasn't, I could not have gone back to work for the new owners as my pride would just not allow

78

me to do so and it would definitely not have worked out anyhow, so there seemed little point in trying. The only alternative, therefore, seemed to be to set up on my own making clogs as this was the only thing I really knew that seemed to offer any real prospect for the future.

Having made up my mind, the first thing to be done was to try to find some suitable premises to start up in. After looking at various empty buildings I was eventually able to find what seemed to be a likely place on the opposite side of the road on Northgate, perhaps some hundred yards or so from the old shop. This opportunity came about because Mr Hays and a Mr Joe Rushworth had both had similar working-class footwear businesses on Northgate for a long time and, though in competition, were very friendly and would help one another out if there was a shortage of any particular line that they both stocked. On occasions like this I had been sent along to Rushworth's pre-war to collect pairs of footwear, so Mr Rushworth had got to know me. As a result of this situation Mr Rushworth offered to let me use his boot repairing premises situated in a separate building from his shop on the opposite side of a small yard. Unfortunately from a retail selling point of view the premises were out of sight from Northgate, being down a yard, but as I thought at the time, I would rather start down a back yard than finish up down one. I jumped at the chance offered and was happy with a rental of just £1 per week. At the far end of the yard were the toilets for both premises and a house next door. A flight of stone steps led from the yard to the cellar door.

One advantage of the agreement to rent the property was that as Mr Rushworth had not been actually using his repair workshops for some time, he did still have an allocation of bend leather which I could use myself for whatever purpose I wanted. Having obtained a business address, I applied for the necessary licences to buy upper leather and to make clogs; all types of leather were in such short supply and strictly controlled after six years of war.

No. 110 Northgate had originally been a house with a cellar and three floors above. The repairing had been done on the top floor and still contained the usual boot repairing machinery,

79

including a finishing machine which I had already used, a two-man cobblers' bench and the heavy brass rollers used to firm up the leather after wetting. The rollers formed a convex shape on the leather soles, which helped them to fit better onto the shoes whilst being riveted on. An iron fire escape was reached by walking out through a very large window and down into the yard below. It was also handy to drop anything unbreakable down to save walking up and down two flights of stairs. The ground floor room was about 12 to 14 feet square, with an old iron fireplace used to burn solid fuel for heating purposes. Stone steps led down into the cellar, which had for some reason been extended through under another house in the next yard along the road. Why this should have been done I did not know but it doubled the space for storing clog soles at a low temperature. At first I decided to use the ground floor room to make the clogs, the top floor for boot repairing and the middle room for the storage of anything not needed in the other two rooms. Considerable changes had to be made, including making a two-man cloggers' bench in front of the window and putting the heavy sewing machine in the middle with hand punches and eyeletting machines fastened on one end of the bench.

Fortunately, being rather a methodical type of person, I have always kept the petty cash book from the day I started so I am now able to refresh my memory on a lot of the details of these early days. The opening page of this book lists all the expenditure incurred prior to officially commencing business on 15 November 1946. Among sundry items are the 45K heavy-duty second-hand sewing machine at a cost of £10, an old desk for £1.50, Bunsen burner and piping for 30 pence, a stithy for 62½ pence and a deposit of £3 paid to Huddersfield Corporation Electricity Department as I had not previously had an account with them. This was the ruling before they would connect a supply or provide the supply to an existing one if a new tenant took over. A letter box, hammers, electric globes, postage, ready reckoner, Factory Act forms, buckets, brushes etc. produced a grand total of £80.10 expended in order to start up.

It will be remembered that our pre-war trade of making and selling clogs had been virtually all retail over the counter. On returning after the war this situation had changed completely with clogs, in common with other wearables such as aprons, overalls, gloves, kneepads, helmets etc., having come under the classification of 'protective clothing', being supplied by employers for the use of their employees whilst at work. This presented me with no option but to build up a wholesale trade, selling in bulk to any likely buyers. Firstly I had to be fitted up to make the clogs, and in view of the fact that it was to be industry buying them, it seemed prudent to design patterns as economically as possible rather than the more eye-appealing patterns used in the former retail trade.

Accordingly, having bought a size 8 wooden last and a small quantity of leather, I sat down with sheets of brown paper to draft out a straight-sided style to be used for all types of lace-up derby clogs, with a lower-back version exactly the same but having only four eyelets, for pit use. The shape at the base followed the contours of the clog sole welt, with the sides designed to nearly meet over the instep. From such a basic start the only method to achieve eventual accuracy was by trial and error, getting progressively nearer each time until a perfectly satisfactory shape for the back and vamp evolved, the tongue and stiffener presenting no problems at all. To produce a pattern from a flat piece of paper which, when cut out of leather and lasted to shape, would fit perfectly was no mean task and it was with some quiet satisfaction that I eventually managed it. Having made a size 8 man's size it was relatively easy to grade 9s, 10s and 11s upwards and 7s, 6s and 5s downwards as each size in footwear represents one-third of an inch in length, to be divided up between the back and vamp patterns.

Having applied for my licence some time previously I queried the apparently undue delay in receiving it, and it was here that I was to receive my first real dose of stupid red tape. The application to obtain leather for the uppers met with a refusal because I did not have a licence to make clogs, so, according to the logic of officialdom, I did not need one. But wait, my application to make clogs was refused because I did not have a licence to buy upper leather and so could not make them. Naturally I was furious at this crazy situation, which reminded me of the saying that common sense is one of the most uncommon things there are. From the early age of 20 my hair (like my mother's and grandmother's) had started to go white, and no doubt gained quite a boost from this experience in dealing with the civil service people.

In our area we came under the control of the Leeds office, from where the Leather Controller came to visit me as a result of my applications. No doubt he also wanted to see what the premises were like and if I was a suitable person for the granting of licences. On his arrival, seeing that I was trying to make patterns, he greeted me with the question, 'What do you think that you are doing?' to which I replied that I was making clogs, adding that I couldn't live on nothing as the army pay to cover the first three months had expired. This portly self-important bombastic type of man made unprintable thoughts pass through my mind as I cannot stand arrogance, especially after seeing my fair share of it in some sections of the army. Any fair-minded person would have taken an instant dislike to this official. Gradually he seemed to calm down when I had stood up to him and explained the ridiculous position of the two applications, which was patently obvious to him. On departing he agreed to see what he could do for me but it seemed to me that his impression of the situation was that I did not actually have any trade and to that extent did not need supplies of leather. That certainly was one way of looking at it, but from my point of view I couldn't get any business for clogs if I had nothing to make them with, apart from not having official permission to manufacture anyhow. None of the clogmakers in the trade had any of this bother as they were already trading and I felt penalised for having been in the services.

It was to be Christmas Eve before my first licence was received, Christmas boxes come in strange packets sometimes. Apart from a small amount of repairing brought across from Rushworth's shop which I was able to do with the allocation of sole leather, I made full use of this material in the making of ladies' sandals, the upper leather for these being available from Fairburns in town. As footwear was still supplied only on coupons, it was possible to sell every pair that could be made without the necessity of dealing in coupons when made on an individual basis and in small quantities. Besides making these, I also turned my hand to men's slippers, where again the patterns were reasonably easy to design, or at least they seemed so after what I had done previously. The large allocation of leather in stock at Fairburns, in a wide selection of colours, was instrumental in helping me to make the shopping bags I had made in the army. One type of leather used for this purpose was upholstery leather with a rich brownish-red colour, which looked very attractive when made up. A further line introduced shortly afterwards in time for the 'back-to-school' trade was the leather schoolbags from shiny brown 'shoulder' leather provided by Fairburns and sold back to them wholesale, along with the shopping bags. This situation worked quite well for both of us.

By this time Mr Rushworth, a sufferer from Parkinson's disease, had sold his retail shop to a Mr H.D. Carter, a former shoe firm representative who had called upon him many times and could see the potential the opportunity offered. He carried on bringing any repairs to me as before and was interested in clogs as he also acquired another shop at Penistone, some 12 miles or so away. Any clogs that he collected from me were either sold immediately in the shop or brought back, so he actually received payment before buying the goods himself. Good business if you can get it. As I had not had much actual experience in doing the boot and shoe repairing myself pre-war and did not really like the job anyhow, I was not disappointed when eventually this stopped altogether. It was not really worth while doing with such a small amount coming in, besides charging trade prices to Mr Carter for him to sell retail.

Whilst working all hours in the autumn of 1946 in a determined effort to succeed and make a living, there developed a situation one evening about ten o'clock when I started to see 'double', due to overwork and being tired out. As I could see two rivets instead of one and didn't know which one to hit, so to speak, I simply had to stop work. I was very frightened at this sudden development, so I went down into the middle room and sat there until I felt all right again.

It was about this time that I was to have one of the most infuriating and annoying experiences of my life. Two men in civilian dress arrived at Northgate, having been sent there by my mother, as they had naturally gone to my home address, obtained from the army records of release. Apparently they were investigating stolen lino from Catterick camp, about which, of course, I knew nothing. They stated that two witnesses, one in Scotland and the other in the Midlands, both said that I had taken this lino. By now it had transpired that they were from the SIB, the army investigation branch. Whether this tale they were telling me was true or not I did not know, but I felt sure that if my three month's release leave had not expired and I had still been officially in the services, they would have taken me back to Catterick. Fortunately, it was too late for that now, but it could have had devastating effects on the work that I was trying to do to get going in business. They eventually left. When I arrived home I found my mother really upset by the events and we were both incensed at what had happened. I remembered that one of the last tasks given to me shortly before leaving the army was to lay a Tarran hut out with lino. The hut was so big that it took three widths and a whole length of roll to cover it, but whether this could have anything to do with the present loss was not clear. I was ready to sue for defamation of character etc. but Mr Hays advised me to ignore the matter completely, saying that if I knew nothing about it then there was nothing to worry about, but I did not see it in that light at all. Human nature does not always accept the obvious when wrongly accused of something. Many weeks later I heard that the culprits, a NAAFI girl and her soldier boyfriend, had admitted to the theft, but I heard nothing directly from the SIB or indeed received any apology from the army at all.

Nearing the end of October the clogging room was ready for use and I made a long shelf for clog stock, sufficient to hold 18 pairs of each size on each shelf, running from size 6 to 11 inclusive. The Bunsen burner had been piped up to the gas supply and a cradle fixed up to take the slickering iron. Having decided to set one boy on right from the start, I placed an advertisement in the local paper and made my choice from the applicants. Nelson Rush became the first employee and as from 15 November 1946 I was able to start the books, even though no licences had been received at that time. The making of shopping bags on a regular

JUSTICE TO THE TOILERS

LABOUR WITH HONOUR

THE AMALGAMATED SOCIETY

OF

JOURNEYMEN CLOGGERS

BY COMBINATION

WE SHALL SUCCEED.

CLOGGER

THIS IS TO CERTIFY

THAT

THE HOLDER OF THIS CERTIFICATE COMPLIES WITH
ALL THE RULES AND CONDITIONS IMPOSED
BY OUR SOCIETY AND AMALGAMATION
FOR THE BENEFIT OF ITS MEMBERS AND IS
DESERVING OF THE SUPPORT OF THE PUBLIC.

(COPYRIGHT.)

85

basis, together with the trade from Rushworth's next door, would enable me to have a weekly wage of £3 and pay Nelson £1.15, a fair rate for a 14-year-old at that time. I approached the same bank, accountant and the suppliers that Mr Hays had used before the war and opened the business account with Midland Bank, using the £225 that I had received on leaving the army.

Although it was my intention to build up a trade large enough to be called a wholesale clog manufacturer, in the early stages this was obviously impossible and I decided to join the Amalgamated Society of Master Cloggers, who were mainly in the Lancashire area and held meetings quarterly in a pub at Burnley. Having been accepted into the society, I cycled to Burnley to these Sunday meetings every three months, which was a distance of some 30 miles or so. Looking back, I think that I must have been very lucky with the weather on these occasions as I cannot remember arriving there or back wet through. There were no less than 20 local associations in the society, each sending a representative to the meeting who would no doubt report back. The roll call, in alphabetical order, started off: Accrington, Blackburn, Bolton, Burnley, Chorley, Darwen, Nelson and Colne, Oldham, Preston, Rochdale, Rossendale, West Cumberland and Wigan. Individual members were listed as Anglesey, Tyldesley, Garstang, Cleethorpes, Manchester and Sheffield.

The 48-page handbook issued to me contained the revised rules and objects of the society, wage lists and agreements and other useful information, and was published not long before I joined in July 1948; the original Society was formed in 1894. Among the 13 rules which were agreed to at the formation meeting Rule No. 8 makes very interesting reading and is well worth quoting.

Should it occur that a journeyman cannot be employed in his own locality and shall have occasion to take out a card for tramping, then shall the town from where he first takes out his card pay all his expenses so long as he remains on the road, and not to have less than one shilling [fivepence] per day and a bed at night and that each locality shall provide its own stamp for stamping tramping cards.

A price list drawn up by a local association in 1871 regretting that prices would have to rise (was inflation on the way then?) states under the heading public notice:

Men's Best Dandies   22$^1/_2$ pence.
Women's   17 pence.
Children's, varying between 12 pence and 7$^1/_2$ pence.
Re-clogging: Men's 7$^1/_2$ pence, Women's 6 pence,
                    Children's 5 pence.

The trade at that time must have had a very low opinion of itself, as these prices did not reflect the high degree of craftsmanship that went into the making of clog soles by hand, apart from hand-sewn clog uppers and the ensuing making up.

With the Amendment of the Rules on 29 April 1947 Object 2B enabled members to join the 'mutual accident and death benefit scheme'. Later as more and more older members died, the position arose where it was impossible to pay out what should be paid under the rules because membership was decreasing rapidly, and in the end it was decided to abandon the society and pay out the remaining balance of the fund to the few remaining members. With my share I bought a clock as a memento of the time I had been a master clogger with the society.

Page 19 of the handbook lists the rules of the mutual accident and death benefit fund rules, pages 30 and 31 list wages for clog sole making, seat work and jobbing work, with wage rates quoted per dozen pairs, all piece rates to be plussed by 20 per cent. It is to be remembered that the issue of this handbook coincided with the introduction of the new Health Service Act on 5 July 1948.

I contacted the clog sole manufacturers at Snaith near Goole, who agreed to supply me with what soles they could, bearing in mind the severe shortage of timber supplies. Mr Hays always had bought their soles pre-war and this no doubt had some influence in the decision at that time. The local leather merchants, Denham Bros., situated in Pack Horse Yard at Huddersfield, stocked all the other items needed to make clogs, including the various shapes of clog irons, tip nails, welt nails, toetins, thread, eyelets and the other make of clog soles, by John Maude & Son Ltd, of

Hebden Bridge and also Barnard Castle.

In order to actually make a start I managed to obtain a small supply of waxed split leather from Denhams as they used it themselves in the making of clog uppers for re-sale to their boot repairer customers, who invariably did a bit of clogging as well. At this time Denhams employed both a full-time clicker and a lady closer who also did the machine skiving etc. All sizes of children's uppers were made, using a soft brown grain leather.

Apart from the shop next door, probably my first real customer for industrial clogs was Frank Fairburn & Sons Ltd, on Victoria Lane, Huddersfield, who were also, like Denhams, leather and grindery merchants, but they had a large shop selling retail whereas Denhams had no shop at all. Fairburns had a large stock of all types of leather goods from small purses to large suitcases and trunks. Naturally, this type of trade included clogs, which they had always bought from the manufacturer who supplied Mr Hays with men's clog uppers pre-war, William Lamb, whose works was at Bottomboat in Stanley, outside Wakefield. Fairburns shop was able to supply me with the types of leather needed for shopping bags and Denhams supplied me with a whole range of clog-making materials in these initial stages of the business.

My first licence arrived at Christmas and it was not long before the other followed, and I was now in a position to concentrate on building up a wholesale clog trade. As my potential market was in the heavy industries, I made lists of likely users of my clogs from the classified directories which I obtained for all over the UK, such as steelworks, chemical works and breweries. I produced a circular letter, printed at a cost of £7.55, to send out to all on my lists, offering my services as a supplier of clogs. This method of introduction, a rather time-consuming exercise, was definitely not a success, possibly because by addressing the envelope to the company itself it would simply end up in the waste-paper basket as most post rooms would simply throw such items away. I soon found out that it was the individual responsible for buying that I needed to contact, although this was not always the case. Personal contact, in effect knocking on doors, was needed to both find out who actually did the ordering and introduce myself to that person in order to attract business.

Accordingly, I had a bicycle made to my own specification (at no extra charge) incorporating both the highest and lowest sprockets made, and with a third one halfway between the two called a cyclo-derailler, I think, which allowed me to ride up the steepest gradient at a slower than walking pace but with virtually no physical effort. This cycle was to be my means of transport for quite some time and paid for itself many times over. In order to carry samples of clogs I made a saddlebag to fit them and this was attached to the saddle at the back. I was now ready to take on the world, or was I?

In late February I joined the Huddersfield Boot Trades Association, which was not very helpful in my case as I was trying to specialise in clogs. I remember one member from Milnsbridge saying to me, on hearing what I was trying to do, 'I would rather you do it than me,' to which I replied that if he had no repairing work in he had to be idle but if I had no work on order I could make clogs ready for when they could be sold, thus having no idle time. He took the point but was not particularly impressed with my argument. I was hoping that joining the BTA would spread the word around that I was in business and, hopefully, bring in some trade from boot repairers who might have a small demand for clogs and found that it simply was not worth their while stocking all sizes of the various components needed to make them.

I was now working all hours to teach Nelson clogmaking, cutting the uppers during the day, and having taken one sewing machine home, stitched anything up to 18 pairs during the course of the evening. By passing a length of string through them, I carried them on my back as I cycled to work the following morning. It was soon evident that I could actually buy men's split uppers from a Cumbrian upper maker cheaper than I could make them myself, which would enable me to spend more time on the road looking for trade. This maker used a higher back pattern than I liked, so I decided to cut about an inch off the top part to make them look more like my own patterns, and then these were sewn all the way round the top again. The quality of the leather was not to my satisfaction either but the clog trade was changing and I had to change with it. Looking ahead, it seemed to me that a combination of craftsmanship and mass production had to be the answer in the days to come. However, for the present, buying these uppers was serving its purpose.

Clogs were now considered by a lot of companies to be an expendable item to be purchased as cheaply as possible, worn to destruction and discarded on being replaced by a new pair. In many cases this made economic sense as the time and cost of repairing was not a viable proposition, bearing in mind that to reclog meant both taking the wooden sole off and putting another back on again, entailing more work than when making them new, and in any case the upper might not be good enough if a cheap clog had been bought in the first place. Had the clogs needing repair been sent back to us for this work to be done, it would have meant that two pairs of clogs would need to be supplied to each employee so that one could be worn whilst the other was away being repaired. It was a complete non-starter, and the reasoning, when explained to the buyer, was very plain to see, so no one ever asked to have repairs done once they realised the disadvantages and cost of carrying out this work.

Because of this trend to cast clogs when unserviceable, I found that once a firm had decided which type and quality of clog were best for their particular usage, they were not interested in seeing me every month or so but were perfectly happy to send in their orders by post or telephone. This was a most welcome situation as it is very time-consuming and expensive travelling round calling on customers, especially if your mode of transport is a bicycle. One of the pitfalls of calling unannounced at any likely works was to find a notice in the office foyers stating that travellers would only be seen on a certain day or perhaps two days in a week. The idea was obviously to allow the buyer to get on with his work uninterrupted on some of the days and was quite understandable, but galling to me after cycling up to a hundred miles or so.

By June I still had not been able to attract new clog customers but was again able to sell shopping bags to the Middlesbrough department store which had bought my bags when I was stationed at Catterick. Another line that came my way out of the blue was when a man called from a local mill-furnishing firm asking me to make beam garters. After I said, 'What are they?' all was revealed and explained to me. Apparently they were fitted round a roller on some machine or other used in the textile trade and I was, of course, willing to have a go at anything that could be done. It was helpful to do this work as there was no cash outlay, the materials all being supplied by the customer himself, apart from the eyelets, which I had in stock anyhow. A beam garter is a length of webbing-backed perforated metal strip with hundreds of holes in it, very similar to a cheese grater and just as rough on the hands. Three rows of stitching were needed but it was quite easy to carry on sewing from one to another in a long length until the thread ran out and the spool was refilled and put back into the sewing machine again. The garters were cut to their lengths at each intersection and then needed three eyelets to be inserted at each end to complete the work. With the stitching being done through the rough part of the metal strip, it was amazing that the thread was not constantly breaking. Anyhow, I now knew what beam garters were and was quite happy to have made their acquaintance. Orders for these came in regularly and were much welcomed at this stage of our progression.

It was during the summer of 1947 when things were really bad and I had only sold 57 pairs of clogs in four months that I contemplated closing down completely, but on thinking it over carefully I decided that there was nothing else I could do apart from clogging and there was just no alternative, I had to clog on. Besides this I have never been one to give in if there was any hope at all; the hard times of my childhood had given me a determination never to be beaten by events however bad things appeared to be at the time. The crisis had reached its climax when I paid Nelson his wage and went home with nothing for myself. In such a situation many thoughts pass through one's mind and the will to work and succeed against all the odds becomes almost an obsession.

Winter was coming along and clogs were always more in demand then than in the better weather, but not nearly so much as in pre-war times. I obtained a Wakefield customer who was willing to collect all the clogs I could make for him each

Wednesday, which was his half-day holiday, and he was willing to pay for them on collection, which was just what is needed when capital is limited. This was exactly 12 months to the day from when I had started, and it was the quantity of clog soles that could be obtained which dictated the number that could be made. This Mr Sowden, from 133 Doncaster Road, Wakefield, was to become a regular customer and his weekly payment ensured that wages could be paid without worrying about it again.

In December 1947 I cycled over to Hebden Bridge to John Maude & Son Ltd, clog sole works, to try to persuade them to supply me direct, which I knew was contrary to their policy of only supplying through leather merchants. I pointed out that I was trying to build up a wholesale clog manufacturing business and had no intention of being a 'one-man band' making a few clogs along with other work. My argument was accepted by Maudes, who agreed to let me have a quota each month, which would enable me to increase sales, provided they could be sold, of course. This seemed to be the case following Mr Sowden's visit earlier in the year. The difference in cost between buying direct from the clog sole makers and the merchants was 15 per cent, quite a saving for me.

My accountant had advised me to have a 31 March year-end, which meant that my first 'year' would actually cover a period of some 16 month's trading. When completed, this first trading account shows, among other interesting items, £1.12$\frac{1}{2}$ for the chimney sweep (we had a coal fire) and phone calls at eight pence (I had no telephone of my own at that time). The profit amounted to £440, that is only about £8 a week. Sales were £2,295, stock £507 and total assets £790, including £14.50 for a second-hand typewriter. These accounts, my very first, together with subsequent ones up to 31 May 1987, are still in my possession and most helpful in compiling and documenting the events over 40 years of clog making. They most certainly provide a unique record of the whole period and the vast changes that occurred in the industry during this period of progressive automation. I had only obtained a handful of customers, but on the buying side I had been able to cut out all middlemen by buying direct from all my suppliers, mainly by assuring them that I was intent on building up a manufacturing and wholesale business rather than a sideline selling clogs as an offshoot to other retailing, as had been the case pre-war. Of the many clog iron manufacturers operating at the time, I naturally turned to the one Mr Hays had bought from and which rejoiced under the marvellous name of The Calderdale Co-operative Clog Sundries Manufacturing Society Ltd, which, apart from being a real mouthful to say, was most difficult to squeeze into the space provided on a bank cheque when payment was being made.

During the 1948–49 financial year I bought a second-hand Fortuna skiving machine at a cost of £30.50, which was an advance on the old hand-skiving method that I had originally been taught, and it was more accurate, time-saving and easier.

The next customer I was able to get was the Prince of Wales Colliery near Pontefract, where I met a Mr Harry Dixon, who was the Baths Superintendent there. On going into his stores I was astounded; I had never seen so much stock of every item of clothing one could think of, except in a large retail shop. A person could literally have walked in there naked and been able to buy everything needed to walk out again completely clothed. There were socks, shoes, vests, underpants, shirts, ties and made-up suits, apart from the inevitable stock of clogs. I was to find out through experience that clogs were sold at collieries in the stores, or the pithead baths where these were provided. Actually the lockers where clothing was kept till the next working shift were not a good place to keep clogs as the wooden soles tended to crack more easily in the warm conditions always prevailing in warm baths. Having said that, in the case of the 'wet' pits, any surface cracks in the wood could close up again on getting wet. However, Mr Dixon was suitably impressed by my knowledge of clogs and my presentation in general and decided to order from me for his future needs. Probably the fact that I was cycling round the area the hard way helped to make his mind up as it was obvious that I was keen to succeed and would be a dependable supplier.

Having made this one of my regular monthly calls as time went on, I arrived there one very foggy day with my face black with fog and only two white eyes peeping through. On seeing how I looked, Mr Dixon immediately allowed me to wash and make myself more presentable for my next and subsequent calls on the way back, which was much appreciated as I did not know just how black I really looked until I saw myself in the mirror at the colliery. I tried to make several calls round the area, with Pontefract being about the farthest point from Huddersfield, and by going one way on the outward journey and returning by a different route to eventually build up a round for each area.

Whilst cycling round the Teesside area, some hundred miles from home, having left Dorman, Long & Co. at Middlesbrough, I was making my way back via Stockton-on-Tees when at the side of the road I noticed a sign for a clogmaker and was curious to see what was there. Propping up the bike, I cheekily went inside to find that a man was running a business combining the making of shop blinds with clogs. This seemed quite a variation from anything that I had seen before; clogs were usually part of general footwear sales. However, this man could certainly teach me a thing or two in clog making. He was sitting there in the normal manner, making clogs on his thighs, where all the hammering took place, but the difference was that he was using left and right feet wooden lasts fitted with hinges, making the clogs complete and then taking the spring-loaded lasts out afterwards. Naturally with no two-inch nails ruining the lasts that we had always used it was such a vast improvement on the way that I had been taught. I could see a way of increasing production by at least 50 per cent using this method, and making a better job of it at the same time. I left his shop and Stockton-on-Tees a very happy man with this idea running round in my mind all the way home. I had certainly learnt something that day and quite by chance too. Arriving back, I immediately enquired about these new-type lasts and bought a range of sizes from 5s to 11s and from that time dropped the old way of making clogs like the proverbial hot brick.

With each new customer came the necessity of having more and more capital to finance the credit given to customers in the normal way of doing business as there were no companies willing to pay on a cash on delivery basis, as Mr Sowden did. On 23 September 1948 Mr Hays loaned me £50 to help solve this ongoing problem.

On going round the Sheffield area, I met up with a Mr Swann, who was impressed with the craftsmanship and quality displayed in the making of our hand-sewn shopping bags and was keen to try to sell them in bulk to the hospitals in the Sheffield area, with whom he apparently had good contacts. Although this was to turn out disappointingly insomuch that our high hopes were never realised, I did sell quite a lot of bags to him for his own shop.

Whilst in the area, I was fortunate to obtain business from the English Steel Corporation, as it was then called, for use in the River Don Works, where the head office was situated. The buyer there was a Mr C. Morgan, who must rank as one of the nicest buyers I ever met and with whom it was a real pleasure to do business. As time went by I was to receive many hundreds of orders from him and his signature is still in my mind as I saw it so many, many times. Having been successful at the River Don works, it was a natural progression to supply their other works in the Sheffield area, and as Mr Morgan dealt with orders for their Darlington Forge, this one customer was increasing to several different works.

Things were improving to some extent and whilst on my Pontefract round I received my first order for one gross (144) pairs from the Castleford chemical works of Hickson & Welch Ltd. Trying the Sheffield area again, I met with success at William Jessop & Sons Brightside works and the huge Firth Brown steelworks in the same area of Attercliffe. I was now building up an enlarging Sheffield round, and by going via Chapeltown and Rotherham way I tried to get new trade in the steelworks there. I was surprised to find, calling at the Izal works at Chapeltown, that they were buying their clogs from the Sheffield blind people. I had no idea that this was the case but decided there and then not to call on Newton Chambers & Co. again so long as they were happy with their present supplier.

In February 1949 there was a show at the Huddersfield theatre featuring Larry Macardi and his Dutch serenaders, who needed clogs for their act and had been recommended to contact me to make them. What they needed was some pattern of upper laced up but with the eyelets to be invisible to the audience sitting at a lower level than the stage. I drafted out a whole front pattern to cover up the lace-holes but the clogs were awkward to make as this had to be done without the use of wooden lasts as there was nothing to hold them in position. In the event they seemed happy with my efforts and the show went on.

Another new customer, Lepton Edge Colliery, was added to my Pontefract round. It was my first call, being only some two miles or so from Huddersfield on the Wakefield road. Here a Mr Ellis held his stock in the stores as there were no baths at this colliery. He regularly ordered 50 pairs every time I called on him and became a valued regular customer. Nearly all this type of trade was the rubber leather clog, price being very critical in this type of trade.

Now at the end of my second financial year, sales were £1,541 and the profit a mere £21.72, truly a hard year and no wonder I had earlier felt like packing up. The debtors on the turnover were now £206, an indication of just how much capital would be needed if ever I was to really expand into a large business.

It was during the next year that I was to have a most rewarding experience. One day a lady came to me with her little girl at what should have been something past the walking stage, but in her case she could not even stand up on her own as both her feet turned inwards so much that they met, with the result that she had no balance. Her mother had been recommended by her doctor to obtain some clogs to support the insteps as the rigid wooden sole is so contoured to provide this in the normal course of walking. To make the clogs for her presented me with quite a problem as up to that time we had only made men's clogs and had neither soles, lasts or patterns to make children's clogs. Obviously something had to be done and I took what foot measurements I could and designed a very high lace upper to go well above the ankle towards the knee and give support to the ankle and leg besides the feet. The time needed to do this type of work was considerable but, as usual, I was determined not to be beaten and eventually produced a pair of clogs with reasonably soft leather. Quite some time later the lady arrived with her daughter again as she was outgrowing the first pair of clogs that I had made and needed another, larger pair. Having already made one pair it was relatively easy to grade the pattern larger and I derived some encouragement from the fact that there did seem to be some slight improvement after wearing her first pair. She seemed to balance a little better when trying to stand up, whereas it had been absolutely hopeless on her first visit to me. Eventually they came back for a third pair and the improvement was dramatic and the look in the little girl's happy face said it all as she walked towards me. Delighted at this somewhat unexpected result of my efforts to date, I made a third pair and just gave them to her without any charge, doing something really worth while was all the reward I needed. There are many things that money cannot buy and I had just had the experience of one of them; happiness can certainly come from giving.

During the following year I cycled into Lancashire looking out for new business and was well received at the Warrington Steelworks of Monks, Hall & Co. Ltd, who decided to buy my split leather clogs. I was to find out that in this area they were quite prepared to pay better prices or buy a better quality of goods than in West Yorkshire, where the further east I went, to Wakefield, Barnsley and Doncaster, it was exactly the opposite and one penny per pair lower than a competitor's price would get the business. There were several clog makers in the area then, all competing for the colliery trade and using second-hand leathers. With more collieries being canvassed, I worked my way round No. 6, 7 and 8 areas of the National Coal Board, trying to recruit new accounts.

In the June of 1949 I must have made the impression that I was in business to stay as my electricity deposit of £3 was refunded, along with the princely sum of seven pence, presumably interest accrued on the deposit.

On my next round of the Sheffield area I again went by way of Rotherham and called on another steelworks, J.J. Habershon & Sons Ltd, where I actually was able to see the steel being rolled, which was quite interesting to me and showed me at first hand just how much heat was generated working there and the most suitable type of clog to make for their working conditions. From there I called on Steel, Peech and Tozer's steelworks, which had a large stores and besides safety clogs sold hundreds of pairs of safety boots.

Here I should mention the three different methods of providing employees with safety footwear. Some firms gave them free of charge, probably for essential usage; the second way was to subsidise the cost to encourage the wearing of safety footwear as some of the men were wearing the most ridiculous and unsuitable footwear for their work; and finally the third way was to supply it at cost as a perk of the employment. Steel, Peech used the second method of subsidising sales and all their footwear was sold at below cost price. In some cases this method, like the cost price system, could be subject to abuse when safety boots were sold to men at the wholesale prices and resold by the men to their friends at a profit or as a favour. The retail trade were up in arms at the huge and increasing trade conducted at works and collieries, resulting in a motion being carried at some annual conference deploring this practice but to absolutely no effect. Resolutions made not one jot of difference and the trade continued as before. The manager of Barnsley Co-operative Society gave me figures of what footwear they used to sell, both clogs and working boots, prior to them being available at the pitheads and what their current sales were, which was only a small fraction of the former. He was the man who told me about the resolution condemning this type of trading as he had been present at the time.

Travelling round the Leeds area, I was fortunate to obtain the business of the Yorkshire Copper Works, my first encounter with an extremely efficient lady buyer, the Yorkshire Tar Distillers Ltd nearby, and the Tetley brewery, where I was given a chit to have a pint of free beer. It was the practice there at that time to have a daily allowance for employees. Beer was served at one end of the counter and tea at the other. The person who dealt with ordering clogs here was the welfare officer, which was a change from the usual buyer or safety officer in most works. Shortly afterwards Heys brewery at Bradford joined our list of brewery customers but they only seemed to have comparatively small requirements of clogs. However, they all added up and I found that firms which did not buy many would be quite happy to pay a marginally higher price to compensate for the smaller amount ordered. I was now learning from practical experience that every customer had to be treated in a different way, just as I had to do pre-war with our shop customers buying retail.

It was in August that I made my first sample for ICI, for which I quoted 80 pence a pair for that type and quality. Nothing happened for a long time, which was probably because they had been issued out to someone to wear and test how long the life of the clogs would be compared to their other footwear.

Slow but steady expansion was helped by a loan from Mr Hays for £100, which I was able to repay within the same financial year. I don't like debts and avoid them whenever possible.

Taking another ride round the Warrington and Widnes area brought in Joseph Crosfield & Sons chemical works, where Persil was made. When I first noticed the building I thought it looked like the offices of a steel works. By now I was simply riding round looking for any likely works on my way to or from a definite target area. W. J. Bush & Co also had a chemical works at Widnes, which tried out my clogs and became a regular customer but again they needed only relatively small quantities, although they were prepared to pay a better price for them. At the Clayton Aniline Co. Ltd at Manchester I was surprised to find that the works had their own cloggers shop where repairs were carried out whilst the workman waited, thus making one journey necessary instead of two from plant to workshop. This was one of the few places where management considered it to be a viable proposition to carry out repairs.

For well over a year I had been experimenting with the idea of making a safety clog to compete with the safety boots and shoes which were becoming increasingly used as time went on. Unfortunately to do this meant buying cases in bulk, each containing one size and 250 pairs, and having them shipped from America, where the original patent had been taken out by a Mr A. A. Williams of Massachusetts. From the correspondence I had on the subject with America, I found out that the original patent had become public domain, as it was called in 1917, but the steel toecaps were still being made there. I believe there was some connection between one of the large manufacturers of safety boots in the Bristol area and a certain George Denton whose initials GD were stamped on each toecap. To my mind the turned-up end of a clog sole did not have any eye appeal whatsoever when these steel toecaps were used and almost gave the impression from their appearance that there was insufficient room for the toes underneath.

Having made a few and completely disliking them, I decided that it would be a good idea to have a specially designed internal steel toecap made for use only in clogs, and with this in mind I approached the Bradford firm of James Horsfield Ltd, who had the necessary plant for doing this work and had for a long time been making a 'miner's capill' of somewhat similar shape but fitted externally, merely to save wear on the leather clog upper and having no real safety protection at all. These were simply nailed into the side of the clog sole using ordinary welt nails for the purpose. Unscrupulous, or perhaps ignorant people often described clogs fitted with No. 222 external caps as 'safety', which they were definitely not as the metal was so thin it could be squeezed almost double by hand. The overall shape, though, was what I had in mind for an internal safety cap. Horsfields agreed to make these in two sizes, the smaller would fit sizes 6 and 7 and the larger size for size 8 and upwards. The wooden clog soles were double gripped at the toe end to accommodate the extra thickness of the steel toecaps at a cost of one penny extra, which helped to pay both for the extra work and the fact that one size larger of clog sole was needed to allow for the thicknesses of both steel and leather toecaps. The extra length of the clog toecap was about half an inch compared with the small internal boot toecaps, which gave much more protection over the toes compared with the coverage of the big toe and a little of the second toe provided by the boot toecap.

I was convinced that the new cap would be a winner, especially after seeing the photograph of an X-ray showing just how little of a man's foot was protected by the cap in safety boots and shoes. In order to see this I had to visit the British Boot and Shoe Research Association at Rushden in Northamptonshire, where research into all aspects of footwear and materials was conducted.

The clog safety toecap, being made from mild steel instead of the harder carbon steel, had difficulty in passing the Grade 1 test of British Standard 953, which was essential in order to stamp the footwear with the 'Kitemark'. Accordingly the caps were made using a heavier gauge of steel until sufficient to pass the drop test, which was equivalent to a three-ton drop if I remember correctly. There were other tests of varying strengths but I was only interested in the Grade 1. Incidentally, it is perhaps worth noting that when experimenting with inserting the carbon steel toecaps a crack could often appear at the toe end in the centre just by the action of one or two hammer blows knocking it into position, which I found rather surprising at the time. The English Steel Corporation at Sheffield were very helpful to me at this time by calculating the various component parts of material in the carbon caps. This was fascinating to watch as a camera about four feet long photographed the spark produced on the outside of the cap, after which the proportions and components were immediately available rather reminiscent of a forensic laboratory.

Safety clogs had now come to stay and I registered the trade mark 'PREVAX' as a suitable contraction of the slogan 'prevent accidents with Prevax'. This was later changed to 'ELIMINAX', meaning 'eliminate' accidents with Eliminax'. Suitable literature was produced to publicise the name and I had my business cards printed with the red triangle of road safety design fame as a background for the name Prevax or Eliminax as the case may be.

With safety clogs very much on my mind, I went down to London to the National Coal Board headquarters at Hobart House intending to sell them to their collieries. On being interviewed I was instantly and completely rebuffed by some individual who curtly told me that they were seeking to raise the status of the miner and didn't want clogs. So that was that, or was it? From my experience to date I knew that a lot of pits did use them, and having got to know their way of thinking to some extent, I decided that if the miners wanted clogs they would have them whatever the NCB might say in London, so I simply wrote off my visit to London as a sheer waste of time and carried on going round the pits as usual. In fact, I extended my areas by going to the Potteries, where the pits in that coalfield preferred a different type of safety clog altogether, fitted with copper welting like the London manufacturers made. Altogether I was able to get four new customers by touring this area.

The last new account I was able to open in the 1949–50 year was to prove another good regular one in the Manchester area of Swinton, or specifically Clifton Junction, where the Chloride Batteries Ltd of Exide fame had their factory. The results for the year showed that sales had nearly doubled on the previous year, from £1,541 to £2,865, and although the profit was only £309 I had acquired assets of machinery including an eyeletting machine for £33, weighscales for £3 – which were much needed for weighing rubber leathers – and a Jones sewing machine costing £18.

One of the most important purchases to me personally was a 'minimotor', a newly introduced device for driving the back wheel of a bicycle by means of a metal roller driving hard against the tyre. This invention was a great boon to me when negotiating steep hills or long inclines. Both Lancashire and Yorkshire had their fair share of these. The motor itself ran on a mixture of 50 per cent oil and 50 per cent petrol and it helped greatly when starting from cold to shake the tank from side to side to mix the two together.

The other details on that balance sheet showed that the debtors figure had gone up by half to £304, because of the increased trade and higher turnover generated. This increase enabled me to engage a full time clogger in addition to Nelson, who was learning as quickly as he could and was most reliable at all times. The new man was a Mr Duke Hellawell from Holmfirth, who although about 50 years old or so and with only one leg, was a craftsman who could not do a bad job and was just the type of man I wanted to recruit. Actually Duke was to stay with me for the rest of his working life, but that is another story.

The middle room had now been fitted out to be a clicking and closing room with the clicker's bench in one corner near the window. The first woman to join us was called Alice Fenton. Her husband worked on the railway and she lived only about five or ten minutes' walk away off Bradford Road. She had always been a machinist and was absolutely first class at the work and would herself check every piece of stitching, turning it over to examine the back and make sure everything was perfect. As Mr Hays remarked to me, 'You must look after Alice, she is a treasure.'

Later another woman living on Bradford Road was employed to do both the sewing machine work and the getting ready and finishing off of the uppers. The time needed to prepare them included marking, stamping the size on the backs, skiving and eyeletting and afterwards hammering down the seams and riveting them. It took just as long for these operations as the actual sewing of the uppers.

Soon afterwards we needed another girl as well to help with all these parts of the work in making clog uppers. The old method of clicking, using a cardboard sheet placed on a marble slab, had been replaced by a proper clicking board. These boards were specially made for hand clicking and comprised lots of small blocks of wood two inches wide and square, with the grain of the wood upwards for the knife blade to cut into or through. The same principle applies to the traditional butcher's blocks but these usually had a wooden band round them to hold the blocks firmly in position because the action they use is a chop and not a gradual cut. Incidentally, the clicker's boards used in conjunction with a power clicking press have strong bands of steel round each side, secured by metal nuts. To keep a clicker's board in good condition needed regular scraping to clean off any debris from the underside of the leather, to be followed by an application of linseed oil, which fed the wooden blocks and helped to preserve it. Cricket bats were often treated with linseed oil for the same reason, although willow was never used for clicking boards.

The old cardboard patterns had now been replaced by brass-bound fibreboard ones similar to those used in the clicking rooms of boot and shoe manufacturers, and were reasonably priced. They would last for quite a while until ultimately the one and only joining of the brass binding would come apart and render the pattern useless. Whatever the shape of the pattern, it must of necessity have one joining somewhere in its shape, but this was usually made at a point where there was a right-angle corner, if possible. Clog vamp and back patterns invariably came into this category, with my straight-line designs. I have already mentioned that Denhams in town employed a full-time clicker for this purpose. This man was willing to work an hour or two at nights or weekends besides doing his full-time work, so from that time onwards he did most of the clicking for me, particularly the waxed split leather uppers. During the days when Mr Hays was in Huddersfield he came in and cut rubber leather uppers during the day for a few hours as well.

The 'office', if it could be called one, consisted of one boarded-off corner of the clicking room to take the desk on which now stood the newly acquired telephone, one solitary chair and the typewriter. Not being satisfied with Midland Bank, I changed to the Co-operative Bank, which in Huddersfield offered me the twin advantages of being open till 5 p.m. and on Saturdays all day and, as the bank was also the office, it was even open on so called Bank Holidays.

It was during the course of the 1950–51 year that I broke into the Scottish clog market by tendering successfully for the prestigious Scottish Gas Board contract to supply all their large gasworks in the Glasgow area. The orders were big ones and came from and were delivered to all the separate works. This was where the rubber leather had the edge on price. Although I spent three days cycling round the Glasgow area, the only other customer I got was the brewery of J. R. Tennent Ltd, who seemed to employ girls as their sizes were mainly from 2s to 5s. Brown grain soft leather was used on these uppers and the heavy brewer's soles were fitted with one of our specialised rubber soles and heels. On my list of potential customers in Glasgow was an animal by-products firm and I remember asking the way there until when quite near it was not necessary as I just followed my nose; there was no mistaking the final direction. There seemed to be only one clog maker in the area and he was based in Edinburgh. He had a large trade in hand-made boots, which were his speciality, and perhaps he was not too much interested in clogs as a result.

By this time I was having some limited demand from ICI but was unable to secure their contract in spite of a visit to Earlsfield on the outskirts of London, where their head office had been moved during the war. To prepare for this tip to London I treated myself to a Homburg City-type hat and a top-quality black barathea overcoat and made a new briefcase for myself, but all to no avail. Miss Wilkinson was not impressed and I returned empty-handed and quite disappointed as I could ill afford wasting money going to London and back – obviously the bike was out of the question on this occasion.

In November I obtained the Shell Oil business and my first small order from David Brown Gears, a far cry from the days when I stood outside their gates every day asking for cigarette cards. David Browns also had a foundry at Penistone, where they needed the 4676 Foundry regulation safety clogs, a special pattern of upper with a flap over the laceholes to prevent anything hot penetrating to the wearer's foot.

The saying that you never make your name in your own town certainly seemed true in my case, as although I knew all the local works who bought clogs and had approached them at different times, I always seemed for some reason to be unlucky. Enquiring at the Deighton chemical works of L. B. Holliday & Co. Ltd, the answer I received there was that they had to look after those who had supplied them during the war. Pointing out that I had been away in the army all those years made no difference at all so I had to get on my bike and go further afield.

Shortly before the end of the 1950–51 year I had the opportunity to buy the premises instead of renting them. As the back cellar was underneath No. 120, a house in the next yard along the road, this meant that I had two options – either to brick up the way through into the back cellar or buy No. 120 as well and continue to have the use of it. So I decided to buy both No. 110 and 120 and was thus able to have my printing done with the heading 110 & 120 Northgate, which sounded far more impressive because, as Mr Rushworth pointed out to me, a lot of people glancing at the heading would read the address as being 110 to 120 Northgate, which obviously meant quite a different thing. The occupants of No. 120 were a couple with no family. The husband was employed as a postman. The initial rent of 35 pence per week appears in my book for the first time on 23 March but was increased to 37½ pence some two weeks later. The cost of buying both properties was £550 and legal fees were £12.14.

Sales for the year are shown at £4,412, an increase of 53.94 per cent over the previous year. Debtors rose from £304 to £585, reflecting the higher turnover and, once again, emphasising to me the importance of capital requirements needed in any expansion of trade. The profit of £470 for the year helped somewhat in this direction, after paying £33.75 in income tax.

I answered the telephone one morning to hear the very agitated voice of Mr Dixon calling from the Prince of Wales Colliery. He complained bitterly that he had replaced five pairs of faulty clogs within the past few days and asked me to go over and inspect them for myself and replace them. I immediately rode over there, examined all the clogs in question and agreed with Mr Dixon that they were very badly made – in fact, in my opinion they were absolute rubbish. Having satisfied him to some extent that the clogs were far below standard, I then went on to point out that not one of these clogs had been made by us and showed him the difference in the style of the uppers compared with our straight-sided ones, the two rows of stitching we always had as against the single row on the faulty clogs, the bifurcated rivets on each side of our patterns to ensure the uppers held together even if the thread broke down and finally the fact that all our clogs supplied to him had five lace-holes. All these details proved to him beyond any shadow of doubt that they were not of our manufacture and were, therefore, not our responsibility in any way. In other words he had been conned and he knew it. The clogs had all been purchased from a local shop and taken in to him for exchange when they became unserviceable. He had simply replaced the faulty clogs in good faith, expecting me to do the same. Realising what had happened and muttering just what he was intending saying to the men concerned next time he saw them, he apologised for bringing me over to Pontefract on a wild-goose chase.

The nicest sort of complaints are those concerning other makers' products, but nevertheless ill feeling can easily be caused and if Mr Dixon had not reported the matter to me and simply stopped buying I could have lost a very good customer through no fault of my own.

The next financial year saw more than a double of turnover, resulting in needing more staff in order to cope with the increasing demand. I advertised in the Halifax *Courier* stating the piece rates that I paid and was inundated the following morning by telephone calls from virtually everybody working for our Halifax competitor as, apparently, the wages that I was paying were far in excess of those they were receiving for doing the same work. It nearly caused a riot when they all descended on their office asking for similar rate of pay to those I had advertised. I had no idea at all what other employers were paying for this work and simply worked out what I thought was fair, bearing in mind that I could do every job myself and knew from my own experience what was involved. In the event I set on one of these cloggers and a second one some time later.

Being something of a realist when starting in business, I had asked myself the simple question as to why should anybody want to buy my clogs as opposed to other makes, and came to the conclusion that it must be either price, quality or delivery or some combination of these three. This matter-of-fact approach was to be my watchword for the future. Perhaps one other considerations should be included with the foregoing and this was to be 'choice'. As I went round all sorts of works it was apparent that they had different problems and needed variations of clogs accordingly, and these had to be explained and demonstrated to potential buyers. The choice I was able to offer included the various upper materials, such as rubber leather, corrugated leather, waxed split, grain leather and the specialised rubber canvas material to combat chemicals. The overshoe clogs could be made in either leather or white canvas backs to customers' requirements.

The range of upper styles that I had developed up to that time were the traditional derby lace-up with varying heights of backs, the flap and buckle blucher, a flap front, apron front and the low lace pit clogs. By now I could offer a wide range of soling materials suitable for nearly all types of works floors, which were attached to the wooden soles to provide the wear as the wooden soles themselves, even made from beech, would not last long without some form of soling material on them.

Whilst the clog irons were still the most popular, the demand for these declined as other materials were proving far more beneficial. Several kinds of rubber or neoprene were available, the cheapest form of which were known as 'clog rubbers' or even sometimes 'rubber irons', but we knew what they meant. This type of sole and heel was nailed round the edge of the wooden soles in the same way as the clog irons but had a much wider shape all the way round. A black rubber half-sole similar to those used in boot repairing covered the whole of the tread of both sole and heel, with the latter, where there was more wear, being made from a much thicker material. The circular pattern on some makes helped to grip better than a smooth surface and most makes of these soles and heels used some kind of pattern in their moulds, often including the maker's name or trade mark.

Heat-resistant rubber soles and heels were becoming increasingly popular in the steelworks especially and would stand up to 180 degrees centigrade, which might not seem a lot until it is realised that no one would be standing still on this heat but probably passing over it as quickly as possible. This type was riveted onto the wooden soles in the same way as the No. 3 ordinary rubber just mentioned.

Some works liked to have strips of neoprene rubber nailed across the width of the soles and heels, but I personally never recommended this as in my opinion by merely walking along in the normal manner the movement was totally against the direction of these strips and could easily have caused a man to trip up. However, if customers insisted on this method we had to oblige, but we pushed other types wherever possible.

The longest wearing and most time-consuming to be fitted to the wooden soles was the 'Commando' heavy-duty cleated soles and heels made in both standard and heat-resistant qualities. The soles and heels had first to be roughed up to take the shiny surface off the back and the wooden soles also roughed, taking away the waxed finish, making both suitable for an application of a special 'infra red' solution, so called because the solutions had to be heat-activated before sticking the two together. The solution was applied by brush, usually doing a dozen pairs at once so that by the time the last ones had been solutioned the first would have become semi-dry and tacky, ready for the heat activation under the infra red-ray heater.

A hand press of the Tellus make could only accommodate two soles at a time, so whilst one sole was setting the other could be taken out of the press ready for the next stage in the process. The infra red-ray heater could also only take two soles at a time so the wooden sole and its corresponding rubber Commando sole and heel would both be placed under the infra red-ray electric bulbs at the same time and left there until the timer rang a bell to indicate they were ready for the press. The normal time needed for each sole was three minutes, and leaving the soles in the press for a similar length of time meant that only ten pairs could be stuck in an hour, even taking one out as quickly as possible and putting another in on a continuous basis. When set, the soles were taken out of the press and no less than 28 screws were hammered into the wooden sole between the cleats of the sole pattern, and finally the soles and heels were trimmed round to the shape of the wooden soles to make a neat clean edge, which was done by the drag knife that I had used in boot repairing; it was ideal for this purpose, being made in varying widths of blade.

The enormous length of time needed to fix Commando soles and heels naturally made them the most expensive type to make, but there was no quicker way of fitting them so that they would give completely satisfactory wear in rough working conditions.

In some foundries where the 'flooring' was sand, the clogs would be made with just the plain wooden soles without any kind of soling materials at all. This was the only exception to the rule that wooden soles always needed some form of wearing materials, but sand did not cause undue wear. Originally when clogs fitted with irons were used in these conditions, the heat gradually warmed up the tip nails holding the irons in position to such a degree that eventually the nails burned a small hole round them. This caused the nails and then the irons to become loose and presenting a real danger to the wearer working with molten metal being poured into the moulds in the sand, so this material was quickly discarded in favour of the plain wooden soles.

With all the permutations of clogs that could be made from the combinations of all the different styles, upper materials and soling materials, it was impossible to accurately compile a sensibly understood price list, and I decided that it would probably be meaningless to any potential buyer as he would not know just what all the descriptions meant. In order to overcome this problem I made a suitcase of brown shoulder leather as used for schoolbags, and backed it with plywood, to hold a sample of each and every material, style of upper and soling material, all of which could be carried together and displayed as required. Incidentally, I was surprised how easy it was to sew through three-ply wood, but only when the grains of two of the three thicknesses were parallel, otherwise the stitches rested on the top of the wood.

With this case of samples, together with a boot safety toe cap and my new clog safety toecaps, I could easily show anyone just how much more protection was offered by the clog cap as opposed to the small boot toecap. None of my competitors had anything like the variety that I could offer and all the time I was plugging the point that we specialised in clog making and nothing else, which was a good selling point accepted by all. We were at all times prepared to make whatever a customer wanted.

I now made out a yellow card index, using two metal folders made for the purpose with a wire passing through two holes in each card and fitting neatly into the heavy folder. Each held 200 cards and could be used as required to record details of costings of the various popular types or details of the types bought by each customer, in which case these were always in alphabetical order for easy reference. As orders came in, I was able to refer to the datacard for all relevant details to ensure making the correct type, and in the event of any new enquiry it was easy to look up some other customer's prices to quote for a particular style whilst the customer was on the telephone.

During the 1951–52 year I was successful in breaking into the North-Eastern Gas Board area, and here again different gasworks had their own preferences as to the kind of clog they wanted. Making up clogs virtually to the customer's specification helped to both build up goodwill, kept the competition out and made for a better selling price. With the further expansion in trade, the shortage of capital to expand became somewhat critical again and I obtained both a private loan of £50 and another of £75 from my uncle, who had helped me once before in similar circumstances. Being in business himself, he was aware that increased capital was essential. Orders from what had now become regular customers arrived by post almost daily, with ICI now taking larger quantities of safety clogs. Knowing the requirements of some customers, it was quite possible to anticipate their orders. To mention just one example, a stock of 18 pairs of every size of the most popular style would enable despatch to be made by return ex stock. Delivery could possibly be considered even more important than price or quality, as if the clogs were not there at the works when needed, both price and quality become irrelevant. Bearing in mind that a lot of works storemen had to requisition supplies through their buying department, it could well take ten days for us to receive the order. Delivery was, therefore, more important than at first realised.

A more impressive trading account for 1951–52 showed sales up 121.76 per cent to £9,784, with a profit of £1,404 after paying out wages of over £2,000 for the first time in any year. This had only been £1,125 the previous year, such had been the effect of increased sales. Income tax took £43.60 and the £75 loan was repaid. Debtors rose from £585 to £1,228, reflecting a more than doubled turnover. Assets now included a one-half horsepower electric motor which had been fitted to one of the sewing machines to speed up production and make it easier at the same time. Treadle machines can be quite hard work after a few hours, although they were always kept well oiled and ran very freely. If I had to travel a long distance, such as to London, I was able for the sum of £1.50 to hire a car for the day from a man at Crosland Moor, which was a vast improve-ment on the minimotor and could, of course, accommodate the case of samples that I had made and which could not be carried on any type of cycle.

With the advent of safety clogs, the safety officers at the large companies had to clear these and worked in conjunction with the buyers. When a new safety line came on the market I cycled over to Runcorn in Cheshire, where the General Chemicals Division of ICI had no less than 15 works in operation. Having hidden my bike with its bag of samples out of sight round the corner of the building from the safety office, I handed in my card and was taken to meet the safety officer for the division, a Mr Ben Halfpenny, who, along with his assistant safety officer Mr Harrison, was responsible for all safety aspects of these works, which they visited on a rota basis. After I introduced myself and had some conversation of a general nature, he asked to see my samples. I was just on the point of leaving the room to collect them when Mr Halfpenny most politely insisted on Mr Harrison accompanying me to help bring them in, which was the last thing I wanted to happen. However, it was hopeless to even try to get out of the situation as I could not refuse their offer although I said that I could manage easily. So, putting on a brave face, or more probably a very red one, I walked out to the bike, with Mr Harrison, the rather astonished assistant, and duly collected the few samples. When Mr Halfpenny realised what the situation was regarding my method of transport he said, 'Mr Walkley, you should have come over in a car.' Taking the bull by the horns I replied, 'If you'll buy me one, I'll come over in it.' This rejoinder seemed to break the ice and from then on we both got on fine as he soon realised that not only could I do the job myself but knew what I was talking about, whereas so many representatives have no practical knowledge of the products they are trying to sell. Huge orders followed to these various works and it became quite common for a single works to order 200 pairs of just one size, such was the usage at that time.

Eventually London head office heard about these orders being sent to me instead of the company at Halifax who had been awarded the contract and there was an almighty argument between Mr Halfpenny and London, the words used by the former are not for printing and far more extreme than I ever envisaged, but having heard his words myself there was no doubt that he was determined to get his way. The last I heard was when he roared into the telephone, 'I want Walkley's clogs and I'm going to have them.' Their orders continued as London apparently backed down until such time as a reorganisation took place, with divisional safety officers being allocated certain commodities to deal with. Mr Halfpenny became glove controller, and had he been appointed footwear controller instead I am sure we would have had all the ICI clog trade. Such can be the effect of luck (good or bad) in business. Each ICI division had their own specification to which the clogs were to be made, with about six different ones in all on the contract. The Dyestuffs Division at Huddersfield bought the safety clog with a bend leather sole and heel fitted with brass rivets, whilst the Blackley works at Manchester in the same division preferred our No. 3 studded rubber soles and heels, also to be fitted with brass rivets. Both types had to have non-ferrous grindery throughout, meaning copper or brass welt nails, copper welting and copper toetins. By some strange chance leather laces, or indeed any type of laces, had never been included in the price of clogs, resulting in them having to be ordered separately. We ourselves bought the leather laces in 20-gross pair lots in half-gross (72 pairs), bundles and these were sold to our customers either in bundles as received, as was the case with ICI, or in dozen pairs or multiples of a dozen.

In Scotland the Nobel Division making explosives also needed a non-ferrous sparkproof clog and bought the same type as the Huddersfield works.

With the introduction of the Commando type soles and heels, which provided much longer wear than any other soling materials, there was an obvious overall saving in cost compared with clog irons, although these were much cheaper to buy. In this respect the Clayton Aniline Company at Manchester, who had always employed four men doing clog repairs, changed over to Commando soles, resulting in the demise of the clog shop there. For some time the management had been concerned about the actual cost of clog repairing, not least because of the time spent off the plant when a man had to walk quite some distance, wait for his clogs to be repaired and then walk back again to his workstation. The loss of time and production would far outweigh any increase in the cost of the original safety clogs fitted with Commando soles, but on the downside from our point of view buyers did not need to buy in the same quantities as before.

Travelling down to the Midlands and in particular Birmingham and the Burton upon Trent areas, I called at the Ansells' brewery in Birmingham, where it was not the usual safety officer or purchasing officer that I had to see but the all-powerful Brewer, whose office was at the very top of several flights of spiral staircase, such was the secrecy in which the brewers operated when putting into the beer whatever it was they did put in. Certainly a most effective way to keep any ingredients secret. Here I was fortunate to sell my clogs, but I was unlucky at the next brewery as the person that I should have seen had been suddenly taken to hospital, having had a heart attack that same day. Obviously I would have to try again next time I was in the Birmingham area. Whilst in the city, I called at the offices of the West Midlands Gas Board as I had heard that they had quite a large contract to be tendered for on an annual basis, but here again I was unlucky as this had been placed a little time earlier, which meant waiting almost a year before being able to tender. At the Burton-on-Trent group of breweries I was well received at Truman, Hanbury, Buxton and Marston, Thompson & Evershed, before visiting Ind, Coope & Allsopp, as these three breweries were then called.

Following the Birmingham visit, a merchanting firm called the General Engineers Supply Company contacted me enquiring about factoring our clogs in their area. They had quite a useful trade and subsequently sent regular orders to us. This practice of supplying to both factors and direct to industry can easily cause unintended problems for both as I did not know to whom they were selling our clogs and could quite innocently call upon their customers and upset all concerned. But naturally they did not want to tell me who all their customers were.

Partly because customers were now buying longer-life clogs, the sales for 1952–53 actually showed a 15.9 per cent drop in value, with commensurate pairage sales also being down. The higher prices for Commando-soled clogs did not cover the smaller pairage demand. However, a profit of £787 is recorded and at last I felt confident enough to buy a second-hand car.

A Ford Consul cost me £675. The thinking behind this purchase was the knowledge that the Ford Motor Co. Ltd was one of the largest buyers of clogs in the UK, if not actually the biggest, and I simply dared not go down to Dagenham in any other make. Actually one of the first things I was asked on arriving there was what sort of car I was running, and I was thus able to give a satisfactory reply. Thinking about this later on when we were to supply Reliant, Vauxhall, Leyland, Rolls-Royce etc., it would have cost a fortune to have been able to call on all these carmakers in one of their own make of car, especially the Rolls!

Having bought the car and obtained permission to build a

garage for it on a nearby site of some ten garages or so, I was able to keep the car under cover and locked up, even though it was only a corrugated-iron and asbestos structure. Shortly afterwards I sold the minimotor, incurring a loss on cost of £4.20 on the transaction, but I did not regret this in the slightest as it had given me excellent service – the only snag perhaps being a tendency for the back tyre not to grip too well if wet and the tyre itself showed some degree of wear, but this was only to be expected and certainly not a legitimate grumble.

The time seemed to have come when we had outgrown the Northgate premises and I started to look for larger, more suitable buildings for further expansion. Nelson, who had started with me as a boy of 14, was now a fully trained man and had recently married. On this occasion, having acquired a car, I was able to help by taxi-ing around for the wedding guests.

Duke and the two Halifax men were also making the clogs, and Frank Wright, the clicker, had to work as much as possible to keep the three women with a good supply of cut uppers. Although he was able to use the new brass-bound patterns which speeded up the cutting, it was touch and go whether he could cut enough in his spare time, but in any emergency I could always fill in myself. Clicking was the part of clog making that I liked best as it was a challenge feeling at the leather and knowing just what shape to be cut out of any given part of the sides of split. There was a retired naval man living next door to the workshops in Northgate and he came in every day to pack the clogs up into cartons for me and make them ready for the carrier's daily collection.

Taking it all round, we had assembled a first-class team with a good 'family' atmosphere, as so often happens in small businesses. This situation was rewarded at Christmas time and on the various production or sales milestones, when we would adjourn to the pub across the road to celebrate. The first of these achievements to celebrate was when we made 1,000 pairs of clogs in one month, and some time later it was 2,000 pairs a month, this latter being no mean achievement in such a relatively short space of time.

Before clogs were despatched, I personally put my hand inside every one to check, so that in the rare event of anything not being 100 per cent, it could be rectified straight away before being sent to a customer. By doing this, we hardly ever had a genuine complaint – apart from the splitting of clog soles, which could occur after despatch when drying out further, timber being a natural product and prone to hundreds of surface cracks if standing in sunlight for even a short space of time.

The March 1954 year-end saw a further 27.84 per cent increase in turnover, assets up to £4,125, a wages bill of £2,848, but profits only £470 for a very hard year's work. Income tax took £70.15 and debtors were £1,901. The hire-purchase debt on the car was paid off.

Having been on the lookout for better premises for some time, I was attracted to a town centre property comprising Nos. 22, 24 and 26 Upperhead Row, which was just two streets away from the main road of Huddersfield in a southerly direction. No. 22 was a double-fronted shop previously known as 'Todd's china shop' before that business closed down. Separated by a yard giving access to the rear was No. 24, previously used as a dwelling house, whilst No. 26 was a combined shop and house, the living accommodation being on the first floor and at the back. Number 22 and 24 were joined together above the yard giving access to the upstairs rooms by the original staircase in both properties. At the back of the yard was a large unused mill type of building for which I had no use myself but which formed part of the overall property sale. Negotiations seemed to be getting nowhere so I finally delivered an ultimatum at 2 p.m. one Friday to the estate agent that if my offer was not accepted by 5 o'clock that same day it would be withdrawn. The agent could tell that I meant what I said. He went to see his client at his home, and before the deadline, came back with acceptance, verbal of course.

One snag to be overcome before I could think of moving in was the electricity supply to the premises. In order to operate a power clicking press, which I was now determined to buy – and possibly for other machines in the future – a three-phase supply of electricity was needed. Investigations revealed that the nearest cable was some distance away, which would make installing a supply for us a very big job and quite expensive. However, this just had to be done, and it was.

116

The cost of acquiring all the aforementioned properties in Upperhead Row was £2,343 in the summer of 1955. The fitting up of the clogging room on the first floor of No. 22 entailed making a very long clogger's bench to accommodate seven or eight men, and this was divided up underneath the bench for a full set of each size of men's lasts to be available to each man without having to get up from his chair. It was the normal way of working to have the clog soles on the floor at one side and pile the clogs up on the other after making, which needed the space that we could now plan for compared with the Northgate premises. A very long shop counter was bought second-hand from a 64-year-old boot repairer who joined us as a full-time clicker. It was ideal in length, height and width to put the finished clogs on top, ready for checking and tying up in pairs.

As clog soles and clog irons in particular were always delivered to us in heavy sacks, I had a large square trapdoor made in the floor above the yard so that they could be lifted up by means of a block and tackle fixed to the roof supports. This chain operation took all the work out of carrying each bag upstairs on the back but was not particularly quick to use and needed two to operate, with one person downstairs fastening the sacks onto the hook and chain and the other taking them off upstairs. All stocks were carried on the first floor to give easy access to the clogging room.

When planning the layout of the premises I tried to work out all the best and easy ways of working so that there would be a minimum of time wasted moving anything from one place to another. A wooden-framed rack, with five rows of dowelling fixed horizontally and with a suitable distance between each row, enabled hundreds of clog sole irons to be easily available by simply lifting a bundle, always containing six pairs of sole irons, from the rack. Different sizes and shapes were easily separated by the simple method of facing them in opposite directions where two types met on the same level of racking. The drawers under the counter were most suitable for storing the different sizes and the two shapes of clog heel irons, and by cutting away the top half of the front of each drawer a man simply put his hand in to get them. Heel irons were also in bundles of either a dozen or half-dozen pairs held together on a wire. Also, it was easy to empty a full bag of heel irons directly into the drawers when a delivery was received. The smaller drawers at each end at the top took the two main sizes of iron toetins, and again there was easy access at standing height, which merely meant getting a handful as required as these were delivered to us in bulk. Each man had his own little stock of toetins in his nailbox on the bench in front of him and constantly replenished them in the same way as the clog welt and tip nails. To complete the preparation of the upstairs rooms did not take a lot of doing, just making wooden shelving to store everything that was needed in the actual clog making.

The reader will now have realised the three Cs of making clogs: clicking, closing and clog making, each process being dependent on a steady flow of production from the previous one.

Downstairs a clogger's bench was made to fit into one of the two large shop windows, and this was where Duke worked, which saved him having to climb stairs on his crutches, but in any case he much preferred to be where there was something of interest to see from the window. I had long since realised that everybody likes to see other people working, especially if some article is being hand crafted, and there was an ongoing attraction for passers-by stopping and watching the clogs being made.

The other half of No. 22 was large enough to take three similar make sewing machines, the skiver and the eyeletter, with a small bench on which to place the uppers before and after making up. There were rows of shelving already installed all the way round the shop so I had about 200 glass-fronted wooden boxes made to fit into the shelf space and these were filled with various tongues, stiffeners, eyelets, thread etc. so that each machinist could simply stretch out an arm to the shelf at the side of her sewing machine and take out the various parts as required. The heating for this room was provided by a paraffin-type heater placed in the middle of the room on the floor; this was to prove ideal, and could be moved out of the way in warmer weather.

At the back of this closing room was the clicking room, fitted up on one side with the normal clicking bench for hand clicking, the other side by the passage window letting light in from the yard and taking the power clicking press, which was supplied with a table at each side to fit round the press, on which to place the leather and clicking knives. At the end nearest to the closing room I obtained a small stamping machine, which was operated from the sitting position by the down-stroke of a circular head in conjunction with specially made cutting knives almost five inches in depth which were very heavy to use, needing both hands for constantly lifting the knife onto and off the leather. Round the top of this type of knife was a very heavy-duty rubber fluted edging, and the height of the knife was such that both hands were safely underneath out of the way when the machine was operated, which was done by a foot pedal. All small pieces of leather could be cut, and stocks of each size and type were thrown into their respective boxes as cut, ready to go from the clicking room into the closing room as each box was filled.

The main press was operated in the standing position, with the swinging beam several inches wide, and clutch-operated, so that the beam came down with a three-ton bump to cut the part out of the leather. The knife itself was of forged steel less than an inch thick, and it cut through the leather onto the wooden clicking board already described. In order to trip the machine, both hands were needed as a safety measure to avoid the many accidents that had previously occurred in clicking rooms when the machines were operated by one hand only. Many men had lost either a finger or part of using the old-type machines, either through lack of care or simply by familiarity breeding contempt. Either way, it did not bring their fingers back and the new presses eliminated the risk completely.

The press knives were made for every size of clog and the whole back pattern needed a strengthening plate in the middle to avoid bending due to the extreme pressure of cutting. The vamp knives had prickers screwed into the frame of the knife wherever they were needed to allow for the overlap when sewing up – this had previously been marked in a straight line by hand. The two operations were now done in one cut.

At the rear of the clicking room there was a small passageway leading to the yard and toilets outside, and this was fitted with facilities for washing, with both hot and cold water available.

Number 24 was fitted up as the office, with desk, two steel

filing cabinets, safe, blue carpet to match the fireplace, telephone and so on. At the side, a narrow passageway led to the front door. Behind the office was a large room with a stone floor with one door leading down to the cellar and another to the yard. A staircase led upstairs to the storeroom. This back room was to become the 'shaving room', as I needed a shaving machine to enhance the appearance of the rubber leathers by clearing off oil and any accumulation of grease. A shaving machine is one of the machines specially made for the tanning section of the leather industry and was a floor-mounted belt-driven machine with a covered roller some five inches in diameter which moved towards a cylinder-type cutting roller with a V-shaped pattern of knives about an inch in depth that periodically had to be replaced when worn down. A man operated the machine by holding the leather in both hands and letting it move backwards and forwards by use of a foot pedal moving the two rollers together and shaving off the underside of the leather in a cloud of leather dust. Incidentally, this was excellent for compost. I did not know of anyone able to operate this shaving machine in the Huddersfield area and persuaded a man from Hartshead to come in his spare time at nights or weekends to do this work for me. Shaving leather as opposed to splitting leather is as different as the proverbial cheese and chalk, although they both thin the leather down. The weighscales were placed in one corner of this room to check the weight of rubber leathers and there was adequate space at one side to pile rubbers up high against the wall.

All the planning had now been completed, the work necessary to provide the three-phase electricity authorised, machinery not already acquired was ordered, press knives and an Ideal clicking press arranged and finally the name 'Walkley's Yard' was painted over the archway at the yard entrance. On completion of these things we would be ready to move in.

The author on the farm at Galphay near Ripon, 1936

The author with his friend Eddie Doggrell, May 1942

Hebden Bridge Sawmills

The author in the office, Birkby Works

The Clogging room, Birkby Works

Birkby Works Closing room, with the eyeletting machine at the far end, and four sewing machines.

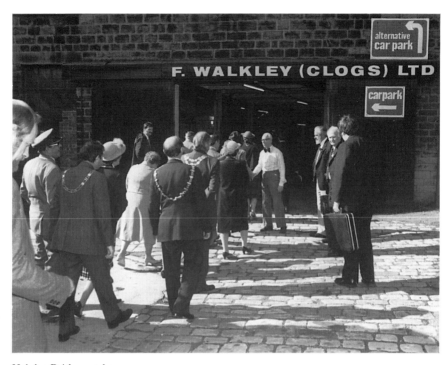

Hebden Bridge works

Brenda and the author behind the Cloggers' Bar in the restaurant, Hebden Bridge works

6

Further Expansion

The move to Upperhead Row attracted the attention of the media as it was certainly unusual to hear of anyone in the clog trade expanding at a time when the overall trade was in decline. The Huddersfield *Examiner* devoted a half-page in their issue of 12 November 1955 to an article about us and supplemented it with no less than six large photographs showing the various stages of clog making, including the machines used in clicking, closing, skiving and eyeletting and two showing the handwork of clog ironing the wooden soles and nailing round the welting. The *Yorkshire Post* also followed this up by visiting the new works to do a similar article for their readers but, unfortunately, caused me quite a lot of unintentional bother afterwards, as so often happens with the press, through inadequate knowledge of their subject. The journalist asked many questions for their article including the inevitable 'How much do clogs cost?' I most carefully explained that we were wholesale manufacturers supplying all our production either direct to industry or through merchants and retailers who sold them on again, and so all our prices were based on a minimum carriage-paid order of 24 pairs, with smaller orders being supplied at the same price per pair but with carriage charges paid for extra. Although this was quite a detailed explanation of the position that our cheapest price was 75 pence, rising to over double that or more for safety clogs made from new leathers and varying soling materials, when the article appeared in the paper it included the bland statement that 'Mr Walkley's clogs sell at 75 pence per pair' with no mention of any other prices at all.

The end result of this was that I received letters from farmers all over Yorkshire wanting to buy a pair of clogs for that price. The time taken to explain the true position was quite considerable but it was amazing to me at that time to realise just how much a few words taken out of context can give a completely inaccurate impression on any given situation. Later on, I experienced this with television crews who repeatedly tried to put words into my mouth and, when I would not fall for it, abandoned the project. I had had enough of propaganda from Lord Haw Haw in Germany during the war and did not easily fall into the trap of saying something just to suit the interviewer. In this case, just the inclusion of the one word 'wholesale' would have avoided all the trouble which ensued for all concerned.

With increasing trade, a regular supply of cartons became necessary for sending orders out to customers and in some cases it was stipulated that goods must be supplied in non-returnable containers. I was fortunate in being able to arrange for a daily collection to be made from Marks and Spencer's town centre stores, where their fire precautions insisted on all inflammable materials, including paper and cardboard, being removed every day. This suited me admirably and I cleared the lot, irrespective of sizes, and never missed once. Previously, when only smaller quantities were needed, adequate supplies had been obtained from one or two local town centre wholesale grocers whose Weetabix cartons were perfect for holding 15 pairs of clogs. Kellogg's cartons held exactly 24 pairs, which was the most popular-sized order as it was carriage paid.

Having bought all the Upperhead Row property as one lot and not needing the building at the back of No. 26, the house and shop combined, I sold both these, recouping £950 in the process, which had the effect of acquiring Nos. 22 and 24 for my own use at a final purchase price of about half the total cost.

The property at the back of the yard was ideal for making fireplaces, especially on the ground floor. The purchaser had been able to bring an experienced 'slabber' from the Stoke-on-Trent area to begin and build up this type of business for him. The work of making fireplaces was done on billiard table slate tops and was quite interesting to watch, as are most productive processes. Bulk orders were supplied to local authorities, who had a large requirement for them.

Besides buying the shaving machine, it was necessary to have a second riveting machine so that one could be operated on each floor, the ground floor needing one in the closing room to rivet the uppers after stitching up, whilst the one upstairs was needed to rivet the flaps onto blucher clogs after they had been made up which ensured that they were perfectly positioned to fasten in the middle hole of the three.

Another improvement was to rent an automatic eyeletting machine, these being impossible to buy outright as only one maker held the original patents, giving them a monopoly over eyeletting machine production and sales. The machine itself was rotary fed by pouring the eyelets into the open revolving container at the top of the machine, which fed a vertical raceway down which the eyelets moved by gravity, with the last one held in position horizontally by a spring ready for the actual insertion into the leather. The action of both punching the holes and eyeletting was all done together, regulated by a cam on the machine making one revolution each time the foot pedal was depressed. There was an adjustment for the spaces between the eyelets, which were fed rapidly into position, sounding rather like a machine-gun in action if the foot pedal was held down to insert more than one eyelet at once. With practice, it was easy to keep the foot on the pedal just long enough to run six eyelets through at one go when eyeletting the normal height Derby pattern, or for four in the case of low lace and blucher clog uppers.

The recent newspaper publicity had come to the attention of Granada Television at Manchester, who invited me over to their studio for a talk on the trade in general and myself in particular. The suit that I happened to be wearing on arrival there was 'throwing' the picture, so they lent me an old jacket from their wardrobe room to wear instead. On first seeing this coat it looked really shabby, but on screen it looked brand-new, much to my relief. Even with the high technology available today I have noticed the moving effect of the herringbone pattern and a small diamond-type pattern still causing problems. However, I thoroughly enjoyed the afternoon at their studio, found that the payment for appearing and travelling expenses were quite generous and left hoping that some more business would accrue as a result of the broadcast.

By now I had decided to take a stand at the Royal Society for the Prevention of Accidents (ROSPA) safety exhibition, which was held in conjunction with the annual safety officers' conference taking place at the Spa in Scarborough. This opened on the Friday and continued till Sunday but necessitated being there in advance to set up the stand. I made some pegboard displays with wooden frames and painted the board yellow to contrast with the mainly black of the clog uppers. Suitable wire holders held each clog in position sideways, with two ends of the wires bent backwards and passed through the pegboard holes, so they could be easily put in or taken out again, the width being the requisite five inches or so to hold a man's size clog sole. One interesting exhibit I took was a safety clog that had been cut in half to show the construction of the clog and at the same time demonstrate the greater coverage of the foot when the internal clog safety cap was used, compared with the small boot safety cap.

Leaflets printed in English, French and German gave a rather professional appeal, supplemented by a humorous picture of a man laughing his head off wearing safety clogs on which a huge steel girder was supposed to have dropped with no adverse effect. This picture, suitably framed, was rather eye-catching and had been drawn and painted for me by a lifelong friend who was a local teacher. To complete the stand a few black and white photographs of different styles of clogs formed a background to the display, with all the sizes of toetins in iron, brass and copper, together with parts of uppers and soling materials.

The exhibition was actually open till midnight and in my case this was a very tiring experience, most of the other stand-holders had at least two or three representatives there who could man the stands in rotation and have a few hours off in between, but as I was a one-man band I had no such luxury and needed to be there just about all the time.

To transport all the equipment for the exhibition, I bought an old ex-army steel-sided trailer from a Wakefield scrapyard, which served its purpose apart from being awkward to load and unload as everything had to be lifted over the sides or back.

Talking to other exhibitors on my first experience of the safety exhibition, it soon became apparent that very little business in the way of actual orders resulted from being there and to a lot of those attending it was more in the nature of a glorified booze-up, with conference sessions in between for the more conscientious types present, although some of the subjects for discussion would not necessarily appeal to all the different people attending. In the event, I learned a lot from going, and in my case did pick up business from the other exhibitors who were dealing in safety footwear and sometimes received orders for safety clogs as well as boots or shoes. Probably my best contact as regards future clog trade was a firm called Crookes' of Gateshead, who bought our clogs for resale and became both permanent customers and friends as well.

At the end of the first year at Upperhead Row the 1955–56 sales totalled £14,926, profit £1,881 and debtors £2,268. Our supplier of waxed hide butt splits, J. H. Grimshaw & Sons Ltd of Hunslet, sent me a very nice complimentary letter on 23 November 1955:

> We must offer you our sincere congratulations on the publicity your business is receiving on the manufacture of clogs. The article is a very interesting one and we would like to take this opportunity of wishing you every success in your new premises. You are certainly showing much more foresight and enthusiasm than some of the cloggers we have known over the years. With Compliments, Yours faithfully.

This letter was typed in blue, which caught my eye as being far more attractive than the usual black/red typewriter ribbons, so I changed my own notepaper to red and blue afterwards and used the blue ribbon to match. I still have this letter, which certainly made my day when I received it. The red triangle, of course, was the safety symbol overprinted with the trade name and also matched nicely with the new notepaper heading.

One of my personal grudges against what I considered was unfair competition in clog making was the action of allowing prisoners in Wandsworth gaol to make clogs as part of their rehabilitation during the final months prior to being released. These were sold, so I was informed, at cost of materials plus five pence. This really riled me as in my opinion many other items could have been made instead of clogs without the adverse effect it had on our tiny industry. Production of all types of footwear including clogs was supplied to the relevant government department by means of quarterly returns showing the breakdown of types, sizes etc., so I was able to see the total UK production, the prisons' production and so on. The actual number of pairs of clogs being made each day by the prisoners would not be more than three or four but it was the principle of the thing that annoyed me, even though, looking back, it was not particularly damaging. Taking the matter up with the Home Office I eventually received a reply signed by 'Rab' Butler, the then Home Secretary, to the effect that in their opinion the prison production of clogs did not constitute any threat to the clog trade and in any case production was only supplied to the nationalised industries, mainly the gas boards and railways. So that was that, but I continued to grumble as the decline in the clog trade continued, and the proportion of the prison trade increased. However, I heard that in the fullness of time clog production ceased at Wandsworth for the simple reason that the instructor had either retired or left the job and that it had not been possible to recruit anyone willing and able to replace him. So that was the unexpected end of the matter.

Two trade papers, the *Shoe & Leather News* and the *Shoe & Leather Record*, were in competition for the weekly business of keeping the leather and footwear trades informed and, of course, obtaining advertising revenue. Of these two, I took the *News*. This ran an article on the clog-making position in prisons with the heading 'Queen in competition with clogmaker', much to my amusement, and was certainly one way of putting it. Anyhow, it aired my grievance and no doubt made me feel a little better at the time.

One of the London clog makers, J. Moon & Son, had gone bankrupt, so I went to see him, hoping to pick up some trade from his former customers, but it was a rather wasted journey as they had probably already arranged for one of the other three remaining clog manufacturers in London to supply them. I did, however, visit the Admiralty whilst in London and my impression of their offices was that they were the most dowdy and dingy ones I had ever seen or could imagine. I found it almost unbelievable that people in London were working in such places and conditions. It was like going into another world for me after visiting so many offices up and down the country. In the event, I came home with the two page foolscap-size papers giving the specification required for both safety and non-safety blucher clogs. The actual details were ridiculous in the extreme, particularly the specification for the leather to be used in the uppers and the stated proportions of wax, fat etc. to be used in making the leather etc. The nailing of the welt had to be so close together that in my opinion it was quite possible that there would be a crack opening up all the way round the clog, weakening it due entirely to being nailed too close together; this was just too extreme to be practical. Later, after tendering, I did receive some orders for the southern naval dockyards, one aspect of which surprised me insomuch that the sizes ordered included quite a large proportion of 11s, 12s, 13s and 14s, certainly not what one would have expected from a normal range of men's sizes. It appeared that a lot of these large sizes were actually destined for Africa, where the natives had apparently very large feet compared with our own. Incidentally, my experience in supplying the Scottish trade was that in general their feet were smaller than those south of the border. Similarly, because children growing up during and after the war were much taller than pre-war, the average size 4 for women had risen to at least size 5 and the men's from the average of size 8 to at least size 9, which added to the cost of the materials used in making the footwear.

One pattern bought by the Admiralty and hardly ever seen in the north of England, except for gardening, was the Baltic, which was the usual height of the Derby pattern but had no eyelets at all, a flap being sewn all the way down the instep and fitted under the vamp. Two short straps and buckles formed the fastening for this type. The uppers usually had a felt lining, and in the case of the navy was worn by both cooks and women.

The largest user of clogs in London apart from the Ford Motor Company was the North Thames Gas Board, at whose stores on the Great West Road I saw the largest stock of clogs in one place that I had seen in my life. All the London gasworks were supplied from there, with the huge Beckton gasworks on the road to Dagenham being the biggest of them all. Supplies, apart from the prison proportion, were bought on a tender for contract basis.

Steady progress during the 1956–57 year resulted in sales increasing to £16,019, debtors very similar to the previous year at £2,241 and a profit of £1,765, slightly down from £1,881.

It was always difficult to obtain good cloggers for the simple reason that there were very few in the country. Having trained Nelson and his younger brother Gordon myself, I had to look further afield. Following the successful acquisition of Daltons' of Sheffield in February 1961 it was to be another year before an opportunity of similar nature presented itself. This was in the case of the Hemsworth Leather Co. Ltd, who besides making clogs at Hemsworth had a shop in Leeds. On 5 February 1962, exactly a year after my first take-over, I was able to acquire their clog making section and persuaded their clogger living in Hemsworth to leave that area, move to Huddersfield, and make clogs here, virtually bringing his own trade with him. He certainly was far better off financially over here and bought his own house on a new estate at Fartown. A suitable agreement was made to take all stock of clog materials, existing orders for around a thousand pairs and to circularise their former customers informing them of the sale of the clog business.

In an effort to reward good men and women, I took out a non-contributory illness and accident policy for all suitable staff, which paid out £1 per day with cover, excluding the first week of illness, for one year and in the case of accident full 24-hour cover for a period of two years. Whilst £1 a day may sound only a paltry amount, in the 1950s £7 weekly in addition to any other benefits payable by the government was very much appreciated, especially as the employees had to pay nothing themselves to the scheme.

Later on, this insurance, in the case of Duke Hellawell, the first clogger I ever set on, was particularly helpful. Having been to the

128

races, Duke was returning home via Leeds when he tripped and fell and was unable to walk to the bus station, having hurt himself in such a manner that he could not use his crutches. He was taken into hospital at Leeds and was later transferred to the Huddersfield Royal Infirmary. He was unable to continue to make clogs after this accident as his one and only leg could no longer stand the strain of the daily hammering that clogging entailed. At the time of the fall he was over 63 years old, and the insurance company offered to pay out the £1 a day from the date of the accident right up to his sixty-fifth birthday, even though this was many months ahead. Accordingly, I was able to take him a cheque for over £500 in settlement of the claim.

A footwear exhibition was taking place in Leeds one day at an hotel in the centre of the city, and on mentioning this at work on the day in question one of the machinists, who had originated from there prior to marrying a Huddersfield man, asked if she could go with me in the car in order to visit her mother whilst I was at the exhibition. Obviously I was happy to take her and dropped her off at her mother's house before proceeding into Leeds centre. The arrangement was that she would make her own way back to the exhibition hotel and then come back to Huddersfield with me afterwards. It is always the custom at exhibitions and similar gatherings for a bar to be provided for invited visitors, as was the practice at the ROSPA safety exhibition, and this was no exception. However, on that particular day most people seemed to have come during the daytime and gone by the time I arrived, so that when Betty came later we were the only three people there and the representative of the footwear firm had packed up ready to go himself. Apparently, unknown to me, Betty's favourite tipple was gin, which the rep poured from the bottle in a very generous measure. After a while, with absolutely no prior warning whatsoever, Betty gracefully slid under the table – out for the count. I had heard of people drinking others under the table but had never in my wildest dreams imagined anything like this happening myself and I was quite lost as to what to do with her. Obviously we had to get her back to Huddersfield somehow or other, and as she did not make any move towards coming round I had to bring the car to the hotel and give the doorman a good tip to carry her into the back of the car and prop her up at one end. I don't know what the doorman must have thought but I had enough to worry about wondering what Betty's husband would think when he saw what state she was in.

Although the evening was rather cold, I drove all the way back with a window open, hoping that the fresh air would bring her round during the half-hour journey. I became more and more concerned the nearer I came to Huddersfield as she showed no sign of improvement, so I eventually arrived at her home and knocked on the door to explain what had happened. Anyhow, her husband came to the car, lifted her out and carried her inside, to my great relief. I did not stay any longer than necessary to see her inside and set off for home as quickly as possible. This was one of the most embarrassing moments of my life, and was only caused by trying to do a good turn for her. I found out later that she had had nothing to eat, having gone straight from work, and this was no doubt at least partly responsible for her passing out as she certainly was not drunk, by any means. If her husband had been a different type of person there could easily have been a very uncomfortable situation, but thankfully that was not the case on this occasion.

During the following year, 1957–58, a substantial increase in trade up to £22,022 was achieved, mainly due to having obtained half the Ford contract, which required weekly deliveries of a specified amount and then any extras as ordered separately. Rocketing trade debtors from £2,241 to £3,836 again demonstrated to me just how much capital was needed for expansion. The profit of £2,321 helped somewhat in this direction. The Northgate property was sold at a loss of £281, but a profit of £18 accrued from the sale of the garage.

Purchase tax, one of the taxes in force in the 1950s, was levied on a whole range of goods at varying rates. The top rate of 100 per cent was levied on luxury items such as fur coats and jewellery with other commodities at lower rates. Suddenly out of the blue with no warning or mention beforehand the then Chancellor, in his wisdom, decided in his Budget speech to put a 5 per cent purchase tax on clogs excluding safety footwear. It was the normal practice when alterations or additions were to be made in any Budget that notices would be sent out the same day to all those concerned with implementing them as they were operative immediately. So they duly arrived in the morning's post following the Budget statement.

I was absolutely livid. I contacted the local MP, Mr Wade (later Lord Wade) to take the matter up in the House and had large posters made saying 'Abolish the tax on clogs'. These were displayed prominently on each and every window of the upstairs clogging room, where there was an uninterrupted view of them from the town centre direction facing down Macaulay Street. News of my battle against the tax soon got round and again I took full advantage of the media interest to publish my efforts to have the tax abolished. For several reasons the purchase tax on clogs was ill thought out and unfair, no doubt formulated by someone with no actual knowledge of the true situation in the trade. First of all, nearly half the production of clogs in the UK at that time was being done by small family firms, with boot repairing as the main trade, often along with footwear retailing, all of whom would be excluded from the purchase tax regulations owing to their individual clog sales total being under the specified level for compliance. The cumulative effect of them all added together was considerable, bearing in mind total UK sales. This was obviously flagrantly unfair competition as far as I was concerned. Secondly, although safety boots and shoes stamped with the British Standards Kitemark were to be excluded, as also were safety rubber boots, there appeared to be no actual mention of safety clogs being similarly exempted. Thirdly, the actual purchase tax receipts to the Treasury would not really be worth collecting.

Apart from these very valid reasons for not taxing clogs, an anomaly arose insomuch that although the purchase tax was supposed to be levied at 5 per cent in actual practice I was instructed to charge 6¼ per cent as this was considered to be calculated on a fictitious factor's price. As a result of this stupid instruction telephone calls came in every day from irate customers who were expecting to be charged a 5 per cent rate, complaining bitterly and most unfairly that I had calculated the tax wrongly. This caused endless time and money to be wasted explaining the lawful position to them.

By the time the Committee stage of the Finance Bill was being discussed in detail, the regulations had been effective for several weeks. Mr Wade moved an amendment to abolish the tax on clogs at this stage, which was accepted by the House, and the relevant clause was deleted. So we did win eventually and the tax was abolished. This being the case, all the tax charged to our customers had now to be refunded, which consumed more time and expense before the matter was finally laid to rest and became just another memory of nasty red tape experience.

Sales for the year 1958–59 were slightly down, as also were the figures for both debtors and profit, possibly due to some extent to the confusion over purchase tax.

In an attempt to break into the export market for clogs, I contacted the Board of Trade in London, who circulated their overseas offices to ascertain which countries, if any, would be interested in importing our clogs. I was already aware that New Zealand was buying clog soles and clog irons separately and I wanted to supply them with our safety clogs if possible. Unfortunately, regulations in their country prohibited the import of goods which they considered should be produced by the home market, with the result that although we wanted to sell and they wanted to buy, permission was not granted. It was even suggested to me that I went over there and set up clog manufacturing myself, but I had enough with UK red tape and had no desire to go there.

A similar situation had occurred in Ireland, resulting in the Bolton Clog Company being driven out of business for the same reason as they were 90 per cent dependent on Irish trade. These tend to be things that one reads about in the press, but when it happened at Bolton I went over there to see if anything could be salvaged from the situation. This met with no success as the damage had already been done and all the information that I could glean was either from the trade press or from others in the trade.

As time went on I was to find that nearly all the clogs worn in Ireland were being imported from one or other of the Scandinavian countries, which, so I was informed, were able to provide very extended credit as regards payment, partly because

132

by sending one large shipment annually the stocks would last a very long time but be cheaper for the sender consigning in bulk. In any case, it was impossible to make a similar clog as the machines used in Norway, Sweden and Denmark were totally different from our own and produced a clog sole shape with an open back having a slightly raised rim round the heel part. The wearing material was an iron ring round the heel shape with a wooden insert, and on the sole part a single strip of wood about half an inch wide again had an iron or steel band round it, secured in the middle of the sole. The first time I saw this type of clog I realised immediately that it was impossible to copy the pattern in the UK, and my friend at Snaith, John Townend, confirmed that they could not make that shape of clog sole with their existing machinery.

Having drawn a blank with the New Zealand and Irish markets, I decided to show at the Dusseldorf exhibition in November 1959 and polished up my German as best I could in the meantime. As mentioned, I already had brochures printed in French and German with illustrations of the various styles available. In order to share expenses and hopefully to increase trade for both of us, John and I made an exhibit of both the clogs and tool handles, the latter being quite important to Snaith in their efforts to diversify and use their existing timber for products other than clog soles which needed to be made from beech.

On 10 November 1959 we arrived by boat at the Hook of Holland, to be greeted by torrential rain and a thunderstorm, which did not help me in my first attempt to drive a car abroad. However, after staying the first night near Arnhem, I found it very easy to follow the yellow A13 road signs all the way to Dusseldorf and thoroughly enjoyed driving on the right-hand side of the road for a change. This was my first real introduction to colour identification on road signs, conspicuously absent at that time in England, and I found them most noticeable and extremely helpful to a driver not knowing his route.

The huge halls of the Messe contained many stands with products of all kinds on display, including safety boots and clogs. On examining the German safety clogs, I found that the leather (*rindleder*) was of excellent quality but the workmanship and the

133

clog soles were just the opposite. This was explained by the fact that the clogs were not made by clog manufacturers but by safety boot manufacturers, who also made some clogs using the same uppers as for boots, which did not really even look right to me. The wooden soles had only been roughly shaped by bandsaw and the samples on show had 'flats' on the sides. As far as prices were concerned, there was no real difference between ours and theirs, comparing like with like so far as this could be done. Thus there was no special advantage to any German in buying our product and having the bother of dealing with the paperwork involved in importing. Most of the visitors to the exhibition were engineers, a highly respected band of men in Germany and a far cry from the British safety officer or buyer. I got on well with all whom I met, with the exception of the hotel porter who, on noticing the silver tank badge on my blazer, took an immediate dislike to me, which was both unfortunate and unnecessary but made no difference businesswise.

I had to man the stand myself most of the time as John had an attack of malaria and had to sit in the car. Service in Malaya had caused this illness, which seemed to flare up once a year for a while. However we had tried and at least knew what the position was as far as exporting to Germany was concerned. I was coming to realise that in most countries where clogs were worn, the trade could easily be made there and there was virtually no incentive for anyone to import clogs particularly bearing in mind the relatively small quantities involved compared with all other forms of footwear.

Having returned from Germany, bringing a sample of their safety clog for exhibition purposes, I had news of an Italian firm which had expressed interest in our safety clogs through the Board of Trade, and I wrote a letter in perfect Italian to Assiende Riunito e Figlio in Milan. The outcome of this was that they expressed delight at my perfect Italian, of which I did not know a single word, having prevailed upon a local ladies' hairdresser to compose a letter for me, and wanted to buy our safety clogs at 50 pence per pair, which they said was the maximum that they could pay for them. As our costs to produce the clogs were far in excess of this low figure, there was no chance of any trade at all, so another country dropped out of my list.

Several parts of the United States of America sent reports on the sale of clogs in their particular area, as a result of which I wrote to a lot of oil refineries in Texas and some steelworks and motor car manufacturers in Detroit, but all to no avail, so the United States joined my list of lost opportunities. Canada seemed for a while to be a likely place to sell our clogs and I sent samples to various firms in an effort to break into their market. Here price was not particularly the problem but the duties imposed by the Canadian government on imported clogs were so high that it was a complete waste of time trying to sell there. There was absolutely no way at all that anyone making clogs anywhere in the world could have been able to overcome such high tariffs and sell at an economical price.

All other countries I tried to supply were non-starters. Even an attempt to sell through the World Health Organisation to thousands of people suffering from leprosy who needed clogs badly proved hopeless. The main reasons for this was the fact that the lepers would have two feet not alike, needing individual cutting of each sole using the stock knives the old-fashioned way as pairs of clogs made in the normal way were just useless. I had real hopes of being able to help a good cause and at the same time sell in bulk, but again it all fell through, although there was one clogger from Lancashire who went to Africa to teach the lepers how to make the clog soles and the clogs for themselves. Sadly, I gave up completely trying to export clogs for the many reasons already mentioned. What the cost had been in financial terms and time expended I cannot say but at least I knew what to tell people when they asked me why we didn't export clogs.

A happy event took place when Phyllis, one of our machinists, remarried, having been widowed some years before. Again I was able to taxi around for her wedding, which was much appreciated as she lived at Scammonden, several miles away from work. Phyllis was invariably early for work every morning, had a ready smile on her face, and was a pleasure for anyone to work with. Obviously she was extremely popular with all of us.

Proposals affecting Upperhead Row in respect of the Huddersfield Inner Ring Road had been laid by the local authority and revealed by the town planning department, resulting in the possibility of a compulsory purchase order hanging over our heads from that time onwards. This was not unexpected, with the five-year original suggestions being reviewed on an annual basis. Accordingly the accountant wrote the property value down to a nominal £2 in that year's accounts and I found myself again on the lookout for other premises.

In 1959–60 we saw a fantastic rise in turnover, with sales up from £20,850 to £29,124, trade debtors rising to £5,190 from £2,868, leaving a profit of £2,056. In spite of the continuing overall decline in UK clog sales, our own sales graph proudly displayed on the office wall showed a persistent healthy upward trend with only very minor small reversals.

The following year, 1960–61, revealed another increase – a modest one this time to £31,197, but for the first time we had reached a figure in excess of £30,000 and, of course, it was a good excuse for a celebration at the Plumbers' Arms a few yards away in Macaulay Street. Although sales had only risen by some 7 per cent the profit was £3,468, the best to date. Various competitors whose clog businesses had declined dramatically could not foresee any recovery ever taking place, which was perfectly true, and nothing could be done about it as demand could just not be falsely created in the clog trade on anything like a permanent basis. On the other hand, there should be a good business for anyone still left at the end of the day and I was determined to be at least one of them.

It was as a result of this appraisal of the clog situation for the future that I had discussions with Dalton Bros. Ltd of West Bar in Sheffield, who had been quite substantial makers and suppliers of clogs in addition to their other ancillary merchanting trade. I was able to come to an arrangement with them to take over the clog-making side, together with their machinery, stock of materials etc., which was signed in February 1961 and their former trade transferred to me. A list of their customers was provided, with the types and prices for each one, so that I could ensure continuity of supply before they had any chance to be looking elsewhere. All former customers were circularised by Daltons, introducing Walkley's as 'one of the largest producers of clogs in the United

Kingdom'. Daltons, like Millers of London, had been quite large makers of wellington clogs made from both leather of various types and from rubber canvas as well, this process needing no less than five different machines or equipment of which I did not have any at that time. These were brought to Upperhead Row and the making of wellington clogs attempted. This was a complete failure and I decided not to proceed in view of both the very small demand for wellington clogs and the fact that in any case I could buy them from Horsfields' of Bradford. They had been making these uppers for years and had all the tackle and patterns necessary, besides the expertise gained over a period of years.

One innovation on taking over Daltons trade was to make a ladies' three-lace clog using blue leather specially obtained for the purpose. Apparently Daltons had at least two local customers, Batchelors Foods and Bassetts sweet manufacturers, who had supplied all their female staff with blue nylon overalls and simply wanted clogs to match. I was happy to oblige as both were quite good buyers at the time. Their other accounts were, like our own, nearly all industrial works, mainly in their own area of Sheffield.

The most important new customer acquired whilst at Upperhead Row was William Walker & Sons Ltd of 45 Montrose Street, Glasgow. On receiving an enquiry from them for clogs, I was in Glasgow the following morning with all my samples and was congratulated on my promptness by the two directors, Mr Cattanach and Mr Joe Shaw, who both interviewed me in depth about the clog situation. I soon found out that they had virtually a monopoly of the Scottish clog trade. This reminded me of the three days that I had spent cycling round that area with little result. I could now see the reason why I was so unsuccessful. Scottish buyers in general preferred to buy from a Scottish supplier even though the actual maker might not be Scottish. We all got on extremely well together and I returned to Huddersfield with one of my biggest successes to date. From that time onwards orders arrived almost every day, and to keep their customers happy and at the same time encourage them to think that the cartons had been sent from Montrose Street, I was supplied with hundreds of their printed labels to use instead of our own. We typed the customer's name and address on these and sent them direct, making a saving on carriage charges by just one handling instead of two. The main buyers in the Glasgow area were the huge steel works, dominated by the famous Ravenscraig works, who bought the grain leather Derby safety clogs fitted with our No. 7 heat and oil resistant rubber soles and heels. Whenever I received any enquiries for clogs from anywhere in Scotland I posted them on to Walkers for attention as they had by now been appointed our official agents for all Scotland, and this was printed on the back of our brochures. Later on, visiting Scotland when we had been having an excellent trading relationship for some time, one of the directors took me out to lunch and the other in the evening for dinner. In between I remember lying on the bed in the hotel trying to sober up for the evening session as their Scottish hospitality was so over-whelming.

With the trade having risen from £12,932 on leaving Northgate to £31,409 at the end of the 1961–62 year, we again needed more space and I personally was having far more to do then than could satisfactorily be undertaken so I decided to employ a manager. He was Hans Kruger, a pilot in the German airforce during the war who had stayed over here to marry a Halifax girl he had met. His English was excellent, with one exception. He never mastered the word 'and' but invariably used the German '*und*', much to the amusement of everybody else. However, he was well liked and quickly picked up the managerial side of things.

Some property at Birkby, just over half a mile from the town centre, seemed ideal for our purpose. It had been used as storage for the large drums of dyes needed in the textile trade, which left the walls and floors easily cleared for alterations and improvements. After so many years running up and down staircases at Northgate and Upperhead Row, the idea of being able to work all on the ground floor was absolutely marvellous. After negotiations, which included a refusal of an offer that I made for the property, the vendor rang me up and actually asked me a price lower than that which I had already offered and been refused. I was absolutely staggered by this development but immediately accepted the lower figure. Whether he had been expecting me to offer more when he refused my first offer I do not know, but this seemed to me to be the most likely explanation.

138

The purchase is shown in the accounts at £4,601 and I sold Upperhead Row for £3,480, having typed out the binding sale agreement myself. My solicitor told me afterwards that my typed-out agreement was actually more legally binding than their own would have been, so I must have done it right, but I knew what he meant as any solicitor's document would be subject to some conditions and get-out clauses.

During the year I changed the Ford Consul for another similar but more up-to-date model. Fixed assets on leaving Upperhead Row are listed at £7,396 before depreciation.

The Birkby premises consisted of three long parallel rooms, with a fourth at the end joining all three together. A smaller, squarish room built on at a later date for mixing colours adjoined the end room. A 600-gallon tank for the gas oil central heating system could be filled up from an outside yard which led back to the main St John's Road for access. Alterations to the premises included the installation of two 30-feet-long skylights and new windows which let in so much daylight that electric lights were not necessary for a large part of the time. All woodwork was painted summer blue, the girders and central heating pipes were aluminium, a new flooring of yellow Roxana material was laid on the top of the existing concrete floor and the inside walls painted in white. The whole inside was then a really pleasant place to work in and looked fresh and clean throughout.

Being a single-storey building it was easy to plan the layout for best production and ease of working. The method chosen was to work in an anti-clockwise direction, with raw materials going in on the right-hand side of the building and finished clogs leaving by the front door on the left-hand side.

At the top end of the middle room, which had originally been an open space in between the other two rooms and now had a covered glass roof, were the weighscales for incoming rubber leathers or corrugated ones. The room itself was only used as a garage to keep four or five cars inside away from bad weather. The right-hand-side room became known as the shaving room, where this machine was installed near a side window at the end nearest to the clicking room. Doors from the shaving room gave access to both the yard and the clicking room. A table, known as a mender's table, was sited in the shaving room, near the machine where the rubber leathers were prepared ready for use. The joining strips of the rubber leathers ran the whole length and had to be cut away, as had each end where the metal and leather washers had been fitted when making new. From this table a long low bench ran the whole remaining length of the room, at the far end of which was placed the infra red-ray heater, the Tellus press and roughing machines – in other words, all the equipment necessary for fixing the Commando soles and heels onto the wooden soles. All the dirty work of roughing rubber and leather was thus done in this same room. The original toilet at this end had been divided into two for separate sexes and fitted up accordingly.

The clicking room occupied one corner of the building and was much wider than the shaving room, to which it had access doors beside the closing room next door. The closing room itself led through to both the canteen and the clogging room. After making a square-shaped office near the door leading into Common Road, the remaining area was shelved and used to both pack up cartons for despatch and to store them as well. A telephone system was installed to enable any room to contact the office or any other room to save a lot of running about, and it was also possible to have different rooms all connected to each other and speaking in conference. A carpet, desk, table, chairs and filing cabinets made it look like an efficient office, with the ever-rising sales chart on the wall. The clock that I had bought as a memento of the Amalgamated Society of Master Cloggers stood proudly on the desk.

The clicking room was to be further modernised by the installation of the then latest 'hytronic' clicking press with a very wide beam. This was to be sited in one corner near the outer wall at the side of a large window, with the other Ideal clicking press to serve as a back-up in the opposite corner next to the shaving room wall. The principle on which the hytronic worked was by a 13-ton squeeze as opposed to the bump of the older press. The press was operated by using two hands as before to trip the beam, which started the downward motion which in turn was stopped by the action of the beam pushing the press knife through masking tape on the aluminium sheet forming the lower surface, resulting in the electric circuit being completed. The oil would then flow in the opposite direction, which raised the beam back to its original level.

The wooden clicking press blocks had been dispensed with in favour of the aluminium pads which were necessary to perform this new way of clicking. The aluminium pad itself was only about three-quarters of an inch in thickness and the black masking tape was applied to both sides so that when one eventually became unserviceable the pad could be turned over to use the other side. Eventually, when both were no longer working satisfactorily, the pads were sent away to be recovered for use again.

The hytronic was so sensitive in its operation that it could be tripped with an egg underneath without breaking it. This was achieved as a salesman's gimmick by using the aluminium pad without tape on it and covering an egg with silver paper, so that when the machine was tripped and the beam lowered onto the egg, the circuit was completed and automatically the beam moved up again without damage. The actual time-saving using the hytronic was not very much as the squeezing operation was certainly no quicker and possibly even slower than the method of the Ideal clicking press.

To complete the fitting-up of the clicking room, a large free-standing metal shelving stood behind the clicker. Each of the four very wide shelves held a different type of leather or rubber canvas, all easily accessible within arm's length. A hand clicker's bench was made to fit into the third corner (the door leading to the closing room being in the fourth) and was really another mender's table with a shelf underneath filled with rubber leathers ready for use after the shaving had been done.

The two windows in this room provided ample light during the hours of daylight. The closing room was fitted up with all the machinery brought from Upperhead Row and so arranged in the same anti-clockwise order that each process in turn worked its way round the room, ending up by the clogging room door. This started with the skiving machine and the eyeletting machine on the back wall behind the machinists, the closing machines in one line alongside the windows and a central bench for hammering and trimming the stiffeners on a 'ranger' at one end of it, from where the uppers would be riveted on the machine against the other wall, with a table on either side to take the pile of uppers before and after riveting. Ample shelving for the boxes brought from Upperhead Row covered the wall by the machinists.

Leading from the closing room to the canteen was a passageway in between the gas oil storage tank, which was enclosed by a brick wall all round, and the central heating boiler, which we installed new opposite on the other side of the passage. There was a connecting pipe to feed the oil to the boiler running underneath the floor, covered by a loose plank set into the floor to provide easy access.

The former colour mixing room and now the canteen was fitted with four or five tables, chairs, gas cooker and hot and cold water, nearby which was a double door into the back yard for use in emergency such as a fire. In practice these doors were only to be needed when there was a delivery of oil from the yard outside, where there was plenty of room for a large tanker. The door itself was fitted with a normal handle for opening but had a steel bar resting on two holders, one at each side of the doorway easily lifted off when needed. This made the doorway more secure from a break-in point of view.

In the clogging room one long clogger's bench ran the whole length up to the doorway leading into the middle room and toilets, with an extension at right angles at the other end for two more men or for sticking Commando soles and heels on after preparation in the shaving room. Underneath the clogger's bench a shelf held a full range of sizes of lasts for each man exactly as before, with the windows all along the room giving daylight in front of people working there. I was fortunate to be able to buy a lot of metal racks on wheels and about six rows of shelves each, which were absolutely perfect in size for putting the clog soles, irons, uppers etc. on so that each order could be made in rotation. These could not have been designed better if they had been specially made for us and cost only 50 pence each. The long wooden counter holding the clog irons was placed in the middle of the clogging room with easy access either side to collect the clogs after making and ready for checking. The clog soles were to be stored on a long wooden rack the length of the clogging room at the back, with several shelves as before to separate the sizes and styles; the free-standing clog iron rack stood nearby.

When all preparatory work had been completed an inventory and valuation was carried out on 9 April 1962 for insurance purposes. This was done on a replacement value and showed a total figure of £13,743.61. Two copies of this bound valuation were provided so that the insurers could have one in addition to mine. Although this exercise is never a cheap one and the sort of thing that tends to get put off, I had always been insurance minded, possibly because my grandfather had taken out the first Co-op insurance book in Huddersfield, and it had been carried on by my mother during the war years before I was born. In the event of any future claim, the figures would not be disputed and showed to a bank as certified evidence of business assets.

In order to obtain the maximum publicity for the official opening of the Birkby premises, I tried to think of someone who would make the best impact. I came up with the idea of trying to get Alfie Bass to perform the opening ceremony and cut the ribbon. Alfie Bass was known as 'Bootsie' in the *Bootsie and Snudge* television series and seemed ideal for the job. I was delighted when he accepted the suggestion, which resulted in a very happy time with journalists and photographers in attendance and the inevitable gimmicky headline in the papers 'Bootsie opens clog factory'. This was just what I had been trying to achieve in the first place. He himself thoroughly enjoyed it and wished that he could have stayed longer, but something else had also been arranged for him. The opening day was a huge success, with suppliers, customers, friends and a lot of spectators turning up to see what a good job of fitting up the factory had been done. A large barrel of beer stood on a gantry in the canteen, where staff and visitors could help themselves to celebrate what was then a real milestone and achievement in the 16 years since starting on Northgate.

7

Taking over Maudes

The shape of Maudes clog soles varied considerably from the Snaith pattern in two main respects. The width of the heel together with its smaller depth was in the region of half an inch in difference, resulting in a much smaller heel iron being needed compared with the wider and longer Snaith heel. This was especially noticeable in the common toe patterns, with others not quite so pronounced. The difference was very little in making new clogs in the first place as clog heel irons were made in every width with sizes in each eighth of an inch from children's sizes up to the largest men's. But when re-ironing took place away from our works at any of the customers' premises, they quite naturally expected heel irons ordered to fit, say, size 6 to do so in all cases, not realising the shapes varied between the two makes of clog soles. Whilst the smaller iron would go onto a Snaith sole, albeit with a poor fit, the converse did not apply as the correct size for a Snaith sole would be far too big for Maudes and would hang over the edges.

For this reason one very irate customer rang up virtually accusing me of not knowing what size of clog iron fitted a size 6 sole, which I found extremely embarrassing, and I was furious because in his eyes it made me look stupid. I explained the position as best I could – that we were using two different makes of clog soles, and obviously some weeks after despatch to a customer we had no idea as to which clog soles had been used on their orders. I had previously tried to prevail upon both the solemakers to standardise their patterns but to no avail. However, I was determined if at all possible, not be made a fool of twice by

144

being placed in this ridiculous situation through no fault of my own, and contacted Maudes on the matter.

Mr Sam Morgan, the manager, came over to see me and I explained to him that I was sick and tired of this silly and unnecessary situation and was determined to end it one way or another. Although he must have understood my position, Mr Morgan refused to do anything at all about it, possibly because they had hundreds of thousands of pairs of soles already made and in stock, and anyhow his words were 'We have always made them that way', to which my very swift answer was that I looked forward and not backwards and if they did not change to the other pattern, which in the case of the London clog sole shape had a heel which fitted all the various alternative soling materials that we used, then I would not buy any further supplies from them, so it was deadlock on the matter.

The larger Snaith heel on their soles was, in my opinion, far safer to wear as there was more area to stand on and I had personally known of a case where a man wearing the small Maudes heel on his clogs had fallen down a stone staircase as a result of not having enough grip on the surface, resulting in injury to him. The galling point about this was that from a manu-facturing point of view the wood cut away from the short heel simply went to waste, so there was no saving in that respect.

Having had this exchange of views with Mr Morgan, I could not help thinking what some of my own customers would have said to me if I had tried to supply a different product to the one required, and could well imagine, say, Ford Motor Company's buyer commenting on a situation like that. However, Maudes had from that day lost my business and had only themselves to blame for not moving with the times. As I have often said, business is constantly changing and to be successful we have to change with it even though we may very often not like to have the change imposed on us by events or others.

However, as mentioned, there were two problems with Maudes soles from a wholesale clog manufacturer's point of view, and this was in the gripping of the soles. Maudes, quite sensibly in theory, cut their grip slightly inwards at the bottom of the cut into the welt, which they contended would help to make a more waterproof joining when nailed round, but unfortunately in so doing the top of the grip tended to have a feather edge, quite sharp at times, which would easily either break or split when the leather or copper welting was being nailed round. This made Maudes soles very unpopular with the cloggers who were on piece work and wanted to get on with it and not be held up by having to smooth off any inside cracks with emery cloth. Conversely, the grip on Snaith soles was almost a right-angled one and far easier to nail round and with very few cracks appearing in the welting process. This problem of Maudes gripping was, of course, immediately solved by not buying any more of their soles, much to the delight of all the cloggers, who felt that they were making a better job using Snaith soles anyhow.

Having taken over Hemsworth's trade, I soon realised that each clog-making firm of any size had one agent in South Wales who mainly supplied the steel industry but some mining as well. Accordingly I went down there to find out what the situation was like for myself, and as a result of various calls arranged with a firm called Struel Bros. Ltd of Neath in Glamorganshire, as it was then called, to be my agents for Wales in the same way that Walkers of Glasgow represented us in Scotland. Their name and address was also printed on the brochure alongside the one for Walkers. Whilst in Swansea, I was surprised to find that a small shop, Blyth's, were actually supplying one of the huge steelworks with clogs. I had called previously on the steelworks to no advantage as they said they were quite prepared to pay higher prices than mine to have a local supplier who would carry the stocks instead of themselves and be able to give immediate delivery. It was impossible to get them to change their minds and they continued to buy from Blyth's, who in any case were in turn buying from Millers of London.

One of the Struel's customers bought a blucher flap-and-buckle pattern clog made from rubber canvas uppers, nailed round with copper nails, and supplied with the plain wooden soles. I did not know for what purpose these were needed, nor indeed was I told as no one else that I knew used a similar clog, and I was more than curious.

Traditionally, competition in South Wales had led to buying

articles of a poor quality to keep prices down, and in the making of this particular clog we had to use reject clog soles, which I have not previously mentioned although all clog makers did use some at times. All the four Wakefield area competitors used seconds soles to the maximum they could get, and were supplied by both clog sole firms at about one-third of the cost of the standard-quality clog soles. This made quite a lot of difference to the actual costs of production as clog soles, like leather, were the high-cost items needed in their manufacture. Any kind of fault could be seen on these soles, from a shape narrower than normal to a piece of sole still having some bark on it. It was amazing how one foot tended to be faulty and the other quite passable, until it was realised that in making the soles they were made one foot at a time and not in pairs, as once the knives had been fitted to the machines they would only make the one shape, either left or right, with pairing done afterwards by simply putting a left and a right together.

It was some time before I knew that after we had delivered this type of clog to Struel's they, or someone else on their behalf, was actually fitting copper runners to these reject soles before supplying them to their customer. These copper 'irons', as some people called them, were made by the clog iron manufacturers from a flat strip of perhaps one-eighth of an inch thick, but were very hard, and bent over in a concave manner to fit the sole. The holes were circular and countersunk to take screws, which were supplied along with the copper runners.

To my knowledge, the biggest user of these clogs with copper runners was Van Den Berg and Jurgens large Stork margarine factory at Ellesmere Port. For obvious reasons they did not want anything ferrous to be used in the making of their footwear.

Unfortunately, when these copper runners were fastened on, whoever was carrying this work out had no idea at all how to do it, as I found out when a batch of clogs with cracked soles was returned to us. On examining them, I first noticed that the brass screws had been hammered in instead of screwed, which had bent quite a few to start with. Hammering screws into reject soles was simply asking for it, so to speak. Secondly, one clog returned had only been partly fastened on before cracking the sole, and the runner was actually on the wrong foot as these runners, like clog irons, were made in lefts and rights. Obviously if the person did not know the difference between left and right feet he should not have been doing this work and ruining what had been good wearable clogs when we sent them out.

I was so incensed at my clogs being called faulty when I knew there was nothing wrong with our work that I sent a strong letter to Struel's explaining the position and fully expecting that they would never buy from me again. Amazingly, the opposite happened and we were asked to fit the copper runners ourselves on these clogs which, apart from other considerations, was far better done before the clogs were made rather than afterwards, enabling the clogs to be made in the normal way, and if any clog soles did crack they could be replaced before making up.

In order to fasten these copper runners on as efficiently as possible, I fixed up a wooden jig, made from some of the wood that had originally been my bed as a boy, and arranged a drill at a suitable height above it to make holes for the brass screws, which could then be screwed in far more easily, bearing in mind that reject soles always for some inexplicable reason seemed to be much harder than normal ones.

Incidentally, whilst mentioning these copper runners, another material called 'white metal' – aluminium-type clog 'irons' – was in limited use and had to be fastened onto the wooden soles in exactly the same way as the copper runners, even though they were narrower like traditional irons. The main advantage of the aluminium runners was in their very light-weighing quality and non-ferrous spark-proof property as an alternative to copper, and if customers wanted them instead we would willingly make them.

The combination of harder reject soles, softer copper nails and the rubber canvas material of the upper for this particular clog made it the most unpopular style of all with the cloggers, who were always unhappy to make them as the softer welt nails often bent when hammering in and had to be taken out and a second nail used. It was impossible to keep everybody happy when these orders came in from Struel's and I never was able to do this satisfactorily, although I did my best to share the work out fairly between the number of men clogging on that particular day. If an order came in for, say, four dozen pairs, as often happened, and there were four men making them, it seemed on the face of it to be quite sensible and fair to give one dozen to each man to be made up, but this might not seem as fair as might at first appear as some men were actually half as fast in their work as others. The faster men making half as many again as the slower man on the 'best work' must surely make half as many again as the slower man if the work was not as good, as in the case in point, so, theoretically, he ought to be allocated one and a half dozen pairs to make and the slower man only one dozen. I never was able to convince one of the faster men that this should be the case and that the slower man was actually losing out more than ever when making the 'bad' work, so it was definitely to the detriment of the slower worker. However, this argument was never settled and the best compromise that I could come up with was to pay a much higher rate than would have been the case in an effort to please them as best I could.

Holidays had always been a problem to organise, especially as I now had cloggers from Halifax, Spen Valley, Wakefield and Huddersfield, all of whom, naturally, wanted to have their local week's holidays. The solution which worked out best was to keep open all the year round, providing continuity of service for our customers, and let everybody take whatever weeks they wanted. It was possible, of course, knowing when a man was to be away, to arrange production of uppers so that any fluctuation in production could be smoothly dealt with.

There were quite a lot of people looking for work, and once after advertising in the local paper, I had 50 girls or women arriving the same afternoon. As there was nowhere that any of them could have had any previous experience, I had long learned to accept the fact that people would always have to be trained to do our type of work.

Shortly after opening at Birkby I was able to start talks aimed at taking over another clog business, this time at Upton, near Doncaster. On visiting this firm, Cheetham Brothers, I found that the production of clogs was actually being done by four women working from 9 till 1 p.m. at 15 pence an hour and nailing the clogs from a standing position. This was something that I had

149

never either seen or heard of, although a casual glance once gave me the impression that the clog was standing on its side against a large heavy iron shape with the clog sole held up against it somehow. The working conditions seemed primitive in the extreme, with a fireplace piled high with ashes looking as if the whole place could be on fire in no time, and as there were no toilet facilities the women had to go to the pub next door. However, they were somehow making quite a lot of corrugated leather clogs for the pits in the area and I was keen to take over their business if possible. On 21 February an agreement was signed with the now usual arrangement of buying the clog materials at cost, circularising their customers and ceasing to make clogs there. With this takeover the day after my birthday, I was beginning to think that perhaps February was my lucky month as I had now had three consecutive successful ones in 1961, 1962 and now 1963.

Turnover for 1962–63 was £30,997, down about £400 on the previous year.

Again in the February, 1964 saw the takeover of Betts of Bow, one of the London clog makers whose trade had dropped considerably and who wished to concentrate on industrial clothing, particularly donkey jackets for the building trade. This was a very amicable takeover, with Betts helping me all they could to provide continuity of supply to their former customers.

By this time there were three cloggers coming daily from the Halifax area and I bought a second-hand Morris van for £200 to bring them backwards and forwards, with one of the three doing the driving. At Upperhead Row the bus station had been quite near, presenting no problem for travel from Halifax, but at Birkby it became somewhat awkward and the van seemed to solve the problem for all concerned. During the day I could use the van for collecting cartons and so on. The arrangement was for each of the three to pay £3 a week towards the running and upkeep, which was agreed at a time they were working five and a half days a week but shortly after getting the van they only wanted to do five days and considered that as a result they should only pay £2.50 at the rate of 50 pence a day, but I was not happy with this method of calculation as the cost of running the van was almost the same as before. However, I did not press the point and agreed to the £2.50 instead. People have different ways of looking at the same situation.

The year resulted in an excellent increase in trade, with turnover rising to £39,442, trade debtors £5,051 and a profit of £3,330. During the year I changed the car for a second-hand Jaguar as I considered that after so many years of hard work I was due a bit of luxury. In any case, I had long held the view that there was better value pound for pound paying about £1,100 for a second-hand Jaguar than paying the same amount for a new car. At the time, Jaguar cars depreciated rapidly in value after 12 to 18 months, and as most potential buyers could probably not afford the higher insurance costs and larger petrol consumption, this tended to make the second-hand market very attractive to me. That happy band of wealthy people who could afford to have a new Jaguar every year obviously had the money to look after their cars, which were usually in very good condition, having only been used for driving around in and not for any real work likely to have damaged the interior.

On 4 November 1964 Mr John Townend, the managing director of the British Clog Sole Manufacturers Ltd, as Snaith was correctly known, wrote a long and detailed letter to me which I consider was so important that it should be quoted in full:

Dear Sirs, Owing to the overall decline in the clog industry there has been a rapid concentration in the number of firms engaged in it over the past few years. This has affected the leather producers who are now reduced to one, clog iron manufacturers who now number only two and a departure from the upper manufacturers of such well known names as Horsfields. The list of clog manufacturers who have ceased production is well known to you all. In spite of this trend there have been two firms engaged in making clog soles although it has been obvious to all that one could do the work easily and much more economically. With this in mind our Company approached Mr J Maude in *June 1962* to consider either an amalgamation of the two firms or for our Company to take theirs over at a figure of £20,000 subject, of course, to Messrs

151

Maudes' being solvent. We were given to understand that Mr Maude intends to retire at either 65 or earlier. Unfortunately our efforts did not meet with success mainly due to Mr Maude's concern over the question of redundancy though it would appear that this would still arise on his retirement. We would point out however that in our offer provision had been made for redundancy payments and had the offer been successful the trade would have been benefiting by a reduction of 10/- [50 pence] per dozen ever since that time instead of which you suffered a price rise in October of that year. Whilst no-one wishes to create redundancy the plain fact is that if fifty people are carrying out the work of thirty five then the extra unnecessary cost must be paid for, in this instance by yourselves. We bring the above to your notice so that you will know the position between the two sole firms since the break in relations last March. As the price of clog soles is entirely due to the circumstances outlined our Company has diversified in the past year with the object of achieving a reduction. We ask you, therefore to consider the position carefully in the light of the facts placed before you and if you agree with the sentiments expressed, to favour us with as much business as possible to enable a reduction in price to be made at the earliest moment. In this way we shall all benefit. We thank you. Yours faithfully, J E Townend.

Having read this letter carefully two or three times over, there seemed little more that I could do personally to help Snaith with their problems although, following my own disagreement with Maudes already outlined, I had been buying all my soles from them. Every time that I was successful in taking over any other business my requirements for the clog soles would accrue to Snaith, to the detriment of Maudes, assuming that the business taken over was actually buying from both, as was usually the case.

About the same time that I acquired the business of Cheetham Bros. of Upton, another small business at Wakefield agreed to sell out to me. At Bottomboat, Stanley, near Wakefield, the old-established clog manufacturers of William Lamb had been supplying my old boss with clog uppers pre-war in addition to their wholesale clog trade, and it was from there that one of their cloggers, a Mr George Lockwood, decided to set up on his own in a small Nissen hut type of building near his home, not far away from Lambs. He made the clogs himself, with two sisters helping with the uppers, all of which were made from corrugated leather. Sales were made to the nearby collieries – Wakefield was in the No. 7 area. Besides taking over his business, I obtained his skiving machine, which had been cleverly adapted to have a drive on the top in addition to the underneath feed roller fitted as standard. This made the work of skiving corrugated leather much easier and quicker, and was superior to our own Fortuna skiver.

Other clog firms, as mentioned in Mr Townend's letter, were closing down as clog makers got older and retired; no one was carrying on their businesses, as there was no means of making a reasonable living. One or two such situations occurred whereby I was able to obtain extra trade without actually having to pay for the business ceasing production. In Newcastle-upon-Tyne the old established clog firm of Gosmans closed and I went up there, picking up a few customers who still remained on his books, whilst in Cheshire the clog firm of Cleavers stopped production and bought their future supplies from us. In Manchester the old firm known as Woolhams, with the 80-year-old senior director still putting in an appearance, was down to a very small amount of work and was mainly repairing with not much new clog making going on at all. So there was not much trade to be picked up there, but as anyone at all closed down it put ourselves in a relatively stronger position.

The devastating reduction in demand resulted in Gregory's of London going out of business, and this firm had at one time been very large producers of industrial clogs and one of Maudes' main customers over the years. This left only one firm in London still carrying on, Millers of the Boro, situated in Borough High Street, Southwark which had a huge trade in industrial clothing etc. but a diminishing trade on the clog side in relation to their overall activities. I struck up a good relationship with the county cricketer Jack Parker, who was the director in charge of the clog side. We had got to know each other some time earlier, when we

153

were fighting each other for Ford's trade, before arranging not to compete in tendering but to agree prices between us. Originally they had all this contract before I came along. Millers eventually decided to cease production of clogs and did not even bother to try to sell the trade to me, but were most helpful in enabling me to take over all their former customers, supplying me with the details of the styles required for each and the prices they themselves had charged. I greatly appreciated this, especially as in the view of all the previous takeovers I would have been quite willing to offer a premium figure to obtain their clog trade.

One of the factors in Millers deciding to close down production was the position in the fishing industry, where they had pretty well the monopoly at all the docks round the UK coastline and supplied huge quantities of wellington clogs, Baltic types and the traditional high-back Derby all fitted with the inevitable brewer's soles, oil dipped, and copper-welted. The overall fishing industry was being decimated and hit Millers in much the same way as I had been affected by the discovery of North Sea gas.

The policy of the Ford Motor Company was to try always to have two suppliers at least for every item that they bought, which is a sensible and prudent business method of ensuring supplies. This same policy could result in a buyer trying to play one supplier off against another when tendering for contracts came due. Knowing this to be the case, and having found out from actual experience the answer to this mutual problem was for me to quote one penny per pair less than Millers for one type of clog and for them to quote a penny less than mine for another type, we both invariably obtained a somewhat higher price each and the contract was shared equally between us. With the demise of Millers from the clog making scene, I did have the contract to myself for some time as there was only one other firm, our friends at Halifax, who could physically make the quantity needed. In the event they were not successful in obtaining Ford trade.

It was about this time that I was able to provide an improvement to the safety aspect of Ford's clogs. Although it will be remembered that all our safety clogs were fitted with the extended internal steel toecaps, giving more protection than a safety boot, accidents, even though not serious, could occur if

154

anything heavy should happen to fall on a workman's instep behind the cap. After one or two of these minor accidents, resulting in absence from work for a week or two Ford's asked me to produce something to eliminate this problem. Within 48 hours I had designed an instep protector made from concave blue steel or mild steel, turned up slightly at the toe end so as to rest neatly on the leather toecap covering the safety cap. The flap-and-buckle blucher pattern lent itself admirably to this design and was fitted easily, securing each instep protector by four bifurcated rivets inserted through the holes made in the protector, and provided full protection for the feet. Any future accidents could only be glancing blows and certainly nothing serious. Ford's were delighted with this idea and from that time onwards all their clogs were fitted with the instep protectors.

Another problem for Ford's occurred at Halewood, the Liverpool works, where they used a very penetrating type of fluid. It was constantly running over the turning process with some dropping onto the men's boots, making them useless after only two weeks' wear. This situation resulted in Ford's calling in representatives of all their footwear suppliers to see the position for themselves and try to come up with something to overcome the problem. Having seen what was happening at first hand, I made a non-leather upper from the rubber canvas material and had a Commando sole made from a neoprene compound, which turned out to be the only footwear to do the job well enough and last long enough to be a viable proposition. Naturally the newly invented instep protector was used on this clog as well. From that time onwards Ford's Halewood works always bought this type.

Most people have the impression that clogs were the domain of the north of England, mainly because they were seen more on the streets of the cotton towns and so on during the First World War, which was the case in their heyday, but there came a time when there were more clogs being made in the London area than the rest of the country put together. This was in the period after the war when overall demand was falling for all the hundreds of small businesses which just made a few and the wholesale manufacturing side was building up to a peak, supplying direct to the heavy industries, which probably affected Gregory's in

London. The main point is that the clogs were being worn at work and not on the way to and from there, which naturally gave the public the impression that the clogs were no longer being worn at all.

In Scotland the local clog maker at Galloway in Dumfries died, and as there was no one carrying on the trade his widow asked me to help clear his workshop and what stock he had. I paid her the current cost prices for the soles, irons and materials that were there, which were no doubt far in excess of what would have been realised at an auction, but the overall quantity was such that I was just able to pack everything into the car to bring back home. The actual trade had been very small indeed, mainly because in that part of Scotland it was still retail.

At the end of the financial year 1964–65 sales had risen from £39,442 to £45,148, trade debtors £5,710 and profit £2,817. Most importantly, the bank overdraft and loan total was reduced from £9,326 to £7,131 in spite of needing a further £700 to finance the expanding trade debtors.

To round off the year end, my friend Les Revill, on whose shop I had called on many times when in Barnsley town centre decided to call it a day and sold me his clog trade for £550, which included some machinery besides the usual stocks of clog-making materials. He also provided me with a full list of his customers to enable me to carry on as before. I believe he took a post office on or near the east coast on moving out of Barnsley. Mr Revill was one of the nicest men I had met running a small business in the clog trade, compared with the others in that area I had called on, and seemed to me to be cut out for other things.

With the acquisition of Revill's at Barnsley I had now almost eliminated the competition in that area, having taken over four of the five previous clog makers. The remaining one was Mr S Symons of Wombwell, who had a shop besides supplying local pits and works. I called upon him many times but he was reluctant to sell out and was not really near retiring age either. However, he always said he would give me first chance when he did eventually decide to quit. He subsequently moved to Cudworth, near Wakefield, and when I went into his shop there he seemed to have virtually no stock to sell but he was carrying on somehow. Having got four of the five firms, this last one did not pose much of a threat to my own trade as, being a one-man band, his production was very limited.

The year 1965–66 saw a small drop in turnover but I managed a modest £464 reduction in bank lending. The 1964 letter from Snaith clog soles had pointed out, quite correctly, that there was only room for one clog sole making firm in the UK and they had done their level best to take over at Maudes, but without success, although Mr James Maude was nearing retirement age. It was becoming rather hopeless for Snaith to keep going in spite of the larger quantities that I personally was buying, and when a point was actually reached where every sole was being sold at a loss, the increased buying resulted in a bigger loss, such was the ridiculous situation at that time. In August 1966 the inevitable happened, with the British Clog Sole Manufacturers Ltd being sold to Maudes at Hebden Bridge. Maudes' circular letter to the trade ran as follows:

Dear Sirs, We wish to bring to your attention that our Company has recently negotiated the purchase of the clog sole business of the above Company [BCS]. In order to keep the continuity of business we shall be pleased if you will direct your future enquiries to Messrs. John Maude & Son Ltd., Clog Sole Works, Hebden Bridge, Yorks. We should like to take this opportunity of thanking all our regular customers for the business they have given us in the past, and to assure them, and any new customers of our best attention at all times, Yours faithfully, John Maude & Son Ltd.

All Snaith stocks were transferred to Hebden Bridge, and the Mill Street premises at Snaith were put on the market. John Townend had done everything possible to keep the firm going, including making 'squares' for the furniture trade, which also uses a lot of beech, and chocks and wedges for the National Coal Board, working up sales eventually reaching a million tool handles in a year, using the same timber as was needed for making the clog soles. With property on the opposite side of the road where stocks of clog soles were kept, a café was constructed and upstairs accommodation rented out to a bank manager, all these things being done in a desperate attempt to bring in extra revenue to keep the clog sole firm going. In the end he had to take the heartbreaking decision that it just was not possible to carry on and sell out to Maudes.

From my point of view, I had now of necessity to buy from Maudes again but used any stocks of Snaith soles for as long as they lasted. The sell-out was as much a blow to me personally as it was to John, but for different reasons, because we had an unwritten agreement that if Snaith had ended up being the last clog sole maker instead of Maudes, then I would be able to buy my soles at a lower price than the others in the trade, assuming that there were some left at the time. But it was not to be, even though we had both worked so hard to achieve that end.

The year end saw a decline in sales to £39,571, profit £3,377 and trade debtors £4,649, with only a small reduction of some £300 in the overdraft. This was a miserable time for me in the aftermath of the Snaith closure and I felt that a large part of my ambitions had been thwarted. I changed the Jaguar for another of similar make and also exchanged the Morris van for a bigger J4 one. Having consolidated the trade as much as I could, and running out of candidates for takeover, 1968–69 sales steadied at £40,366, profit £4,233, trade debtors £5,793, with the following year rising to £47,556, trade debtors £8130, a profit of £4,987 and a reduction in bank overdraft to £5,679.

A new and disturbing threat was beginning to develop, which proved to be a savage blow to the clog trade. This was the discovery of and gearing up for the production of North Sea gas, with the inevitable result in the closure of hundreds of gas works all over the country. By this time we were supplying gas works from the south coast up to Scotland through the Southern Gas Board, North Thames Gas Board, West Midlands Gas Board, Northern Gas Board, North-Eastern Gas Board and Scottish Gas Board, representing thousands of pairs annually. We did, however, supply a few to the oil rig industry at Nigg but very small quantities were needed.

In the 1971–72 year we suffered a prolonged postal strike, with orders having to be taken over the telephone, to which I attached a recording machine for record purposes and proof of receipt. This was a god-sent opportunity for some firms to delay payment of their invoices, so the end of the year showed trade debtors rising to a fantastic £13,127 and a bank overdraft of £11,021, thus distorting the accounts considerably. With the introduction of a date commonly referred to as 'Doomsday' for capital gains tax purposes, I had another valuation done to establish starting figures of assets.

Some five years after Maudes had bought Snaith out, I received a letter from Mr Norman Smith, who was the accountant for Maudes, which read:

Dear Sir, Mr James Maude has asked me to contact you to see if you would be interested in acquiring the working assets and stocks of the above Company [Maudes]. He feels that the time has come for him to take things easier, although he would, of course, continue to be available if required in an advisory capacity. He realises that the clog sole trade is not an expanding one, but wishes to point out that he holds good stocks which he is prepared to pass over at a price which would be most attractive to you when compared with present day figures. I personally think that this is an opportunity which should not be missed. It has occurred to me that you might wish to carry out this as a joint operation with Walton Bros. Ltd., just in the same way as you co-operated with that firm when you took over the trade of Millers a little while ago. Yours faithfully, N. Smith.

The letter is dated 10 June 1971. Naturally, as the largest buyer of clog soles and wishing to guarantee my future supplies, I was more than interested in the suggestion – except that it would have to be done on my own and not in conjunction with any other firm as had been suggested in the letter. At this time, Walton Bros. Ltd, was the only other wholesale manufacturer of clogs of any size. Their main trade, apart from dealing with some industrial firms, was through the 30 or so retail shops running under the name Walco Leather Stores and situated in many towns in Lancashire and Yorkshire. Time seemed to pass very slowly after receiving this letter from Mr Smith and I wrote to Mr Maude direct about a month later to speed things up if at all possible, as there did not appear to be really anything to hold up any agreement. I suggested going up to Boldron, Barnard Castle, where Mr Maude lived, to have a good chat about the position and hopefully find some solution to the delay. I had already made approaches to the bank for help in the event of buying Maudes and agreed to form a company to take over my business and Maudes as well.

Mr Maude took me to look at the sawmill situated in a field corner on the Raby estate; he had an agreement to buy their beech and to use the land as a sawmill. The equipment seemed to be very old and in any case was duplicated at Hebden Bridge many times over. Mr Maude was still concerned about paying redundancy money as obviously Raby was not needed if the soles were to be made at Hebden Bridge again, but as I pointed out to him he had employed these men over a period of time and it was only fair that he should be responsible for any redundancy payable, and he agreed.

A Northamptonshire maker of leisure clogs who supplied Scholls had become interested in taking over at Hebden Bridge, which worried me quite a lot as I soon formed the opinion, rightly or wrongly, that if he got the mill he would simply sell all the stock of clog soles, numbering perhaps a million pairs, and then close it down, having made a handsome profit in the process. Having the monopoly, he could have dictated his own selling price for the soles, which we would have had to buy or close down ourselves. However, I decided that my best defence against this happening was to buy a copying lathe to make my own soles at Huddersfield, buying in the clog blocks from any timber merchant who could supply. On contracting likely suppliers of these blocks, I soon found that by trying to buy relatively small blocks in bulk, the cost was rising out of all proportion to what could be reasonably paid for them, which was rather disheartening.

In the event, I went down to Northamptonshire to see Mr Walker at his Kettering works. We both got on with each other excellently, having similar outlooks and a common interest in wooden-soled footwear in general. I told him what I was thinking of doing as regards obtaining a lathe to protect my future supplies of soles, and I felt sure that he knew that if I was able to do this successfully then the demand for the stock of Maudes soles at Hebden Bridge would drop dramatically, certainly by over 50 percent, resulting in the huge stock there supplying Waltons and anyone else left making clogs for years. As a result of this meeting, Mr Walker withdrew from the sale, to my profound relief as I personally had no experience in making the soles myself; I had seen plenty of the work involved but that is not the same thing as being able to do it. Neither Snaith nor Maudes had ever thought of making soles from a copying lathe, which was quite understandable, having the original machines and the trained men to use them.

At Kettering, I was able to see Mr Walker's copying machines at work, but these were of the 'vertical' type with a model turning on one shaft whilst the other shafts turned above and below the model. The copying lathe that I had seen in Windermere, where the only British maker had their works, was more of a flat-bed machine, with horizontal shafts producing the same results, but far more sturdy in construction.

Accordingly, an agreement was drawn up by my solicitors, Eaton Smith & Downey, to acquire the land, goodwill, plant, machinery and stock in trade for completion on 1 June 1972. I was not buying the company itself, nor was it even being offered for sale, no doubt because it had other assets of an investment nature which had nothing to do with the actual working assets. The proposed agreement ran as follows:

Messrs. Clarkson, Thomas & Hanson,
25 Harrison Road,
HALIFAX

For the attention of Mr. G. W. Hanson. 28th April 1972.

We confirm our telephone conversation with Mr. Hanson this afternoon when we informed him that Mr. Walkley and Mr. Maude had met today, as a result of which it had been agreed, subject to contract, as follows:-

1). The purchase price for the land, the goodwill, plant, machinery and stock-in-trade should be £19,000 all inclusive, the division of which should we suggest be as follows:-

Goodwill	1.00
Plant and machinery	491.00
Stock	15000.00
Land and buildings	3508.00
	19000.00

2). Completion should be 31st May 1972.

3). £18.000 on account of the purchase price shall be paid on completion, the balance of £1,000 to be paid on or before July 1st next.

It was also agreed, though we think that this need not appear in the contracts, that a). our clients would buy 4,000 pairs of clog soles from your clients at current prices during the month of May 1972 and b). our clients should select such machinery or plant at Barnard Castle as they might wish to take over, (to be included in the purchase price of £19,000 abovementioned), which would be brought down to Hebden Bridge by your clients at your client's expense in time for completion on 31st May 1972.

It seems to us that the Contract for the sale of the land can remain as drawn, with the substitution of the 31st May 1972 as the date for completion and of £3508.00 as the purchase money instead of £3395 as heretofore. This would involve a deposit, we suggest, of £350.00 making a total deposit due on exchange of contracts to exactly £400.00. We therefore enclose the Contract anent the sale of the business, re-typed and amended to accord with the agreement arrived at. We have altered the warranty in Clause 7 (c) to provide for a sum of £20,000 since we are instructed that there has been a substantial rise in the price of clog soles since we were last engaged on this matter.

If you will please let us know that the terms of this letter and our amendments to the Agreement for sale of the business are

162

agreed then there would appear to be no obstacle to a rapid exchange of Contracts. Yours faithfully, Eaton Smith & Downey.

In view of this letter, the financial year 1972–73 was to be extended to 31 May for this and future year endings. The property itself comprised the five-storey mill alongside the River Calder, another part at the side of the main Burnley Road and the two joined together in a 'V' shaped building. A large stone-built house a few yards from the mill served as an office in the middle part but had separate living accommodation at each end. One of the present employees lived with his wife and family on the far side from the mill and had quite a large garden, whilst the other end was rented by the widow of a former employee. Between this end and the mill wall was an electricity sub-station belonging to the mill and built against the mill wall on one side. A small house in Mytholmroyd was also included in the sale and again this was let at a small rental. On the opposite side of the river was a large iron foundry, sometimes called the engineering works, which was full of spare sets of clog sole machines, kept there, very sensibly, as an insurance against a possible mill fire so that production could be re-started quickly in that event. The whole of these properties were bought as per the contract for the sum of £3508, having been written down in value over the years.

One clog firm of any size remained in Ireland, and they were also clog sole manufacturers as well. For some time we supplied them with clog soles after they also ceased production and eventually we bought a 'gripper' from them, along with other machinery, whilst continuing to make any clogs for them that they needed for re-sale. Again this trade was rapidly declining. The firm ran under the name of Parsons & Co. and was situated in Charlestown, Co. Mayo.

The 1971–72 accounts covered 13 months and showed sales of £63,936 trade debtors £9,914 a profit of £6,451 and the overdraft down by over £3,000.

In order to take over at Hebden Bridge, a company was formed under the style of F. Walkley (Clogs) Ltd, with a share capital of some £15,000.

On carefully examining the contents of the mill, it seemed to me that to make it more efficient and also far more safe from a fire-risk point of view, all the overhead line shafting, which had driven the machines in the past by flat belting, should be dismantled, and any of the machines which were still to be used separately motorised. The mill was virtually full of 'sets' of machines grouped in threes, the sidecutter, hollower and shanker, all of which were needed to produce the shape of the wooden soles ready for the subsequent barrelling and waxing. The whole of the remaining space was just one mass of wooden shelving piled high with all sizes and shapes of soles, a large part of them many years old and long since obsolete. all these shelves were likely to be surplus to future use on the top three floors.

By fitting up one long length of shelving on the first floor to take all the stock of clog soles likely to be needed in the future, all other storage could be accommodated on the other side of this same room, which would eventually leave the top three floors empty and allow all work and machinery to be sited and used on the ground floor. In view of the constant loud noise emanating from the waxing barrels, these were to be the exception to the rule and used on the third floor, simply for quietness downstairs.

The original workforce had been in the region of 80 and was now down to only six men and there really was little to do for two of them who had been running the mill up till that time. Mr Maude himself was in the habit of only coming down to Hebden Bridge once a year from Barnard Castle, at the time of the annual audit. As it was my intention to make future supplies of clog soles using copying lathes which were able to do all of the three original processes at one go, the spare sets of clog sole making machines in the engineering works, together with the sets of Maudes machines in the mill, were no longer needed so I sold them as scrap metal for £1,050 and the foundry itself for £3,090, making a total of £4,140. As I had only paid out £3,508 for all the property described, this meant in effect that I had acquired the mill itself for nothing, with the office and the domestic properties thrown in and bringing in rents.

Altogether it took a whole year to dismantle all the old wooden shelving and clear the space, and as I did this work myself, using a hammer and crowbar, I arrived back in Huddersfield every day looking like a chimney sweep with all the dust about.

Shortly after taking over at the mill there was a strike by the coal miners in 1972, and as the mill had always been heated by two solid-fuel boilers, this presented a problem for me. The actual piping of hot water round the five-storey mill was very poor indeed and it took nearly all day to warm the premises up, so after studying the various options open to me I had the two boilers taken out altogether and concreted the floor in the boiler room for storage purposes. A 500-Bthu gas oil fired heater placed in a suitable position near the middle of the ground floor was quite capable of heating the area satisfactorily as too much heat can easily cause problems with cracking timber.

Outside the mill at the far end was the original stackyard for taking delivery of timber 'in the round', meaning in tree trunk form. It was lifted from the delivery vehicle by a huge crane which had one of its jibs literally through the roof of the ground-floor part of the mill and set in a large square concrete base. With the crane no longer in use, this was dismantled and the concrete blocks broken up and removed to leave a flat concrete space where lathes and other machinery could be sited.

As the various shapes of clog soles had long been obsolete, I decided to make a 'standard' sole similar to the London pattern but shaped at the toe end to take the second grip when used as a safety clog sole. When used as a non-safety sole, this would completely replace the former London pattern. At the time of taking over at Hebden Bridge each style was still stocked in substantial quantities in the usual three thicknesses, strong, medium and light, which resulted in huge stock, taking into account the size range from babies' size 2 up to a man's size 12 or 13.

Three copying lathes were ordered from Fell's of Windermere, who were the only makers of these in the UK as this was a rather specialised machine originally intended for turning golf club heads. It was my idea to site these three machines in a row near the road side of the mill, where they would be as far away as possible in the event of a fire destroying the narrow part of the five-storey mill on the opposite river side.

165

On taking over on 1 June 1972, I called the six men together to introduce myself and explain what I intended to do with the mill in the first year, bearing in mind that there were so many soles in stock that even if none was made at all for months there was not likely to be any significant shortage to supply orders. The wage being paid by Maudes to these men was in the region of £17. As I had always tried to encourage my own workers to both do their best and be rewarded accordingly, I offered each man a further £5 per week, which was quite a substantial increase. I wanted a happy and contented workforce, of which these six could be expected to form the nucleus for any future expansion if they proved suitable and flexible in their working. Certain jobs, like in clog making, did not need even one person doing a particular task all the time. People knew and accepted this, resulting in a man doing two or three different stages of work. However, to my astonishment, one of the six refused the rise offered, preferring to have Friday afternoon off instead if I was agreeable.

Having taken over at Hebden Bridge, I naturally knew from the records there just how many soles were being bought by the customers of Maudes and could work out what proportion of total sales were made by ourselves and the scope for any expansion in the future.

Taking into account sales of clog soles besides clogs, and the 13-month trading period to the new 31 May year end, sales of the newly formed company were shown at £85,945 with the bank overdraft rising to £24,598 due to acquiring Maudes and obtaining new equipment. The trade debtors ran at about half the overdraft figures at £13,028, whilst the trading profit was £5,326 after taxation took £4,500. Rental income was £149. Prior to Maudes closing down the Raby sawmills on takeover, most of the actual work in making the soles had been done there for quite some time, and all that was required at Hebden Bridge was to unload one lorryload of blocks each week of the partly made soles to be finished off there. This meant that although there were six men at Hebden Bridge, more were needed at Barnard Castle, which is highlighted in the 1971 accounts showing wages for Raby at, in round figures, £9,500 and only £6,000 for the Hebden Bridge end.

Incidentally, one item in these accounts merits attention even though the cost was only £926.75 for that year. This amount was for the hated Selective Employment Tax, known as SET, which some Chancellor in his wisdom had thought up in an effort to bring in revenue; it was really a tax on employees working in manufacturing industry. I had also had to pay this iniquitous tax for my own men whilst it lasted. No wonder that employers took on as few people as they could manage with, especially when so many others not in manufacturing did not come under the scope of the tax.

Following the takeover at Maudes, 1972 also saw a further impending development in the size of the clog trade. The one and only remaining clog iron manufacturers, Buck & Benson Ltd of Sedgwick Street Works, Preston, were finding that the level of trade had dropped so much as to be hardly worth while making them, in spite of making the copper runners and white metal ones as well. The boot heelplate trade had been quite substantial, with good export orders. Having sent one of my men over to Hebden Bridge to work there as manager, I sent him to Preston as well, as he was halfway there to start with. He was taught how the various clog iron making machines were operated and about the punching of holes in the irons, which was very important. This period of learning went on for three months or so, after which I took over the clog iron making business from Buck & Benson Ltd, finalising the sale exactly one year to the day from taking over at Maudes.

I had to decide whether to make the irons at Huddersfield or Hebden Bridge and finally decided on Huddersfield, where the shaving room proved to be the ideal size for the six machines involved. A 15-ton press had been used to flatten the end of the duck-toe pattern clog irons but was not really necessary, and was not needed for the other shapes of irons, so this was not brought over with the other machines, leaving Bucks to do whatever they wanted with it. All the machines had to be separately motorised as they had been on line shafting at Preston.

I now had the monopoly of both clog sole and clog iron making for the trade, such as was left of it.

Following the demise of Horsfields of Bradford, who besides

167

also being large makers of clog irons in the past had made a whole range of toetins, steel toecaps, uppers etc., their trade on the grindery side had been sold to Heginbotham Bros. Ltd of Stoney Middleton, near Sheffield. As the firm of John Watts of Sheffield was no longer trading, Heginbotham's continued to make these various items and supplied them in small lots to the individual clog makers. As the overall quantity of these small lots was not a good proposition, I suggested to Heginbotham's that if they would supply me with all their products in bulk, I could store them at the mill and by accepting even a 5 per cent margin would be able to send out orders for clog soles, irons and toetins altogether to the trade, resulting in quite a saving in carriage charges and the bother to Heginbotham's of these small lots. This idea was definitely to our mutual benefit and they willingly agreed to do this. A carriage-paid order from the smaller clog makers could now be made up of all the items needed, including soles, irons, nails, toetins, copper welting, leather laces and so on. We had always bought our nails from Hall & Rice Ltd of Birmingham, after the Leeds firm making the 'Hare' brand had gone out of production years before, and by buying nails in bulk had been able to add this item to the list of sundries being sold to others.

After we had been at Birkby for a while, it became apparent that whilst the clicking and closing rooms were adequately heated by the newly installed boiler, the large high clogging room was losing a vast amount of heat through the glass roof, and to solve this problem a partition was made across the end of the room by the office, leaving room to go out by the side door as before. Altogether about 3,000 cubic feet of space were boxed in by plasterboarding in the clogging room, even though only half the length had been shut off in an attempt to maintain a lower temperature at the back of the room where all the clog soles were stored. A doorway through the partition gave access to the clogging room from the front doorway.

As often happens when one problem is overcome, another can be created, and in this case the extra warmth in the clogging room started to crack the clog soles at the back, even though we had done our best to avoid this.

8

Red Tape Gets Sticky

Receiving an enquiry from the Associated Octel Co. Ltd of Ellesmere Port, I went over there to see what the problems were. The company itself was owned by all the main petroleum companies jointly and its problems were twofold, heat and static electricity. Apparently clogs had never proved satisfactory in the past for both of these problems, as whatever material had been used to provide the wear on the wooden soles would either conduct static electricity through the nails or if stuck on would be quickly rendered useless by the heat from the small furnaces. These were individual ones only about two or three feet in height and on which, for some reason which was not explained to me, the men had to stand for a short while. On actually seeing the situation for myself, I realised the huge electrical power being used, which was most vividly apparent when I saw two men with a huge open-ended spanner some 10 to 15 feet long moving a nut to either open or close something well above my sight line, looking upwards possibly some 15 to 20 feet from the ground floor. I had never come across anything like this before and by now had visited hundreds of different works and seen many manufacturing processes.

I realised that I would only face the same problems as the others who had supplied their clogs in the past if I attempted to either stick or rivet the material to the wooden soles; a completely different approach was needed. I decided first of all to use the plain wooden sole as used in the Sheffield furnaces, as there was not really going to be any hard wear on the wood. Then to eliminate the static electricity I would insulate the inside of the clog, a comparatively simple method which no one had thought of before. I obtained some insulating varnish cloth like they used in the old type of wirelesses; this Wellstead material was supplied by a Greengates factory on the outskirts of Bradford. As it was readily available in rolls, I was able to cut out the sole shapes from press knives already in use; and because the insulating cloth was so thin, I decided to stop any roughing up by sticking a similar sole of carpet underfelt to it, so that when placed inside the clog it would fit snugly all the way round and certainly make the clogs far more comfortable than if the varnish cloth had been inserted on its own. In order to stick these two materials together satisfactorily, by trial and error I found that a Casco cold-water cement proved best for this purpose. After all the work for the insulation of the inside of the clogs had been done, these were then made in the usual way and the felt insoles put in afterwards.

The Associated Octel people were delighted that we had overcome both their problems quickly and were able to make a clog which was even more comfortable to wear. From that time onwards they bought this pattern. It was only a pity that there were no other firms doing the same work, otherwise we might have been able to cash in on this innovation.

For some time I had been using three sizes of clog sole knives for internal insoles; there had been a demand for them from pre-war which was now small but steady. The press knives that had to be made for clog insoles were of a much different internal shape than for boots or shoes, especially in the waist and instep. By the simple expedient of turning the material over when cutting the felt, it was possible to cut both left and right feet separately, whilst in the case of the varnish cloth this did not matter as the surface of the cloth was similar on both sides.

The sign on the mill wall on the fourth floor at Hebden Bridge had been quite a landmark for years, especially to the road traffic coming from the Hebden Bridge direction as there had always been a very bad 'S' bend where the road crossed the canal and the words MAUDES CLOG SOLES stood out in white on a green background. On taking over, I had this sign repainted to F. WALKLEY (CLOGS) LTD, which for some unknown reason caused a howl of protest followed by a letter from Calderdale

Council on the matter as no application had been made for my new wording on the sign. I stood my ground on this latest act of bureaucracy, pointing out that the new name was in exactly the same position, same colours, same height and style of lettering and identical in every way except the name. No doubt it was realised by someone in authority that the complaints they had received were just plain stupid, and the sign stayed as it was as long as I was still there.

With the impending resumption of clog sole making through the whole process, improvements were made to the stackyard, which was tarmacadamed. A low wall on part of the perimeter, a double iron gate on the corner by the road and a wire fence on the Burnley Road side were added, thus giving it a neat and tidy appearance.

The sightline coming from the narrow road over the river bridge at the side of the mill into Burnley Road was simply non-existent, being a complete right angle with the side of the mill, and there was only a narrow pavement two feet alongside, making the egress really dangerous. After discussing this situation with the West Riding authority who dealt with road matters, I offered to give them a triangular piece of land from the road to a point where the mill building stood, thus giving far greater egress from the side road into Burnley Road. In return the authority resurfaced that part which cut the corner off.

The new method of delivering timber, as is now common with building materials in bulk, was to use a lorry with a crane fitted to it, operated by the driver. This enabled timber to be lifted off the wagon and over the low wall into the stackyard where the crane used to be.

We had now obtained a cyclone, which stood near the mill wall away from the road, to extract the sawdust and woodwaste which was blown through tubular ducting into a large container. When full, this was regularly exchanged for an empty one and the firm who supplied them were quite happy to pay for the privilege as sawdust could be used in a variety of ways, including making chipboard. In our case, beech was in demand, particularly for the mink farms, which had to use a hardwood sawdust in their revolving drums when curing the pelts. We used a similar type of

171

drum when making boot heelplates, called tumblers in the engineering trade as they revolved so slowly that when the goods reached the top of the drum, they dropped down instead of going round and round the rim. This method took all the sharp edges off any metal products.

All the machines now being fitted up on the ground floor had to have individual sheet-metal ducting attached to them, and the whole installation was quite expensive as every job was on a one-off basis measured to fit the machine and rest of the ducting. A large 25-horsepower motor was needed to operate this system and force the sawdust and woodwaste through the mill wall opening into the cyclone, after which gravity would take over and the waste drop into the container.

After installing this costly waste-extraction plant, another objection came from Calderdale Council following an anonymous complaint, this time about the cyclone, which was only visible to anyone who happened to be approaching on one side of the mill as it was close to the mill wall of necessity; it was only two storeys in height. A planning application was enclosed with their letter for completion and submission for planning permission to be granted. Red tape was rearing its ugly head again and had to be dealt with. Thankfully it is my normal practice to go into things carefully before taking any action to which anyone might possibly object, and so avoid trouble later on; so I was able to reply to Calderdale that the structure was below the minimum height that required planning permission. One would have thought that anyone in authority would have used their common sense, if they had any, to check up first on such elementary details and avoided making themselves look foolish, but some people seem to work the opposite way round. However, the matter was resolved and work continued as before, but I began to wonder why the locals should feel so hostile to me; this had been shown in other ways as well. Perhaps I was a 'comer in' from Huddersfield and not one of them.

The work of fitting up the ground floor was proving both expensive and time-consuming but we had plenty of the latter as the huge stocks of clog soles meant that we could easily work for up to two years without needing to make any more. However,

£5,693 was expended on various items of plant fittings up in the 1973–74 year. With sales of clogs, clog soles and irons now all totalled together, the turnover had risen to a higher level, from the previous £85,945 to £122,450, whilst trade debtors were now £24,875. A tax rate of 42 per cent operative at that time, reduced the profit to £4,704 as taxation took £2,225; the pre-tax figure was £6,929.

The emptying of the three top floors of the mill proceeded on a gradual basis with Arthur, one of our best craftsmen from the original Hebden Bridge six, making a new double-sided clog sole shelving to take a few thousand pairs of soles, a quantity likely to be sufficient for normal needs. This was made virtually the whole length of the first floor of the mill near the river side, giving access to both sides and with a way through in the middle to avoid walking all round. A fire hose was sited in the middle of the room, with the hose of sufficient length to reach to either end.

On one of the periodical inspections carried out by the fire and other services regulating industrial property, I was ordered to have a totally enclosed fire escape made at both ends of the mill as apparently regulation alterations stipulated that this be done, probably following fire experience in similar-type buildings. Although I pointed out that we had no less than three staircases already, one at each end and a third in the middle, this cut no ice with the powers that be. Things were made more difficult by their insistence on the walls enclosing the staircase having to be constructed through the floors with their thick supporting timbers, and not from floor to ceiling on each floor, which would have been much easier to construct. It was plain to the inspector to see that no work was being carried out on the upper floors, rendering the exercise a complete waste of time and money; there seemed to me to be no sense in making more fire escapes for people who weren't there at all. Red tape has to be accepted sometimes, and Arthur did all this work over a period of time with some help from one of the cloggers. The only mitigating factor about this staircase business was the fact that the authorities did not rush us to do the work but let us proceed at our own pace, but of course they must have known full well that there was no fire risk to anybody on these floors, which were only occupied by the odd pigeon or two coming into the very top floor through air vents in the roof. Government grants were available to some extent to help with enforcing these regulations, and on visiting the relevant office on the north-east coast which dealt with these, I obtained the miserly 20 per cent grant allowed under their rules and regulations. The eventual cost of both these staircases, enclosed by breeze-block walls and suitable fire doors, was agreed at £8,000. This had to be worked out to include our own time doing the work, as opposed to having a contractor's invoice for the work.

It is normal practice that when any grant is made by a government regulation, someone has to inspect the work in the first place on completion and then each year over a period of five years to ascertain that it is still being made use of and has not been disposed of by sale or any other way. In the case of staircases this was rather silly as it was rather farcical to look at them every year, but there had been cases where an unscrupulous operator had obtained a government grant to improve a building and then sold it on afterwards for personal profit, leaving the purchaser with the problem of paying back part of the grant or trying to recoup it from the vendor.

The length of the mill was apparently such that a third staircase could have been demanded as the regulations stipulated that no one should have to go more than a certain distance before reaching a fire escape. Anyone standing in the middle of our mill had to travel a very little more than the distance prescribed, but thankfully they did not enforce this in our case.

My own personal view of these two totally enclosed staircases was that in certain circumstances they could be the cause of a fire starting, because any employee knowing that smoking was not allowed in the mill could easily walk into the enclosed staircase out of sight and have a smoke, whereas they would have been seen otherwise. Another possibility was that if this happened and a fire started in the staircase itself, we would not know because we could not see it. But regulations do not always take common sense or human behaviour into account.

During the 1974–75 year, total sales again increased by £45,000 to £167,370, with a doubling of the profit before tax to

£17,316 but reduced by £7,336 tax to £9,980. The improvement had mainly been caused by using and supplying clog soles bought from Maudes at a low price when taking over. Trade debtors only increased by £2,000 to £26,823 and a reduction in bank overdraft to £15,047 was achieved.

The next year saw a slight fall in sales of some £3,000 to £163,812 with debtors down in line by £600 but still another reduction of about £1,900 in the overdraft to £13,157. Capital expenditure of £3,738 was incurred in the ongoing fitting-up of the mill.

Demand for leisure clogs was beginning to be felt as the so-called fashion for wearing them became a real upsurge. Several firms up and down the country starting to make them and, of course, needed the wooden soles. Over a period anything to do with fashion can be good or bad depending on when to get in and, more important, when to get out. In our case the latter could present a serious problem as timber bought fresh-sawn takes weeks to dry out to a suitable moisture content ready for use, but this was a risk that just had to be taken. The alternative was to buy kiln-dried timber, usually from abroad, at many times the cost of home-grown fresh-sawn timber, and be able to use it straight away after cutting the delivered lengths into blocks of the size required.

However, capital expenditure during 1976–77 was £13,170, with three copying lathes in work and a further two on order. Again a time lag of nine months would be the norm for ordering and receiving lathes. A fork-lift, second-hand of course, was purchased for moving the timber in and around the mill, and a compressor installed on the first floor to provide compressed air for various uses but initially for securing the thin PVC soles and heels to the leisure clog soles. A whole range of both men's and women's sizes of cast-iron moulds had to be specially made to turn the soles, and a nearby foundry was able to do this for us quickly.

Our Halifax competitors in the wholesale clog manufacturing field set up a separate factory to make these leisure clogs in a big way and were soon asking for 1,000 pairs a week. This was quickly followed by 2,000, then 3,000 and, at its peak, a maximum of 4,000 pairs a week. We attempted to reach their production targets by employing more and more men and starting a nightshift. Complaints were received about the noise and readings were taken late at night on the number of decibels recorded as being in the valley bottom, and with only one house in sight the noise level tended to be worse at higher levels of the hillside opposite.

In order to turn clog soles on a copying lathe, the mould of the size required was fixed on a central revolving spindle in the lathe. Two spindles on either side of the central one would turn in unison, with two turning clockwise and the other two anti-clockwise, which had the effect of making two left feet and two right feet at the same time, irrespective of whether the mould was a left or right foot. The horizontal movement of the lathe turned the blocks of wood from toe to heel, which is with the grain of the wood, and this operation could take up to five minutes for a large size of men's sole. The action of making both left and right feet at the same time always intrigued those who saw the lathe working for the first time, and this was called a mirror pattern in the trade.

The machine itself, made only in small quantities, was originally designed to make golf club heads, and I was able to see this being done at an Accrington works before ordering my own lathes. Again these heads could be made for either left or right-handed golfers according to which way the spindles rotated, but most were right-handed. The bed of lathes had to be considerably extended to make clog soles compared with the short golf club drivers, and also had to take into account the larger 'blown-up' moulds in the width as well so as to avoid the blocks touching one another. This blown-up shape was necessary because the revolving circular-shaped cutters on the lathe head could not produce a right-angled cut.

The criterion for the cutting of any shape on a copying lathe is perhaps best explained by saying that if an old penny could be rolled over the surface of whatever shape was required without seeing any space underneath it, then the lathe could turn that shape. Very long legs for certain types of furniture needed a different lathe altogether and only turned one at a time. One problem to be overcome using the lathes was to make sure that the four blocks were placed accurately in position at the end of the spindles to ensure correct turning. To do this, our engineer produced both a centering device and a levelling idea so that when the block was positioned in the lathe this was done accurately. This saved a lot of time previously spent on centering by hand and levelling the blocks. Production was thus speeded up considerably.

In order to increase production of the leisure clog soles as demand increased, more lathes were on order and eagerly awaited, and the night shift ensured that maximum production was maintained by keeping the lathes working round the clock. It was now impossible to speed up the actual turning time, besides the improvements in fitting up four new blocks as soon as the others were turned. One man could keep all the lathes going by feeding each in turn with new blocks as the machine finished its turning cycle; they were automatically switched off by means of a metal raised button which closed when the turning was completed. There were eight electric motors on each lathe to operate its various movements, and these were worked by four buttons on the side of the lathe, each operating one pair of cutters.

We soon worked out the best way of making the leisure clog soles after the turning operation had been completed. This was done by sticking the PVC soles and heels onto the leisure-type soles and removing the surplus PVC together with the two wooden end bits where the soles had been held in the lathe on the old Maudes machine – the sidecutter, which really came into its own again. A good outside shape resulted from this work. It was carried out in two stages on the sidecutter, which needed the fore part to be shaped out first, and then the jig was reversed to shape the back part to complete the full outside contours of the sole. One man in particular could use this machine like a dream and, of course, there was plenty of opportunity for practice. This process of removing the two wooden end bits from the soles became known as 'topping and tailing', and was done on the bandsaw before using the sidecutter to give the final shape. The use of the sidecutter was an advantage to us compared with anyone else trying to make these leisure soles, as we were the only firm to both have them and know from experience how to use them.

177

The next process after the final shape had been made was to barrel the soles in the large revolving drums as for the ordinary soles. Large pieces of wax were thrown into the drum, along with the soles, which could roll round inside it for perhaps half an hour or more to give a nice waxed finish. The soles were then gripped to take the leather upper and stamped for size, which had to be the Continental sizes as opposed to our British ones measured in inches.

The gripping was different for leisure clogs in two respects, insomuch that the grip itself had to be narrower for the lighter leathers used on the uppers, whilst the back part had to be left ungripped for the heel to be left open so that the foot could slide straight in and leave a neat appearance from the back. This was not easy as the gripping machine is so constructed that the work has to be held upside down, making it difficult to both start and finish the cut exactly where it was needed. Only practice could make perfect doing this work; the rotary action of the cutters meant that a gradual cut into the grip was unavoidable at both start and finish. The gripping machine itself was foot-operated, with more pressure on the foot pedal producing a deeper grip.

In order to cope with this ever-increasing demand for leisure clog soles, which was coming in from previously unknown firms besides Waltons at Halifax, we had to arrange for timber supplies to arrive every two or three days, cut this up into blocks as quickly as possible and stack them up to dry out in such a way that the air could circulate round them, just like building up dominoes in piles about five feet high. Each batch was given a number, and the size of the blocks was chalked on one of the blocks at the top of the pile, along with the date they were stacked up. This enabled us to know which had been drying out longest, as they could not just be piled up in date rotation in view of the number of sizes that we were making. A most remarkable moisture meter was activated by pushing the two prongs into the wood and simply reading off the result from the indicator on the meter face. From experience, we had found that on certain floors of the mill drying out varied considerably, along with the different times of the year. This could on occasions have the result that after dropping gradually to a satisfactory moisture content, adverse air conditions could lead to this increasing again, which was most annoying.

The stocks of timber in block form and partly made rose to a cost of £80,535 and the overdraft to finance these huge stocks to £44,220. However, turnover rose to £301,370, up by a massive 84 per cent, topping £300,000 for the first time. A fantastic achievement all round, considering that when starting to make leisure clog soles we had no idea of the differing work involved compared with the traditional clog soles. The trade debtors almost equalled the overdraft figure of £42,838. Most unfortunately for me, the bank overdraft rate coincided with a then high of 13 per cent for Bank Rate, or base rate as it was coming to be known, and I well remember telling Lloyds bank manager that we at the mill were working harder for Lloyds bank than their own employees, which was quite true. Paying out between £500 and £600 a month for bank interest was to my mind like having an extra man at the end of the bench drawing a wage and not doing any work, but money is a commodity that had to be bought, just like the timber. However, my comments to the bank manager merely met with a wry smile and, in spite of my efforts, he refused to help me by reducing the penal rate that I was paying.

It was during the 1976 and 1977 years that I tried to satisfy some of my missed aspirations on the educational or academic side by gaining qualifications in various fields such as management, accountancy and so on, apart from my own trade of footwear. Since leaving Huddersfield College I had immediately enrolled at the Huddersfield Technical College for both French and German, having done six years of the former at school but none of the latter as this was not taught there. Before going into the army in November 1940 the results of the Royal Society of Arts examination came through, showing that I had been successful in obtaining the RSA 1st Class Intermediate certificate. I shall always remember the congratulatory postcard from Dr H.D.C. Lee, my French teacher, who had marvellously clear handwriting and signature, which I found most remarkable having been written by a blind man. Dr Lee was a highly respected man who was devoted to his teaching of the French

179

language, and he was most ably supported by Mademoiselle Dejardin, who also taught her native language to us.

Soon after starting in business I had enquired as to what I needed to do to be an ABSI (Associate of the Boot & Shoe Industry) but was informed that this qualification did not at that time extend to the clog trade, and so I had to give up the idea. However, times had now changed and what I had done over the past 25 years enabled me to be considered for this honour.

In the two years I acquired more letters after my name than there were in it, which gave me a sort of individual satisfaction of at last doing some of the things that I might have attempted years before if there had been no war when I was a teenager. Probably the most satisfying qualification for me personally was the CMD, which consisted of two parts, law and accountancy, with both sections having to be passed within a maximum three-year period. The law part of the examinations was set and marked by a London Queen's Counsel, and it gave me great pleasure to pass this law exam with honours and to receive the silver badge and certificate at Huddersfield, having passed the accountancy part as well, of course. The clog trade had been looked down on over the years – and probably quite rightly so, with some of the people involved in it – but it was my intention in gaining qualifications to show that at least some of us in the trade perhaps deserved better.

One of the Wakefield customers whom we supplied with a lot of corrugated leather clogs for his colliery trade rang me up almost in tears as he was feeling so upset. He had apparently been to an NCB meeting or similar and had been informed that a new 'condition of employment' had been introduced for miners, who were to subscribe an initial £1.50 to be supplied with a pair of safety boots, kneepads and a helmet, all of which had to be worn at all working times to comply with this condition. Having stipulated safety boots as opposed to safety clogs, that would mean the sudden end of his clog trade with the pits, which was both very substantial and had been going on for years. He really took it hard, which is not surprising, and having had a somewhat similar shock from North Sea gas, I could tell just how he must feel. The firm, Legards of Wakefield, Barnsley and Doncaster,

180

had the misfortune to have two sudden deaths in the space of a few weeks with devastating results to these businesses due to death duties. Only one branch survived as a result of this.

The 1977–78 year was the peak year for our sales, which totalled £324,084 excluding the VAT and were about £23,000 better than the year before. Trade debtors were £42,024 and stock a record £87,277, up some £6,700. Large purchases of timber forced the overdraft up to a record high of £63,930 and bank interest was £6,006. Boot heelplates made on the clog-iron machinery were exported to New Zealand for £5,329, which was the best export figure we could achieve in view of the previously explained situation with regard to clogs. Capital expenditure was £17,425 for plant, with a further £4,635 to acquire three to four acres of land alongside the River Calder on the opposite side to the mill. I had hopes of making this unused land into a car park as it had no real use, having once been a rifle range at the far end and now designated as No. 3 agricultural land. Anyhow, it was nice to take the dog along the river bank at lunchtimes and this was much appreciated by her although she was otherwise happy to sit in the office all day.

Calderdale Council slapped a Compulsory Purchase Order on the house and office property near the mill as it considered that the 100-year-old foundations for this building were no longer sufficient for the heavy traffic passing so near to it on the Burnley Road. At times of severe weather this was often the only road open into Lancashire and it did carry a terrific volume of traffic. Fortunately, there was so much good stone in the structure that demolition firms were queuing up to bid for razing it to the ground, resulting in a very satisfactory offer being accepted and used towards making a car park. There was now to be a nice space suitable for that purpose, as the house and long garden together had taken quite a large area of land between them. About 20 cars could be accommodated altogether and it was helpful when timber deliveries arrived by the large double doors at that end of the mill, making it far easier for the forklift to bring it in as the doors at the other end were only half the size and not big enough to allow a forklift in.

Having geared up for something like maximum production

with a total of five copying lathes installed and approaching £100,000 worth of timber in various stages of drying and production, the expected and inevitable downturn in demand for the leisure clogs started in 1978–79. Sales dropped by £1,000 a week, totalling £65,000 for the full year. Orders for incoming timber were scaled down quickly but it was still to take two years to get the stock down to a somewhat normal size, such was the effect of the drying time and the drop in demand as time progressed. Capital expenditure on plant previously ordered was £6,656 but a reduction of £16,235 was achieved in the overdraft. Trade debtors, because of the 'leads and lags' of credit, peaked at £52,905, up almost £11,000. Exports of boot heelplates realised £621 for the year.

To some extent a small revival occurred in 1979–80, which turned out to be the calm before the storm as far as trade was concerned. Actually sales increased by £30,000 to £289,452, with the stock slightly higher but trade debtors reduced to a more manageable £34,857. Bank interest was around £6,000 again, at £5,958, but £17,000 was knocked off the overdraft. Capital expenditure for that year took a further £3,011.

The year 1980 saw the arrival of the biggest slump in manufacturing industry since the great depression of the 1930s. Every day hundreds if not thousands of redundancies were announced in all kinds of manufacturing industry. A lot of firms were dependent on one another, which produced a rapidly growing snowball effect all over the country. Within a very short time, as firms either stopped ordering or drastically reduced their requirements, the effect on the clog trade was a drop of half in orders. Often an order would be received with a typed figure for the quantity needed altered in ink by the buyer to a fraction of what the storeman had requisitioned. Obviously in this sort of situation buyers were only too well aware that delivery of virtually anything was almost ex stock, so they in turn need not order in bulk as hitherto. This could possibly have been the start of the so-called 'just in time' policy adopted in the motor car industry in the 1980s, where the manufacturer held the absolute minimum of component parts and relied on either weekly or even daily deliveries to keep production flowing.

After the body blow to the trade as a result of North Sea gas, this depression reduced the demand drastically, especially in the steel industry, where we were now supplying nearly all the works in the UK from Kent to the Scottish steelworks. Our main South Wales trade was by now being conducted through John Liscombe Ltd of Newport, who were in a far bigger way of business than the small firm of Struel's that we had been supplying for some time and who had originally catered for us in that area. As mentioned, some years before, each clog manufacturer had an agent in South Wales, and as we kept taking over the clog makers it was just impossible to appoint all these agents to cover an area for us and we had to make a choice. Certain of Liscombes' trade had been supplied by Millers of London, and it was when they stopped making clogs that we were able to supply them in addition to Struel's of Neath and Blyths of Swansea, all of whom had their own loyal customers of many years' standing.

A small sideline developed for aprons made from the sheets of rubber canvas which were about the size that was needed for this purpose and always in stock. All we had to do was to fix one sail eyelet in each of the two top corners and the apron was made.

As our orders for industrial clogs actually dropped by as much as half in the space of some six months, it seemed that 30 years' work was disappearing before my eyes and, of course, all other clog makers of whatever size were having a similar experience. As a result of this lack of demand in general, the situation at Hebden Bridge was the same, with half the trade just going.

In May 1980 at the end of that financial year half the workforce at both Birkby and Hebden Bridge just had to be made redundant as there was no hope of the lost trade ever coming back again in the same quantity. This was absolutely heartbreaking for me personally as I had known all those who were having to leave for years, and in some cases they had been with me from leaving school and had not done any other kind of work. In all my business life it was extremely rare for anyone to have left me, except in the first two or three weeks when they realised that our kind of work was perhaps not what they had been cut out for.

The provision for costs to be incurred at 31 May 1980 of £5,300 is in respect of estimated redundancy and other expenses associated with relocation. The many happy times at Birkby had come to an end after 18 years and it was there that clog production had actually reached 1,000 pairs a week, no mean achievement with so much hand work involved. The clog iron machinery, together with all the clog machinery, was moved over to Hebden Bridge, to the clog mill, as it was now to be called and which had been agreed with the Post Office for address purposes instead of the cumbersome former Canal Wharf Sawmills, Hawksclough, of earlier days. It was much shorter to say and far more explicit in its description of the trade that was to come. In view of the length of time worked by some of the men at Birkby who were to be made redundant, either 90 days' notice had to be given or paid for in lieu with nothing in return, so I stayed at Birkby for three months with these men whilst everybody else went to Hebden Bridge. None of those leaving were able to obtain other work during this period; they were quite at liberty to leave at any time without forfeiting any money. It was quite easy during this three months for clog uppers to be brought from Hebden Bridge each day to be made up at Birkby and far more sensible to pay the men for working than paying them in lieu without any production in return.

The Birkby property was put on the market, as were lots of others at that time of recession. Although the estate agent suggested an asking price of £40,000 for the building, I considered this too high in the prevailing circumstances but gave way to what should have been his superior judgement. However, potential buyers were put off by that figure and I feel sure that if a more realistic price of £30,000 to £35,000 had been asked, it would have sold quickly, as those people who did come to inspect the property were genuine potential buyers and not time-wasters. One actually told me some years later that it was an excellent single-storey building suitable for many kinds of business. In the event, I was unfortunately proved to be correct in my assumptions as regards price for the works, as it was to lie empty for two years before it was eventually sold to a local printer for only £25,000. A quick sale would have been a godsend at the time of moving out and having to pay all that redundancy money when the income was at a much lower level, due to reduced sales.

All the methods of manufacturing goods of all kinds were changing dramatically with the progression of automation, especially in the motor car trade, where we had been selling such large quantities of clogs. Firms needed fewer and fewer employees, resulting in decreasing demand for all the items of clothing that they had been wearing whilst in work.

With the introduction of the electric arc furnace method of making steel, at the Rotherham works of Steel, Peech & Tozer the men had no further use for the hundreds of sweat towels they had previously worn and were actually complaining of being cold as all the heat was now well and truly inside the furnace, where it should be, and not spreading round the works as before. Safety footwear, whether boots or clogs, was no longer needed either, but it was a strange sight to see such things as canvas-upper boots worn in their place. One initial problem with this change in steel making was the noise, which the men found deafening in its intensity due to the electric power needed in the process. However, there was no point in me calling again at this works and it was with a heavy heart that I said my goodbyes to the storeman, whom I had known for many years now and become quite good friends with. It seemed to me that everything was going into reverse, as some years earlier I had been calling on these works trying to get trade, and now I was just thanking them for that business and losing them for ever,

In the brewery trade, the bottling departments had now set up automated bottling all over and did not need many employees, Nor did the former food factories of Bassetts and Batchelors of Sheffield. The fish dock trade was plummeting with the Icelandic cod war, so that our two outlets at Grimsby could no longer even make up a carriage-paid order of two dozen pairs. Another trade to be affected in the fishing industry was the ice manufacturers, where I found this type of work highly organised, with the big blocks of ice being transported from the floor where they were made and out of the factory by overhead carriageways and finally lowered directly into the holds of the shops berthed alongside. This was quite a sight to see for the first time, and, of course, the men working there needed a good-quality waterproof clog to work in these conditions. The chemical trade, particularly ICI in certain divisions, had changed their methods of production so much that they hardly needed any clogs as the automation of these processes resulted in very few men being employed, and for those that were, it was more a matter of pressing buttons to regulate machines than actually working as we formerly knew it. Another trade quickly hit by the depression, as is always the case, was the building industry, where we had been supplying quite a lot of cement works and, following the end of clog production at Millers, had been supplying the many London Brick Company works which they had previously supplied. The textile trade had not been very large users of clogs for quite a while and even the British Cotton & Wool Dyers Association firms almost stopped buying altogether.

A drastic rethink was absolutely vital and urgent. Having most reluctantly decided to close down at Birkby and move over to the clog mill, I decided that our future lay in tourism and not in industrial clogs any more, so I made three main decisions for the future. Firstly, we would open to the public seven days a week for them to come and see clogs being made; secondly, we would open a mill shop; and thirdly, we would make our own leisure clogs to our own designs to be sold to visitors in the shop, as there was still some demand for these even though the fashion craze had long since gone. Needless to say, a lot of planning had to be done to make the mill a suitable place for the public to walk round safely, with the various machines on show but at a safe distance from visitors, especially children.

9

The Tourist Venture

A large wooden welcome sign about eight feet square was fixed to the wall near to the entrance to the mill, giving information about opening times and stating that admission was free. Under the heading, a notice to the effect that this was the only mill in Great Britain making a full range of clogs, irons and soles to suit all the family proclaimed that 2,000 pairs were always in stock to choose from, to emphasise the variety. A space was left on this noticeboard for a map of the area showing all the other tourist attractions in the vicinity. A spotlight above the board drew attention to it and saved visitors asking a lot of unnecessary questions.

After passing this welcome sign, one part of the mill on the right-hand side was partitioned off, with a rustic bark frontage some three feet high and a window-like opening for visitors to be able to see clearly inside the 'engineer's shop', where welding and saw-sharpening work was carried out. A bandsaw sharpener was on view prominently at the front, but more than an arm's length away for safety when switched on. It worked automatically, as also did the circular saw sharpener sited further back. This room was affectionately known as 'Jack's cabin', being the former workplace of Mr Jack Uttley, who had looked after all the machinery over the years; he did actually start work there on leaving school, so his whole lifetime had revolved round the sawmill and Maudes.

From a doorway in the Burnley road about halfway along the mill, entrance was gained to a small house built into the mill premises and known as Sawmill house, being the rented

187

End of an era as Walkley's moves

WALKLEY Clogs is on the move from Hebden Bridge to Elland, ending a 140-year-old tradition at Britain's last remaining clog factory.

Most of the business, including the sole-making, is moving to the Brooks Mill factory shop in South Lane – although some clogs will still continue to be made up by hand and sold at the Walkley premises.

making since 1852 when production of the famous Maude sale began.

The loss of the manufacturing side of the business to Elland may also have implications regarding the use of mill, which is owned by Lancashire businessman Mr Terry Krell.

It is subject to strict retailing and manufacturing...

shopping centre. Brooks Mill is ideally situated – the customers are there and it has the right environment."

It is also part of the Ponden Mill group at Stanbury near Haworth which already...

years the public had not been able to see this part of the process at Hebden Bridge and she felt they would notice little difference.

Although the manufacturing process is moving out, a new shop is being created for the sale of clogs.

going. It now means we can improve the clog side for the public and therefore the mill in general.

"The only impact will be is that in...

Another chapter for clog firm

Words: JUDY VICKERS
Pictures: GRAHAM LYNCH

MR Frank Walkley, the founder of the famous factory that bears his name, has just finished his autobiography following his 50 years in the clog trade.

But it is a career that almost did not happen, as Mr Walkley was accepted for the civil service in the 1930s.

He only took up an apprenticeship in clog and boot making in Huddersfield when he failed the civil service medical.

But war broke out within 18 months, and...

Opening time for (from left) Frank Walkley, Roger Dower, Susan Jones and Steven Jones

PEOPLE can have clogs made while they wait at a unique factory which has just moved to Elland.

A shop selling Walkley Clogs remains in Hebden Bridge, but the clog making has been moved to bigger premises at Brooks Mill South Lane, Elland.

The new factory will be open every day with the clog making process...

The factory still sells thousands of pairs of clogs a year to industry and a growing part of the business is fashion wear with sandals and slip-ons.

Mr Jones said he believed Walkley clogs were the only...

Walkley road plans rejected

A HUGE question mark hangs over the future of a major Calderdale tourist attraction after new road plans.

Environment Secretary John Gummer has refused to allow a new access road and junction to serve Walkley Clogs, while inquiry last...

By BRIAN ...

magnet which attracts 600,000 visitors a year.

Walkley's growing popularity led to plans to transform the surrounding area so it could cope with the huge numbers of visitors, but the proposals proved highly contentious in the community.

Today, managing director Mr Mark Cyndes said the decisions could have major implications.

And further multi-million pound ...development plans for adjoining...

...the Environment Secretary had ...Calderdale Council scope for that to continue.

The council's group planning officer Mr John Ashton said the council was still awaiting the planning inspector's report.

It had received a copy of the decision letter but officers needed to ...ster but officers with the ...Walkley's...

reached with the council for that to continue.

Mayroyd which houses and industrial units were now scrapped, unless we can face serious issues with C...

because we ...road."

If the development proves too expensive ...ments to...

The Save Mayroyd Action ...re Group said limiting the selling of ...goods, not made on the premises, to ...to 25 per cent, and the rejection of ...an access road and the green belt ...was a tremendous victory for Hebden Bridge.

"The threat of competition from ...unauthorised out-of-town shopping, and not swamped by huge ...numbers of additional cars, might ...now have been lifted," ...esman Mr Anthony Rae-...

Clog firm moves into new factory

A CLOG company founded in Huddersfield is stepping into a new era after completing an ambitious move to new premises.

Walkley Clogs has transferred from H...

Company, British Steel and safety equipment su...plier Arco.

Mrs Jones said: "We are extremely busy w...as safety footwear whi...ds.

...ith the working boot ar...of the feet as well as th...ger.

...t more room to expand ...roduction even further."

...hit by ...etition

...o giant supermar-...or the closure of a

COUNCIL PUTS BOOT IN ON CLOG FACTORY BAR

HEBDEN Royd Town Council called time on a plans for a brewery and bar at the controversial tourist attraction of Walkley Clogs.

Independent brewer, Mr Christopher Smith, of Hoults Lane, Greetland, plans to establish the Black Horse brewery on the third floor of the clog factory producing two bitters, one special and one regular strength beers.

He is seeking a lawful development certificate from the chief town planning officer for use of the top floor of the factory as a bar incidental to the brewery.

If granted by C... plannin...

the certificate through the back door. I was a clear change of use from clo making to a bar.

She said that Walkley's had previous agreed that no retail sales would ta place on the third floor and repeated t at the public inquiry into retailing at mill.

Councillor Mrs Seward said the co tion was set by Calderdale in ord ensure adequate car parking.

"It is essential the proposed cha use can be properly assessed in te impact on car parking and the ment of Environment...

formed ..."

Sh...

Hundred face axe if plans refused, ...ims clog firm

By JAN WINTER

...would not stay open if the Secretary of State ...refused permission for the road.

"This would lead to eviction of a substantial number of small businesses from the premises, with the loss of more than 100 jobs and considerable personal hardship. There is no suitable accommodation for these businesses elsewhere in Hebden Bridge," she said.

Mr Anthony Rae, for the Save Mayroyd Action Group, told the inquiry the claim about potential job losses was being used as a weapon.

"It's an emotive claim," he said. "A constraint has been placed on the planning process..."

Mr Brundell told the inquiry that the Secretary of State would need evidence on several issues before making his decision. The new access road would run across green belt and access to the area and traffic problems should be considered.

He said the inquiry would have to look at other sites in Hebden Bridge would be suit...

Mr Godfrey also told the inquiry that the road would probably be too expensive to for such development unless Calderdale Council gave permis... r development on the Mayroyd site, ould offset the cost.

Council 'failed to take action over clog firm'

...son ...ed yes-...ve

Inquiry puts Walkley future in doubt

THE future of Walkley Clogs was in doubt this week after the result of Government inquiry into Environment Secretary John Gummer, has allowed retailing at the mill but limited it to a quarter of the floor space and rejected the proposed access road.

The rejection of the access road means plans for a hotel, houses and industrial units at land at Mayroyd cannot now go ahead.

The inquiry, ... town hall, was ca... into planning ... by Walkley's ...proved, wou... it the trad... a new acc... k. Owners of ...hey will be f... unless plans ...go-ahead.

Yesterday, ...examination ...the ...Rae of the ...Group, Mr ...plans, Mr ...firmed the ...heard ...been brea... involved ...ractured council

...would be l... 'alk...' enforcement action against ...alli...

...trad-...bden...ned ..., a

ike ...'er ...or

Blaze at clog factory

BRITAIN'S biggest clog makers, founded by a Huddersfield man, was hit by a huge fire at the weekend which caused many thousands

BLAZE WRECKS CLOG FACTORY

Residents and workers clash over clog mill

RESIDENTS of Hebden Bridge and tenants at Walkley Clogs clashed yesterday at a public inquiry which will determine the future of the mill.

The inquiry was called by the government after angry residents protested about Walkley's plans for retail use at the mill and a new access road.

It will consider an application to allow retailers to sell goods not made on the premises — something which has been going on since 1989 despite a planning condition banning such sales, the inquiry heard.

Mr Steven Jones, a partner in the clog manufacturing firm at Walkley's, told inspector Mr Mike Brundell at Halifax Town Hall:

"We are here to ask you to preserve a traditional trade and to secure the jobs of our workforce who, I'm sure, could not get jobs anywhere else."

Mr Jones said if the Environment Secretary refused to give permission for retailing at the mill the shops would close and visitors would diminish. "The clog manufacture could not survive without the visitors."

the plan. "Bad road planning can cost lives," she said.

Mrs Margaret Godfrey, director of a town planning consultancy, who was giving evidence for Walkley's, told Wednesday's hearing that Calderdale Council planners demanded a new access road if retailing was to continue at the mill, which would not stay open if the Secretary of State refused permission for the road.

"This would lead to eviction of a substantial number of small businesses from the premises, with the loss of more than 100 jobs and considerable personal hardship. There is no suitable accommodation for these businesses elsewhere in Hebden Bridge," she said.

Mr Anthony Rae, for the Save Mayroyd Action Group, told the inquiry the claim about potential job losses was being used as a weapon. "It's an emotive claim," he said.

Inspector Mr Brundell told the inquiry that the Secretary of State would need evidence on several issues before making his decision. The new access road would run across green belt and access to the area and traffic problems should also be considered.

He said the inquiry would have to look at the development of retailing in the mill and whether any other sites in Hebden Bridge would be suitable for such development.

Mrs Godfrey also ...

Boss praises firefighters and staff as 40 make great escape

AROUND 40 people escaped unhurt as fire swept through one of ...

Story: MARTIN HEMINWAY Pi...

Clogs of war

Order books clogged

NOBODY would want it to pop its clogs, but Britain's last factory making the footwear is having to tread carefully these days.

Its bosses are certainly not dragging their feet and thousands of pairs are shipped to dozens of countries — including Holland, home of the wooden shoe.

Workers at Walkley Clogs produce 20,000 pairs every year at their 19th century riverside mill in the West Yorkshire town of Hebden Bridge.

But its success as a tourist attraction has plunged the four-storey mill into a struggle for survival.

Around 500,000 visitors a year flock through the factory gates to watch the leather-topped clogs being made.

A record number of cars is pouring into the area, generating a traffic crisis. And Walkley's now faces a huge bill for a new road network.

Managing director

Traffic jams threaten firm's success story

By ROBERT TAYLOR

swimming pool — an idea which would help to pay for a new access road.

But turned council decided Environ

"Clogs have a important the town says Mr have cre of both place wh can thriv visitors to wide rang attraction Times ha founded the 1870 and for fear that th industrial spie Now the put for itself ho

recent years, with special editions and fashionwear for the youth market and leisure in particular demand, says ...

'Clog king' ready to retire

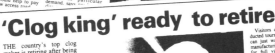

THE country's top clog maker is retiring after being in the trade for 50 years.

Mr Frank Walkley, aged 66, who started making clogs in Huddersfield in 1936, is selling his clog making factory F. Walkley (Clogs) Ltd, at Fallingroyd, Hebden Bridge.

The company is the only clog making factory in the country, making a full range of clogs, irons and soles to suit all the family.

People travel by coach, on organised tours, or just drop in to see how clogs are made and to buy the ...

Visitors can be taken on conducted tours of the factory or they can just wander around. All the manufacturing areas are closed off for full viewing by the public. They can watch the various processes and old fashioned methods of clog making with original tools. They can also watch working machinery and visit an engineers workshop with modern and old tools.

Mr Walkley said people always liked to see somebody else at work.

A mill shop is a big attraction, selling clogs of all shapes and sizes and in various styles and colours.

Mr Walkley said they always had 2,000 pairs of clogs in stock, ranging from working clogs, safety clogs, and fashion footwear.

The mill and restaurant is now open to the public seven days a week.

Clogs are made for the catering trade and the firm can meet orders. The industrial side has a steady turnover.

But Mr Walkley said it was time he had a rest from the trade, although he would still work and would help and buyer of the business.

He is assisted in the business by his family, and the firm has a full time staff of 14, plus three or four part-timers, helping in the evenings.

The Walkley clog factory has been publicised widely on TV and

Booming family clog firm ready to tempt the buyers

BRITAIN'S biggest clog makers, owned by a Huddersfield family, is up for sale.

Director Frank Walkley, of Bradley, founded F ...

off every year and often we are working into the night," said Mr Walkley.

"I should have retired last year when I was 65—so now I am making a serious ...

Mr Walkley said the business was constantly increasing and that there was still room for expansion.

"Because of the huge increase in tourism our sales ...

gone tremendously well but it has been hard work. Luckily I have always enjoyed the best of health.

"We are such a unique attraction that people come ...

accommodation for the boilerman so that he was available to start work before the others to get the boilers going. This house, being an integral part of the mill, was, of course, included in the original purchase but has not been mentioned previously. It was let on rental for a short while a few years before but had not been used for some time, so the ground floor part was altered to make a ladies' toilet area with three separate cubicles, an essential provision for the public visiting the mill. A staircase inside the doorway led to several rooms only used for storage purposes.

From this toilet area an opening was made through the wall into the mill, where a small square room fitted up as a photographic display area showed excellent shots of every stage in the making of both soles and clogs, starting with the original stock knives, which were also on display in the engineer's shop, then the three Maudes machines and finally the modern copying lathes, which could be seen actually working, through the windows at one side of the room. A lot of chairs and two low tables helped to make this more of a rest area where people could browse around and see the photographs at their leisure. They were also able to take refreshment from a drinks machine in one corner.

Outside this small room, an 'L' shaped bench was fitted up for making leisure clogs, with a steamer to soften up the leather before lasting, a jig fitted up to force last the upper into shape by compressed air, and the staple guns and lasts of all sizes placed round the bench, giving a good idea to the visitor how these clogs were made. The method of making leisure clogs, or slip-ons as we called them, compared with making traditional clogs was as different as cheese and chalk, with the stapling of the uppers always interesting to watch.

Opposite this bench where the leisure clogs were made was the long clogging room, partitioned off by a wood and glass framework enabling visitors to see inside clearly to watch the traditional clogs being made and compare the two processes. The handwork in the clogging room was only the last of the three stages of clog making after the uppers had been cut out and sewn up, which the public could see as they walked further round the mill. The cloggers' bench was long enough for three men, and a

190

fourth space at the end had a wooden part extended from the bench and fastened to the floor to enable the clog soles to rest on it whilst being fitted with rubber soles, or whatever soling material it might be, except, of course, the clog irons, for which the stithy was used in the normal way. This was something else to look at, and there was always plenty of this handwork to be done as very few clogs now had irons on the soles.

After seeing both these methods of clog making being carried on, and proceeding further into the mill, the next section on the right was partitioned off in the same way as the clogging room so that the public could easily see all five lathes through the glass windows.

Opposite to the lathes section was an area used for the bandsawing machines for the topping and tailing process, with two of these saws on view.

At the end of the mill where an old clog solemakers' bench was standing with a set of the three stock knives hanging behind it on the wall, a small area was roped off to keep people away when the knives were being demonstrated. One sidecutter machine was in use near the exit door, whilst a second one was positioned in a row of the three Maudes machines forming the set to enable visitors to see how Maudes had made the soles for almost a hundred years. For visitors, having just seen the copying lathes in action and then walked round to the stock knives, the Maudes machines completed the three ways of making soles that had been evolved over the years, enabling them to see at first hand the progress that had been made.

Arriving at the far end of the mill, they made their way back again. Round the far side was the clicking room on the left and the closing room directly opposite. Both these rooms were fully boxed in, with similar partitioning and glass windows all the way round like the clogging room. A vast array of clicking knives completely filled the wall behind and at the side of the hytronic clicking press, with the other press situated out of the way at the other end but ready for use as a standby if needed. In between the presses was a long bench where any hand clicking could be done and where the hand colouring of some of the leathers used for leisure clogs was demonstrated at weekends.

Looking into the closing room, the skiving machine, eyeletting machine and two of the sewing machines could be easily seen from outside in the corridor between these two rooms, so there was plenty of room for up to a maximum of 50 people to see what was going on when demonstrated. Other machines were at the far side of the room by the riverside. At one end of the closing room, shelving held all the various items used in the making of uppers, and one part was divided up into pigeon-holes to take every size and colour of the newly cut slip-on uppers. In front of this rack was the binding machine, which neatly sewed a matching binding round the vamp over the instep part.

The shop next to the closing room had to be further extended, having again been proved to be far too small if a busload of 50 people arrived at once, in addition to the steady flow of other visitors coming on an individual or family basis.

Opposite the shop, all the clog iron making machines were fitted up, taking up all the space from the end of the mill wall to the doorway opening of the lift. A low rustic partition similar to the engineer's room kept people away from the machines for safety reasons and added to the old-world decor of the mill itself.

Leading through the doorway which had been originally the end of the mill was a very large area which joined the two sections of the mill together at the Mytholmroyd end. It now contained the two grippers, standing side by side, with one set up for traditional clog soles and the other for gripping slip-ons. A bench and racks for the attaching of Commando soles and heels was fixed up against the wall in one corner next to the office, and the equipment, such as the infra red-ray heater for heat activating the special solution for sticking these soles together, was placed by the side of the formerly hand-operated Tellus press, which was now fitted up to the compressed air system, making this work quicker, easier and better.

The small room next to the doorway had very quickly proved to be too small for a shop and had been made into a reasonable office. A brochure in the form of an A4 three-fold sheet headed 'Craftsman made clogs' was produced for the public at large and provided details of the history of the firm up to that time since starting up in 1946 and giving information as to how clogs and clog soles were made. Opening hours were printed on the back, together with a small map showing the location of the clog mill in relation to the nearby towns and intended to be helpful for visitors finding their way there for the first time.

We were having trouble in obtaining supplies of 'peg tip', the flat iron strip with which boot heelplates were made, as the quality of this had deteriorated to such an extent as to be virtually unusable. It was essential to buy this strip with the rectangular countersunk holes spaced at different lengths to make the many sizes of finished heelplates. Eventually the quality got so bad that it was returned to the makers, which was most frustrating, bearing in mind that no one else in the UK was still making a full range of men's sizes of boot heelplates, and we had orders in hand for literally thousands of pairs. Strenuous efforts to prevail upon some other firm proved hopeless as it seemed to me that unless a sufficient quantity of iron or steel could be ordered to provide work for one full shift then they were just not interested in making the strip.

In early 1981 ICI sent two men up from London to take photographs and prepare for an article to be printed in their March/April house magazine and which was to cover four or five pages in all. When finally printed there were 12 coloured photographs and five black and white ones covering every section of clog sole, clog iron and clog manufacturing, with probably about 100 of the smaller original photos in the making. Their picture of the shop shows clearly the floral pattern of some slip-on clogs standing on the shelves. Altogether with electric cables and arc lights strewn all over the place it was quite an operation to prepare for their magazine article, at the finish both men said how impressed they were how everybody was always hard at work without any obvious supervision, commenting that if every firm was like ours then Great Britain had nothing to fear, which seemed quite a compliment to all concerned.

Following the ICI article, the house magazine of Ernst & Whinney, who were our accountants at the time, produced their May issue of *Quarterly Account* with an article headed 'A clatter of clogs' and no less than ten coloured photographs showing various stages in the making of clogs and some of the finished ones as well. On the front cover of this magazine was an excellent picture of Jack Uttley demonstrating the hollowing of a clog sole using the stock knife and the part-made sole being cut from a block, and clearly showing the clog sole bench itself with the hollower knife held in position through the iron ring fixed to the clog sole bench.

The turbulent year of 1980–81 ended up with sales down almost £50,000 at £240,373, stock of £72,085 and trade debtors down £10,800 to £24,033. The overdraft was, however, reduced by £21,600 to a more manageable £9,194 resulting in a lower bank charge of £4,569. Capital expenditure, mainly on the alterations to the ground floor of the mill, took £4,832 during this period.

Whilst the shop takings rose significantly in 1981–82 to approaching £100,000 on an annual basis, all other sales continued their downward trend, so the year ended up very little different in total, at £237,109 some £3,000 down on the previous figure. Stock was similar at £70,801 but tended to increase with a larger stock of leisure clogs, at the same time decreasing as timber supplies were being reduced. The bank overdraft was at last eliminated, with interest now at £461. Capital expenditure, though, at £7,517 was high but necessary to attract tourism.

By this time we had introduced two new lines of slip-on clogs for industrial usage. The first of these was the 'hospital' clog, so called because these clogs were used all over the world in operating theatres, mainly for their anti-static electricity properties, and the second type was the 'caterer's' clog, widely used by chefs in their kitchen work. Both these types were made from white leather. The caterer's clog was accepted, among others, by Bolton Catering College as being part of their standard personal protective clothing, so that once a year we had to go there to fit each new student with the correct size of clogs. All leisure-type clogs were always made and stamped in the Continental sizes, which, being measured in centimetres instead of inches, did not equate with one another, so every pair had to be tried for a correct fit. The soling material for the caterer's clog was nearly ten times the thickness of the normal PVC soles used on all other leisure clogs and gave excellent wear until the tread

194

was worn through, at which stage it would deteriorate rapidly and need replacing.

In 1982–83 came what I called the second round of the recession, and as a result of this drop in demand I had to make two more men redundant, with their payments costing a total of £2,650 as both had been employed for a long time.

More publicity came from the Yorkshire Tourist Board, and in particular from Maria Glott, who was doing such a marvellous job for the tourism industry from the unlikely setting of Bradford. She, along with other members of her staff, were featured wearing our colourful clogs in the 7 May 1983 issue of *Titbits*.

Several ways of increasing clog sales were tried, including the popular garden centres. There had always been a 'gardener's' clog made from a fairly soft leather fitted with a warm lining sewn inside, and the wooden sole, of course, being so solid, was excellent for digging and far superior to boots or shoes with their leather or rubber soles. Arthur made some very attractive beechwood stands to display the clogs at garden centres. They held about 30 pairs altogether and were supplied on a 'free on loan' basis so long as our clogs were being sold there, to be returned if clog sales were discontinued.

Having obtained a full list of the names and addresses of every garden centre in the UK, I circulated all of them in an effort to maximise this source of outlet, and for a while I also had the services of a representative who was self-employed and going round the garden centres as agent for all sorts of things that they were buying, including even such items as barbecues and garden furniture. He was paid on a commission basis on actual sales. This seemed a good idea, although in the past I had never been keen on agents selling our clogs as they would not know the trade well enough to be able to give the best advice to industrial customers, but this was a different type of selling altogether.

After an initial surge in sales at these garden centres, this trade slackened off to a somewhat unsatisfactory level and, bearing in mind the cost of making and supplying the stands, could not really be called a success in view of the small margin of profit in supplying slip-on clogs at wholesale prices and paying the representatives' commission.

195

Another possibility that occurred to me was to sell through the mail order houses as I knew that their sales of a black leather slip-on type were considerable. Having approached one of the Yorkshire mail order companies I was very well received and shown what they were buying at that time. Their supplies were coming in from Austria but had what looked to me to be an Italian-made sole on them. At the time my quotation for this black slip-on was exactly £8 wholesale and I was amazed to find that if they bought at that price it would mean them charging no less than £23 selling mail order. Naturally I queried this apparently exorbitantly high mark-up on cost, which was explained to be necessary due to three things. Firstly, the sending out by post of each pair separately and the large volume of returns due to unsuitability or not fitting well resulted in quite a lot of unproductive work being done when a sale did not occur. Secondly the commission paid to mail order agents had to be set at levels high enough to both attract and keep them as they in turn had to deal with their own returns. Thirdly, the sheer volume of bad debts when either customers or their agents failed to pay for the goods received. Naturally they would not disclose to me either the level of bad debts or the proportion of sales lost by returns, but this must have been considerable in both cases for such a high mark-up to be considered essential. The fact that each supplier had to pay for the coloured illustrations in the expensively produced mail order catalogues each time a new one came out was the final straw and killed it completely from my point of view. If they could sell these clogs at £23, surely I could be able to sell fair quantities at the mill at a much lower price.

Another form of competition in this slip-on clog trade was now coming onto the market in the form of substitute materials used by some continental makers. These uppers looked rather like leather in appearance but had been made from a reconstituted leather and board, which did actually last into a very good shape when done correctly onto a PVC type compound material forming the soles. Obviously this soling material had to be able to accept the stapling of the uppers onto it, and no doubt a lot of experimenting had been done in the first place before the ideal mixture of the compound was forthcoming. This material had one

196

advantage over wood insomuch that it did not crack, but from a health point of view did not breathe, as wood or leather does.

The main source of supply for this type was Italy, but anyone else in all the other countries making clogs could easily copy them. The largest manufacturers of slip-on clogs were the Scandinavian countries, where the home demand accounted for a large proportion of sales, with some clog making firms actually making over a million pairs a year, so that we in this country had absolutely no chance of competing on price. Imported clogs from all the Scandinavian countries undercut our prices and completely decimated the trade for both the hospital and caterer's clogs. The trade in both these had been relatively short-lived but seemed worth while at the time, and in any case if one does not try, it is impossible to foresee what the outcome might have been.

With increasing public interest in the clog mill, we started to do guided tours for parties with a minimum of 20 up to a maximum of 50, the largest number of people able to see and hear satisfactorily what was going on. A modest charge was made for tours as to some extent it did interrupt work for a while if the lathes or other noisy machinery were working and had to be temporarily silenced whilst I was giving a talk. The tour itself took about 45 minutes to go round seeing every stage in the making of traditional and leisure clogs, clog soles, irons and uppers, hopefully leaving people with plenty of time to buy clogs or souvenirs from the shop. These tours quickly became popular and widely known, so that every weekend in particular buses would come from all over to have a pre-booked guided tour before going on to the Brontë country at Haworth or the nearby Automobilia motor car museum at Old Town, outside Hebden Bridge off the Keighley road, the Worth Valley railway or the newly introduced canal boat trips. These latter had a stop exactly opposite the clog mill entrance following the opening up of the way under the road to canal traffic. Bus companies were now organising their following year's itineraries on the same basis as the foreign tour operators do, with bookings for their different tours arranged well in advance.

For us, the most successful of all these was Parry's of the Birmingham area, who organised weekends from Friday evening to Sunday afternoon visiting places of interest around these parts. The parties would arrive at an hotel near Huddersfield for a two night's stay for around £40. The coaches would drive over to Hebden Bridge, often for the first call of the day on the Saturday morning, and have their tour and browse round in the mill shop before leaving to visit other places, arriving back at the hotel for their evening meal. Sunday morning might well include other calls before making the journey southwards later during the day. What started off as a single bus of visitors quickly became two, then three and on some occasions at the peak brought four coaches of 50 people in one Saturday morning, resulting in me almost losing my voice during four consecutive guided tours. Everybody seemed to be so interested and attentive to every word said that it was nice to give so much pleasure to the public and to see the enthralled expression on their faces, which really had to be seen to be believed.

It had become obvious that some arrangements would have to be made to provide better refreshments for the ever-increasing number of visitors, so an architect was called in to advise on the best way of providing this service and obtaining the necessary planning permission. One corner section of the first floor seemed to be the ideal place to make a restaurant which would have views of the river Calder flowing alongside the mill on one side and a good view down the Burnley road towards Mytholmroyd and the bend in the river from the other side. The existing fire escape covered in from floor to ceiling would be nicely inside the restaurant area and easily accessible from all parts. We were advised that to complete this project would cost in the region of £10,000 to £12,000, bearing in mind that Arthur would be able to do a large part of the work, such as a new maple floor and pinewood walls all around, along with the necessary partitioning of the area where two sides had to be constructed to enclose the restaurant, and an outside 'cellar' for storing beer barrels and bottles. On this assumption we decided to go ahead, doing the work in between any clog sole making work that had to be done first. The plan was submitted by the architect and passed, having been previously discussed at a meeting on the proposed site between the planning officer, police, fire officer, architect and myself so that everything could be proceeded with in an orderly manner. The plan provided for a staircase to be made and located outside the clogging room on the ground floor and to lead upstairs through a double swing door into the restaurant. It was at this stage in the making of the restaurant that red tape was to become involved in the matter with devastating effect and cost. At the meeting already mentioned, everybody concerned was perfectly happy with the proposals for making the restaurant, and the fire officer in particular was delighted with our concern to have everything executed in a manner to provide maximum protection against fire risk. The already agreed total of seating for visitors ensured that in any emergency everybody in that area could be speedily evacuated through three different exits.

However, everything was to change when a man called to say that he was to inspect the building for buildings regulation purposes. In his view, making the restaurant in one corner of the mill – as had already been approved by the town planning department – constituted a 'separate purpose building' and, as such, came under the separate purpose buildings regulations, of which I had never even heard and most certainly they had not even been mentioned by any of the others concerned. This individual dictated what he thought could or could not be done to comply with these regulations. The staircase treads must now have different widths and heights for each tread, thus increasing the floor space needed to make it and generally getting in the way of other partitions already constructed. If the staircase was now to be made to this new specification but with the back part of it in the original position, then this would increase the floor space towards the office, leaving only about three feet in between them, so that people could not pass through safely. This was just plain daft as I personally would not have allowed this to be done, no more than the fire officer could agree to blocking up an exit path only wide enough for one person to walk through at a time. Alternatively, if the staircase was made the other way, with the bottom step in its originally designed position, then the extra space needed for the base would push this so far back as to be virtually touching the clogging room door, so whichever way it was eventually to be done would be most unsatisfactory from a common sense point of view.

Thus there was only one solution and that was to adopt the latter way to satisfy this inspector. The doorway into the clogging room had to be blocked up as it was to be impossible to open it, and a new doorway made at the end of the room. This was the worst of both worlds and resulted in partially blocking what had previously been an excellent viewpoint to see clog making in progress, and spoiling what had been an attractive layout.

The work on the maple floor and pinewood walls made steady progress over a year, whilst planning for the kitchen and its equipment was eventually done by ourselves, having lost all confidence in the various catering equipment manufacturers, who seemed only to be interested in selling the maximum amount of equipment at the highest prices they could get. Their planning was just plain silly in some cases, such as making it necessary to cross the kitchen with boiling water or hot food in pans whilst other staff were working in the central part. Accidents would be just waiting to happen if we had adopted some of these layouts.

The work on the servery and its equipment was most unsatisfactory and had been contracted to be completed by 24 December 1983, but it became obvious that this was not going to be achieved, which would disrupt our plans for opening the restaurant and for the publicity beforehand. Things were going from bad to worse with the installation of the servery, and some of the work had to be done over again and faulty equipment replaced, so that in the end, with the loss of trade caused by not opening on time, I finally put the whole matter in the hands of the company solicitors, who took the case to the High Court in Manchester, where the company doing the work operated.

As with nearly all legal matters, win or lose, it is very rare to feel satisfied, and the costs of bringing a case can be considerable, especially as it was obligatory to employ counsel to represent both plaintiff and defendant in high court cases. The end result probably satisfied no one except the legal participants, who win in any case by receiving their fees, but it had been necessary in this instance as everything else had been tried before taking this drastic action.

When the restaurant was nearing final completion after 15

months from the original idea being put forward, the building regulations inspector had a final piece of idiocy to enforce. This was the painting of the underside of the restaurant, in other words the ceiling of the floor below, which covered quite a large area and was most awkward to paint, with huge beams supporting the floor above. This had to be painted using an extremely expensive fire-resistant or retardant quality and done in three coats. This special type of paint was quoted for at an estimated quantity to cover the required area three times at a cost of over £1,000, and of course the time involved during painting would be extra. As part of the restaurant was immediately over the shop as well, this meant that part of this ceiling should also be done with this special paint, which would make the shop ceiling look odd if we only did that part which was underneath the restaurant. However, it was insisted that all the ceiling under the restaurant just had to be done and the inspector himself watched that the requisite number of coats were put on.

Not content with his personal verification of the work, to add insult to injury he sent in a bill a few days later for watching it being done. By this time I was livid with all these stupid and unnecessary rules and regulations, which had in my opinion ruined the original expectations. As costs had now rocketed to a total of £48,000 instead of the £10,000 to £12,000 originally expected, I refused point blank to pay for anything else he might make me do. This was the last straw as far as I was concerned, and I would even have stopped the opening rather than give in to anybody else in officialdom telling me how to spend my money and making me look like a fool in the process. The whole building regulations had proved to be a disaster, and as the fire officer had from the beginning been quite happy with all the arrangements, it was ludicrous for someone untrained in his particular sphere to be calling the tune in fire prevention matters.

To help with traffic problems on the Burnley road with so many visitors coming by car to the mill, I applied to have advance warning signs placed some distance from each end of the mill to give adequate time for cars to slow down and indicate their intention of turning into the car park. Calderdale refused to let me do this, so in the end I decided to have two holes sunk into the ground opposite the mill, lined with wood at ground level and had a heavy wooden sign made with two legs which could be lowered into the holes to keep it in an upright position. By carrying this heavy sign across the road each morning on opening and bringing it back in at night, I was able, in spite of the refusal by Calderdale, to make my contribution to safer road conditions outside the mill and hopefully to prevent further accidents. Already several accidents had occurred, mainly involving motor cycles, whose riders seemed to gather together one night a week in Mytholmroyd and roar past the mill like madmen. On one sad occasion when there had been an accident right outside the mill doors one of our employees was called outside to investigate, only to be shocked to find his own child lying dead in the road.

Another problem for us at the mill was the vandalism caused by young people returning from a night club in Mytholmroyd in the early hours of the morning and walking along the canal bank towards Hebden Bridge. For want of something better to amuse themselves, it became the practice when passing the mill to throw stones at the windows from the other side of the road along the canal bank. This became almost a ritual happening on Saturday nights so that every Sunday morning I would arrive to open up wondering just how much damage would greet me. The very worst of these incidents was when I counted up no less than 70 windows broken with stones lying inside on the mill floor, where they had come through at first-floor level. Unfortunately, some had damaged the leisure clogs placed in racks near to the windows as well, to add to the damage caused by these idiots.

Things had got so bad that one night a few of us from the mill waited at each end, hidden in the gardens until the early hours of the morning, ready to catch anyone damaging our property as the police were not able to deal with the problem. (I even asked them to loan us some walkie-talkie equipment for the night so that we could try to deal with the situation but this was refused). However, on the night we waited there was no stone-throwing and very few people about compared with other weeks.

Apart from the weekly vandalism, there were a few attempts to break into the mill and some people were caught in the act as we had installed a very sensitive alarm system which alerted the police at Sowerby Bridge police station. However, although quite effective in its way, the alarm did not stop some items being taken, and on one occasion, after the office door had been forced, a few items were found to be missing, including a gold medal that I had been awarded for war service. It would appear that the mentality of the thief was such that only the gold one appealed to him, as other items were untouched. With those who were caught being dealt with at Todmorden court, certain individuals known to the police had to pay weekly amounts in respect of fines or restitution, and small sums regularly appeared in my morning's post.

As is well known, burglar alarms can be so sensitive that false alarms happen for a variety of reasons, and it was on one of these occasions that I received a telephone call at Huddersfield to say that the alarm had gone off on Christmas Day of all days, which was now one of only three days a year that we had a holiday. However, I went over to the mill and waited for the engineer to arrive and re-set the alarm. One of the snags of these alarms is that they can only be re-set by the alarm people themselves, which is quite a nuisance if you have to wait a long time for somebody to come. However, it is quite understandable from a security point of view as the aim is to stop burglaries being committed by insiders who could then re-set the alarm at their leisure.

The mill burglaries contrasted strangely with a previous break-in at the Huddersfield works when the police rang me as keyholder to go there in the early hours of one morning. Apparently a thief had entered the premises and broken into the office to steal the safe, which he manoeuvred onto our long low level trolley used for carrying heavy leather and so on. Having wheeled this easily round on the level floor to the front door, he had somehow got it down the two steps onto the road which would be no mean achievement. But having done this, his troubles started when the safe, which was full of heavy coins used for change, started to run away from him by its own weight, as Common Road had quite a steep camber, downwards from the office door to the opposite side of the road, where it promptly fell off the trolley.

My next door neighbour did actually hear a noise and could see what was happening, and rang for the police – or at least tried to do so. Quite cleverly, in order not to alert the burglar that she was ringing the police, she did not switch a light on but dialled in the dark. Unfortunately, instead of dialling 999 as she thought she was doing, she had actually dialled 000 by mistake, thinking that the last digit on the telephone dial was a nine and not a nought. When she realised what had happened she re-dialled correctly and of course the police then came quickly, but unfortunately in the meantime the man had gone, having given the job up as hopeless. The police saw the safe lying there and rang me to come down from home, only two miles away, and we carried the safe back in again. It took at least two strong men to move that safe and it must have strained the man trying to do this on his own, which was why he soon gave up. Relieved at having the safe intact, I suggested to the police that all they needed to do was to look for a bow-legged man with a hernia and they would have got him. The joke was appreciated and the incident closed.

Capital expenditure during 1982–83 reflected the work progressing in the making of the restaurant and reached £22,161, with a newly created overdraft due to this situation with the restaurant of £4,363.

The restaurant and kitchen were eventually completed and ready for use, with matching wooden seating and tables. Wooden clogs with a poker work snowflake pattern were fixed to the ends of the tables, making the restaurant look different from any other. Between the newly made windows were three 8 foot by 4 foot hardboard sheets depicting in pyrography the three stages of making clogs and in keeping with the decor. The wood-effect all round was most attractive to see and very much admired by all who saw it.

It was at last possible to decide on an opening date so as to gain maximum publicity for this new venture, and invitations were sent out to the local dignitaries and everyone who had been connected with the setting-up in any way. This did not include the building regulations inspector.

The bar had been named the 'Cloggers Bar', a restaurant licence having been obtained from Todmorden Justices for the purpose of opening it. A lovely pair of red wooden shaped clasp clogs were fastened over the bar to give it effect and draw attention to it.

Several journalists attended the opening ceremony and the monthly journals were well represented and able to write their follow-up articles having seen the result of our efforts for themselves. Various television programmes featured either myself or the mill including, *Hometown, On Location, Swapshop* and *Wish You Were Here*. During the filming of the latter I well remember Judith Chalmers sitting in the main clogging area and musing that the previous week she had been on the banks of the Nile. It was on the tip of my tongue to say that she was now on the banks of the Calder, but I refrained from doing so in case it was not taken in the way intended.

With the opening of the restaurant, a new brightly coloured leaflet was produced in thousands ready to sent out to the Yorkshire Tourist Board information offices all over the area and to many other likely places including airports and hotels. The leaflet was most attractive in its presentation, with a coloured aerial view of the mill, pictures of the kitchen, which had eventually cost some £25,000, the restaurant and the Cloggers Bar. Finally a picture of a man making clogs by hand completed the pictorial side of the leaflet, which was filled with details of guided tours, hours of opening and a small map showing the location of the clog mill on the main A646 Burnley road.

The guided tours in the evenings now took on a completely new dimension as parties could have an interesting guided tour, followed by a lovely meal in the restaurant with a nice selection of wines or other drinks, and finally round off the evening browsing round the mill shop at their leisure. The parties would book to arrive at 7 p.m. or later, according to how far they had to travel and stay as long as they liked, with the bar being open till 11.00 p.m. if required. For me personally it was a bit of a rush once I had finished the guided tour as I had to wash my hands, take my apron off, put on a bow tie on and hurry upstairs to serve behind the bar as quickly as I could as some of the party would be queuing up for their drinks before I got there. Often when the tour was over people would still carry on asking questions when I was wanting to rush off upstairs and I had to be as diplomatic as I could in explaining the situation. Having been at the mill all day till about 4.30 p.m., I had only time for the half-hour drive home to Huddersfield, have a quick bath and shave to be back in the mill in good time to prepare for the evening tour. Certain preparation was necessary, in particular for the making up of slip-on clogs, where the demonstration at the start of the tour needed a supply of boiling water from the steamer to soften the leather uppers ready for lasting.

Bookings for tours were being made months in advance. The most popular groups were the Young Wives who came from all over the area. Weekends, particularly Sundays, were the busiest times at the mill as visitors had naturally more spare time for leisure activities. I have even arrived at the mill early on Sunday to open up and found visitors who had already travelled up from London just to buy a pair of clogs and, of course, to see the mill and the clogs being made. When people had come a long way, we literally made some clogs from start to finish if our stock of 2,000 pairs did not just fill the bill for them. In fact, people liked to watch their clogs being made as both they and their families were most interested, not having been able to see anything like this anywhere else before.

If clogs were brought for repairing, most people would be pleased to make use of the restaurant services, where the home-made scones were much in demand – some visitors enjoyed them so much that they bought some to take away. Doing repairs whilst customers waited saved them having to make two journeys to the mill, and the service was much appreciated.

The slip-on clogs were now being made in all sizes, from the smallest children's to the largest men's sizes in a range of seven different colours of leather. I mentioned briefly the crimping of the clogs that I had been taught pre-war and that most patterns at that time were butterflies or flowers crimped onto the vamps of clogs, with sometimes a pattern on the backs as well. This skill was now to be revived for crimping the ladies' slip-on clogs, and visitors could watch this work being done in the shop in between serving customers. Each clog maker post-war tended to have his own design, which, by an unwritten law, no one else copied, thus

206

giving an individual stamp to their own product. In our case, what came to be known as the 'snowflake' design, crimped onto the flat vamp of the clog upper prior to binding and lasting, showed up well on the various colours of leather. This was an instant success and extended to any colour. Crimping is done by using a hand tool somewhat similar to a pair of dividers or compasses, with one leg turned over at the end and sharpened from the outside to form the cutting edge. This work had to be perfect as any cut done inaccurately would have spoilt the pattern.

Among the visitors who regularly came to the mill was a group called the New Model Army. They came from the Bradford area and adopted our clogs as part of their outfits, making a very colourful party with their hair, both sexes included, of many bright colours and styles. On one occasion the lead vocalist was fitted out with golden leather type uppers to match one particular ensemble. The group played all over the world, sending us postcards from such places as America and China. Invariably on returning to this country they came along to have their clogs repaired or replaced.

The snowflake design was also used on what became known as the Sundiclog, which besides having been crimped in the usual manner of the slip-on types was further embellished round the front and sides in a similar pattern, which made a very attractive clog using the traditional low lace pattern of upper and to make it even more fancy an extra-long tongue was sewn onto the vamp upside down and then turned over to match the other leather. Two rows of brass eyelets in the tongue itself enabled the two top ones to be used in lacing the clogs up and holding it in position. At each side of the back of the clog a triangular pattern of eyelets was made, with five inserted in the normal position, then four, three, two and one, making up the triangular shape. In all 72 eyelets were inserted in these special uppers, contrasting with the black leather and making a very eye-catching style of clog. Sometimes the end of the tongue itself would be cut a short way from the bottom every tenth of an inch, similar to the 'ghillie' pattern in shoe making and looking like a fringe. Some other colours looked quite nice done in the same way, particularly red, but most customers preferred black to contrast best.

207

An article on footwear and fashion in one of the Sunday supplement magazines featured the snowflake pattern extremely well with the coloured picture really bringing out the detail.

All kinds of items were sold in the shop, which was fast becoming the most important source of revenue as the number of visitors increased. For every pair of clogs on display in the shop there had to be a back-up stock of at least five pairs of similar size, colour and design to replace a constantly moving stock from the shelves. As each pair was sold the details were noted, and all day long at weekends one person had to walk round filling up the spaces on the shelves. This system worked very well. As the slip-on clogs were arranged in sizes and colours, it was easy to know just what was required without having to check up individually.

The theme for shop goods was always to have items which appertained to either clogs, or the Hebden Bridge area, or had some connection with handcrafting. An attractive logo was used on all sorts of items from leather bookmarks to restaurant serviettes and prominently printed on the large yellow bags given away with purchases. The logo itself consisted of a clog maker making clogs by hand in the centre, above which was printed 'Welcome to Walkley's', with the address of the mill and telephone number underneath, the whole making a circular motif.

One of the most popular lines in the shop was a whole range of ladies' handbags all made from leather in various colours, which were sold at a most attractive price by the hundreds. A range of miniature clogs was produced with pokerwork on the beechwood showing the snowflake pattern, after which they were waxed and polished. Silver clogs for earrings were attractive souvenirs, and we even made chocolate clogs in the restaurant and served them as a sweet with various fillings. The larger wooden clogs, pokerworked like the miniatures, were made in three sizes and could be used for a variety of display purposes. An attractive pair of these formed the doorhandles on the double swing doors at the entrance to the restaurant at the top of the stairs and were greatly admired. A local artist painted scenes of the Hebden Bridge area on children's small clog soles, including some views of the mill itself, and these could not be produced quickly enough to supply the demand.

Perhaps the most interesting innovation to me personally was the introduction of wall plaques suitably decorated with pokerwork or colouring. On taking over at the mill I came across hundreds of near circular pieces of very light-weighing wood about an inch thick, all piled up in one corner of an upper floor of the mill about seven or eight feet high, and I was most curious to find out just what they were. They were not made from any of the timber used in making clog soles, such as beech, alder or sycamore, and no one I spoke to at the mill seemed to have any idea what they were. Anyhow, at that time, well over ten years previously I could not think of any use for them so they stayed there for years. Eventually, the secret was revealed to me that these were the centre pieces cut from much larger pieces of flat wood when making the old-fashioned wooden toilet seats such as I had seen on the farm at Ripon as a boy. Looking at the plaques on the wall in the shop, I found this an endless source of amusement and wondered what the many happy buyers of these mementoes would think if they knew the history of the souvenir they had just bought.

Although meeting the public and doing the guided tours was a very rewarding experience in itself, working long hours day after day, with only Christmas Day, Boxing Day and New Year's Day when the mill was closed, made me start to think that at the age of 64 the time had perhaps come to contemplate retirement. By now, I was completely fed up with all the red tape and bureaucratic interference that I had been subject to for so many years and was fast losing all patience with officialdom in any form. The restaurant fiasco with its huge cost had been a particularly bad blow to the company finances; after clearing the bank lending completely, we had then had to borrow heavily again when all that had seemed finished, and it had a most demoralising effect on me. The ongoing damage to the mill by louts passing by each week did not help either, as the upkeep of any hundred-year-old mill needed constant attention in some part or other. One year alone we had paid out £5,000 for roof repairs, and this was only to one part as the structure was so large.

There seemed to be plenty of problems, looking ahead, which could perhaps be better tackled by a younger person with more patience. Probably the last straw that broke the donkey's back in my case was when Calderdale sent in someone one Sunday to see what was being sold in the shop possibly in contravention of the universally loathed Shops Act, with the myriad of anomalies that this had produced. I took exception to being threatened in this way, knowing that if we were shut down on Sundays we might as well close altogether. The sales figures showed that this Sunday trading was essential to our survival. However, as I had already had to pay out two lots of redundancy money, which happens at times when the least cash is coming in, I was determined that I would avoid having to pay a third lot. Accordingly, to protect the company and myself, each employee was given a 90-day written protective notice, which brought the matter to a head and was discussed at the council meeting by the people concerned with enforcing the Shops Act. I had previously sent over 30 letters, one addressed to each member of the council, explaining the position as regards Sunday trading and offered to show them the sales of Sunday trading compared with the total to demonstrate just how serious this matter was to the survival of the last clog makers in the UK. My offer was not taken up. As controversy continued we simply carried on as before, but with the constant threat of council action hanging over us all the time.

Having decided that 40 years of interfering officialdom was as much as I was prepared to take, I advertised the business in the *Financial Times* and the *Yorkshire Post*. Over a hundred replies expressed interest and a lot of time was wasted sending the inevitable last three years' accounts to so many, as this is an accepted method of assessing the value of a business, at the same time showing whether the trend in sales is upwards, downwards or stagnant. Several potential buyers either came along personally or sent representatives such as accountants to obtain further details and see the place for themselves. One couple came over from America and were very interested indeed. The main snag in selling was the fact that whoever bought the business would almost certainly not know anything about the clog trade, which naturally tended to put some buyers off, although I was perfectly willing to carry on showing any purchaser whatever they needed to know for as long as they wanted. It was obvious to me that whoever came would want to know all about the business and the clog trade in general, and indeed if they didn't learn about this unique and specialised business they would just flounder about, lost in its complexities, especially on the industrial side, where customers bought such a variety of clogs – often typing an incorrect description on the orders, which would naturally confuse anyone who did not know what each customer actually wanted.

In the event, it was to take no less than three years to complete a sale.

A major roadworks project near the mill on the Burnley road was authorised to enable canal barges to pass under the road, which necessitated moving hundreds if not thousands of tons of good hard-core away from the site. The site engineer in charge of this work approached me to ask permission to put it on the land opposite, which had been bought for the purpose of making a car park and which I was delighted to agree to as this was to the obvious benefit of all concerned. All the convoy of loaded heavy wagons carrying the hard-core needed to do was to load up, drive over the bridge onto the land opposite, deposit their load and go back again for another. Hard-core would be necessary to cover the land for any future development and the cost of buying it would have been considerable. The arrangement was extremely sensible and to our mutual advantage. However, that was before the next dose of red tape arrived on the scene.

Within one hour of the start of moving this hard-core, some official arrived at my office door ordering me to stop this work immediately as I did not have a tipping licence. How on earth he knew about what was being done and so quickly I will probably never know, but as far as I was concerned it was my land and hard-core was needed to form a base for a car park, permission for which had already been authorised – even if subsequently killed off by Calderdale's conditions. The last thing I wanted was for it to be used as a tip, nor did I want a licence for tipping. This common-sense argument made no difference to officialdom in spite of the site engineer stating his side of the story and pointing out that by putting the hard-core on my land was absolutely ideal being so near to their work and saving both time and money for the eventual paymasters, the local ratepayers.

The end result was that the wagons had to travel past the mill for several miles to a so-called recognised tip which had a tipping licence, and, of course, paying heavily for the privilege, thus losing out in two ways. Eventually bureaucracy was satisfied and issued me with a tipping licence, by which time a vast amount of hard-core had already been taken away so that when they were able to resume putting in onto the original land it only covered part of it and had to be levelled out over a much larger area. Another hollow victory over red tape, but only after it had caused so much unnecessary trouble and expense to two businesses trying to help each other in a sensible way. Even after the hard-core had been levelled, a further estimate of the cost of providing a car park for visitors showed it was still uneconomical. The three pages of conditions to comply with the approval would have been laughable to read had it not been so serious to me in trying to cater for the public visiting the mill. These conditions laid down, among other things, that a large number of trees had to be planted as specified on the plan, with their number and Latin names provided. The whole thing would have looked more like a park than a car park. Somebody at Calderdale must have spent hours preparing these plans. They might just as well have said 'No' in the first place rather than waste time drawing up expensive plans which could not be implemented by any small firm. Needless to say, the idea had to be abandoned after all the various bodies such as gas and water had inspected the site and commented accordingly. The new height of the land, naturally, was the concern of the Water Board in view of the flooding higher up the river in the Calder Valley and at first sight appeared to infringe 'surface water' regulations, but after carefully taking readings at various points on the river bank everything was all right to proceed, if we had been able to do so on financial grounds.

Turnover for 1983–84 was similar to the previous year but now included £4,086 for restaurant takings for the part year. Overall stocks were down £6,000 to £63,518 as the very large back-up stock of leisure clogs needed increased the proportion compared with other less-selling items. Trade debtors were £30,176, up £5,600, and the overdraft rose to £39,796 due to the further capital expenditure of £38,465 for the restaurant. However, at long last the Birkby property was sold – after being empty for about two years – for only £25,000 but showing a 'book' profit of £20,291 for accountancy purposes.

The average number of employees for the year was now only 11, which included the restaurant staff, and this made it extremely difficult to put on a good show for the visitors, who naturally expected to see clogs being made whatever time of day they arrived. The seven-day opening stretched resources to the limit, as with the men working a five-day week there never was a time when everybody would be working at the same time. The exception to this was at Bank Holidays, when it was a case of 'all hands on deck', with time taken off the following week, which then made the mill look deserted until things got gradually back to normal.

The last remaining wholesale clog manufacturing firm at Halifax had sold their business to one of their long-serving employees, who came to see me at the mill to ask for supplies of soles, irons, etc. so that he could continue their former business. Although I had always hoped and indeed expected that sooner or later I would be able to acquire their trade like all the others, it was only fair to let this man have supplies of his raw materials, otherwise he could not even start, so I agreed. In the event his trade deteriorated quite rapidly and the premises he had obtained were nothing like suitable for this work, so an arrangement was made for us to buy his business and he and his daughter would come to work at the clog mill, bringing any machinery and stock with them.

I had now been in business for 38 years, during which time for various reasons I had obtained the businesses previously carried on in the trade at Wakefield, Barnsley, Pontefract, Sheffield, Newcastle Upon Tyne, Leeds, Macclesfield, London, Dumfries, Manchester, Liverpool and finally Halifax, thus ending up with a complete monopoly in the clog trade. The few remaining, making a few clogs along with some other type of work, consisted of only one-man businesses. Even taking into account the combined sales of clogs, clog soles, clog irons, clog uppers, nails and toetins, the whole trade was now at a level at which it seemed impossible to

213

increase, even with a contribution of £30,792 in restaurant sales. Everything that could be done seemed to have been tried at this stage.

The news of my suggested retirement was widely reported in the press and on television news of the north. The Halifax *Courier* of 17 July 1986 came out with the headline 'Clog King ready to retire', with an accompanying photograph and article giving details of the history of the firm, commencing on my leaving the army in 1946. The *Yorkshire Post* photograph taken in the shop showed a lovely snap of the 'Sundiclog' with its crimping prominently displayed and a somewhat similar article. The local Huddersfield *Examiner* of 27 June 1986 carried the heading 'Booming family clog firm ready to tempt the buyers' and also gave an account of the history to date.

For the benefit of potential buyers, the freehold land and buildings were professionally valued at £58,000 on 8 March 1985 but not incorporated in the accounts, which only showed a book value of £29,700. Following the acquisition of the Halifax trade the average number of employees in the 1985–86 year rose to 15 enabling the mill to look at least a little more occupied.

In October 1986 Granada television asked me to set the questions for their *Busman's Holiday* quiz as they were presenting the show with three bank managers in one team and three clog makers in the other. This was very successful but entailed me having to hold the telephone earpiece to my ear all the half-hour of the show just in case any answers to the clog questions needed a final decision, which was not really likely to arise and in the event did not do so. For this service I was paid £75 and received the grateful thanks of the producer.

The proportion of turnover in the shop for 1985–86 was £94,540, the restaurant £38,902 and the balance of £134,418 for all credit sales and industrial orders. Up-to-date figures in a half-year ending in November showed a total of £159,395, made up of £60,549 in the shop's increasing sales, £24,706 from the restaurant and £74,140 for other sales to trade and industry. A profit of £15,605 resulted for the six months.

The *Financial Times* had done an article about me in their 'Management Column' weekly article, listing the achievements in the clog trade over the years, and some time later a similar article appeared in the *South China Times*. This latter was brought to my notice when a lady knocked on my office door and introduced herself as having seen the article in the paper in Hong Kong and wanted to see the mill for herself and meet me personally. People literally from all over the world came to the mill and such publications as *Geographia*, with a world-wide circulation, produced a lengthy article about it.

One German teacher brought a party over each year and the guided tour of the clog mill proved to be one of the highlights of their visit to England. Naturally I got to know him quite well and he would translate anything into German if questions were asked during the tour. Having been two or three times he had got to know the routine and could almost have done the tour himself as far as the talking side of it was concerned. At the end of these tours I was able to conduct the last part in German myself, having rehearsed the technical translations, which usually drew a cheer from the students.

Another regular annual party was from York, where the teacher always had a most obedient and attentive class of boys in the 12-13-year-old age group. to whom it was a real pleasure to explain all the ways of making soles and the component parts as we progressed round the mill. Sadly, after about four years this teacher left the profession, unable, like many other first-class teachers, any longer to stand the crazy trendy methods being introduced into education when the traditional ways had been so successful in the past, Too late for one generation – these trendy methods have produced thousands of illiterate and innumerate individuals unable to even spell simple words correctly. Some time later this teacher called at the mill to see me, bringing with him a tree he had just bought at the Todmorden garden centre and which he planted by the corner of the mill near the river where there was a small area where shrubs were growing. Whilst I cannot recall his name, I hope that he might see this book somewhere and accept the grateful thanks of those of us who cherish the type of teaching that he exemplified in his work at York.

Whilst the act of planting a tree gives ongoing recognition to past events, perhaps in my own case a parallel could be drawn with the huge bronze figures of a group of Sheffield steelworkers in the Meadowhall centre, which bears witness to my own contribution; the straight-line pattern for industrial clogs that I designed in 1946 can be seen in detail on the safety clogs worn by these men. The pattern is unmistakable and will probably be there for all to see for years to come.

One of the most outstanding events in the restaurant was when British Railways opened their 'Rose Line' service, so called as it ran from York to Blackpool through the red and white rose country. To celebrate and publicise this event the mayors and mayoresses of each main town on the route were invited to travel along part of it, have a guided tour of the clog mill and a meal in the restaurant. A terrific time was thoroughly enjoyed by all, with bar takings achieving an all-time record. In total there must have been about half a million pounds' worth of gold chains in the restaurant that day and it was an occasion that all who were present will always remember.

My final year, 1986–87, gave a total turnover figure of £285,471 net of VAT with £38,152 coming from restaurant takings.

Some weeks before selling out on 1 June 1987 I had to arrange for my final television programme at the mill, which was for *Treasure Trail*. Anneka Rice was to come to the mill by helicopter, where a suitably hidden object had to be placed near one of the sidecutting machines, in one of the large wooden containers in which we threw part-made soles to be wheeled round the mill to the next operation. With the help of Sergeant Hirst of Todmorden police and some of the television staff, arrangements were made. There was a practice run for the helicopter to land in a field at the side of the Burnley road about half a mile away from the mill, from where she was to be driven by car to the mill. These things have to be timed to fit in with other places to be included in that programme, making a dry run essential to avoid any slips.

Altogether we had now been featured in no less than ten different television programmes at varying times in addition to talks on the radio, including overseas and Irish programmes. The very last broadcast I did was for Radio Leeds on my impending retirement and it went out in most unusual circumstances. To do this I had to go to the underground studio below Halifax Town Hall and obtain a key to let myself in. The broadcasting equipment was all set up, with a direct telephone line to Leeds, from where I was given my instructions on what to do and when. The broadcast itself went as planned, after which I switched off the lights, locked up the studio and returned the keys to the person who had given them to me on entering. During the whole of the time I had not seen anyone at all, which seemed a strange experience, bearing in mind the large number of people who always seemed to be involved in television programmes.

Although at times television crews walked into the mill unannounced or within 30 minutes of a phone call, they always seemed in one way to be in a hurry and could be a nuisance if other arrangements had been made at the mill. However, apart from the filming at the Piece Hall at Halifax, where it was almost freezing that particular morning, I always thoroughly enjoyed television and of course the publicity for the mill was very acceptable.

All this type of thing seemed a far cry from when one of the clog makers had beaten the panel in *What's My Line?* in about 1950. On that occasion one of Eamonn Andrews' stock questions at the beginning of each attempt to beat the panel was to ask where the contestant came from, which was supposed to give the members of the panel some idea as to the likely occupation of the candidate. In this case, unfortunately, the answer given was 'Halifax', which was perfectly true of course but unwittingly gave publicity to our competitors there when it was eventually revealed that he was a clog maker. This was the last thing that I wanted to happen as I was hoping for some publicity for ourselves at Huddersfield. It would have been far better if he had been asked where he worked and not where he came from so that he could honestly have said 'Huddersfield', as I had intended when the arrangements were being made beforehand. Just one word can make a lot of difference.

In the 15 years since taking over at Maudes I had sold over three million pairs of various types of clogs and must take some

217

consolation from this fact, in spite of the decline in the clog trade which had started even before I did in 1937. The final overdraft figure is shown at £6,511 down by £15,000, with the trade creditors included in this figure and totalling £31,841. Net assets after a lifetime's work were £147,297 after providing for taxation, so the original army gratuity of £225 had seen some increase over the years.